James Crouse
and Dale Trusheim

The Case Against the SAT

The University of Chicago Press / Chicago and London

JAMES CROUSE is professor of educational studies and sociology at the University of Delaware. He is a coauthor of *Who Gets Ahead? The Determinants of Economic Success in America* (1979). DALE TRUSHEIM is assistant director of institutional research and strategic planning at the University of Delaware. Both Crouse and Trusheim have published extensively on the SAT controversy.

The University of Chicago Press, Chicago 60637
The University of Chicago Press, Ltd., London

Printed in the United States of America

97 96 95 94 93 92 91 90 89 88 5 4 3 2 1

The University of Chicago Press gratefully acknowledges the contribution of the Exxon Education Foundation toward the publication of this book.

Library of Congress Cataloging-in-Publication Data

Crouse, James.
The case against the SAT / James Crouse and Dale Trusheim.
p. cm.
Bibliography: p.
Includes index.
ISBN 0-226-12142-9
1. Scholastic aptitude test. I. Trusheim, Dale. II. Title.
LB2353.57.C76 1988 87-24404
378′ .1664—dc19 CIP

Contents

Tables

Preface

This book summarizes the results of a six-year research project on the origins and uses of the Scholastic Aptitude Test (SAT) by American colleges and universities. The SAT is sponsored by the College Entrance Examination Board, administered by the Educational Testing Service, taken by nearly 1.5 million persons a year, and used in admissions by more than 1,500 colleges and universities.

Our research grew out of the controversy sparked by Ralph Nader and Allan Nairn in 1980 with their publication of *The Reign of ETS*, a highly critical report on the Educational Testing Service. Our initial reaction to the Nader report was mild disbelief. We thought the report's version of ETS's role in the history and culture of admissions testing was oversimplified, and its conclusions about the usefulness of the SAT suffered from serious technical flaws. But we also felt that some of the charges leveled by Nader and Nairn and the claims made by ETS on behalf of the SAT could bear more careful scrutiny than either side gave them. We therefore set out to correct the technical flaws in the Nader report and to assess ETS's case for the usefulness of the SAT as thoroughly as we could.

As we began our own analyses and started to look carefully at how ETS documented the effectiveness of the SAT, we became increasingly skeptical about the value of the test. We continued to think that the Nader report suffered from an oversimplified version of the history of admissions testing and from technical errors. But we came to believe that ETS and the College Board relied on an equally flawed documentation of the test's effectiveness and an equally oversimplified understanding of the history of admissions testing; and that most psychologists and college admissions officers had accepted ETS's claims for the test far too uncritically. As we asked ourselves how this could happen, we began to have serious questions about how fully ETS and the College Board presented information about the test, and how vigorously and objectively they had tried to assess its benefits and costs.

Midway through our research we began to think that the case against the SAT was far stronger than the case for it, and that the roles of ETS and the College Board in promoting and documenting the test were not what Americans ought to expect from corporations chartered to serve the public interest. When we presented our arguments and analyses to ETS in situations that did not provoke defensive reactions and political posturing, we were impressed with how few counterarguments ETS made. We also received considerable encouragement from colleagues to continue our investigation.

But mostly we were impressed by how little educators, mainstream psychologists, and talented people at ETS and the College Board have thought about how to document the effectiveness of a college admissions test. By and large our profession has been willing to assess the usefulness of a college admissions test on very limited technical grounds—increments in correlation coefficients. Our profession has also been remiss, in our opinion, in not trying to think through the social and economic consequences of admissions testing or to collect the information needed to assess these consequences empirically.

This book focuses on shortcomings in the performance of professional psychologists, college admissions officers, the College Board, and ETS. We have no illusions that we have supplied remedies for these problems. But we do hope that the arguments we make and the empirical data with which we support them will broaden and deepen the national debate over the usefulness of the SAT. We also hope that our arguments will lead colleges and universities that now require SAT scores from their applicants for admissions to reconsider their usefulness. We describe our suggestions for what such colleges and universities should do in the final chapter.

Unlike many critics, we do not question ETS's claim that the SAT measures important abilities that are related to educational and economic success. Rather, we argue that *despite* its ability to predict educational success, the SAT is unnecessary. This apparent paradox disappears when one recognizes that even when a test predicts college success fairly accurately, it may not *improve* prediction much when used to supplement information available from high schools about students' coursework and grades. Our argument develops the case against the SAT as a tool in college admissions, not against the test's validity in measuring individual differences important to educational success.

Some of the data analyses and arguments in this book have been published in different forms previously. Crouse published an early version of parts of chapter 3 in the May and November 1985 issues of the *Harvard Educational Review* and the January 1986 issue of the *Phi Delta Kappan*. Trusheim and Crouse published a brief description of these views in the *Phi Delta Kappan* in 1982. Near the beginning of the project, Crouse collaborated with Christopher Jencks on an early version of parts of chapter 8, which was published in *The Public Interest* and *New Directions for Testing and Measurement*.

We owe a huge debt to colleagues and friends who have read, given us critical comments, and talked with us about the issues and problems in draft after draft of these chapters, especially Christopher Jencks, Peter Mueser, Michael Olneck, David Owen, and Len Ramist. Each of them read all or most of the manuscript in draft form, and read some chapters two or three times. Each has helped in innumerable other ways as well.

We also owe a debt to Henry Bedford, Walt Haney, Barbara Heyns, Arthur Jensen, Leon Kamin, and John Weiss, who read the entire manuscript and gave us helpful comments. Karl Alexander, Albert Beaton, Carol Blumberg, Norman Bowie, George Brabner, Marvin Brams, Kevin Coveney, Ken Eckhardt, Ralph Ferretti, Bob Hampel, Art Hoerl, Saul Hoffman, Dal Holmes, Michael Katz, Robert Linn, Victor Martuza, Samuel Messick, Lou Mosberg, John Ralph, Bill Reese, Robert Taggart, and Glen Thomas all read at least one chapter in draft and gave us helpful advice or consulted with us on statistical or other matters. Bob Shaffer and Sarah Tung gave us much good programming advice. We would also like to thank the University of Chicago Press and Peter Dreyer for their careful reading of the manuscript and attention to detail.

Two of our secretaries, Vickie Porch and Judi Holmes, worked way beyond the call of duty to type the manuscript and make the seemingly endless number of corrections in the drafts.

We also want to thank the University of Delaware for giving Crouse a fellowship in its Center for Advanced Study that released him from all academic duties during 1985–86. The fellowship was instrumental in enabling us to complete this project.

Finally, our wives provided the kind of support and understanding for our work that made writing this book enjoyable.

ONE

Can We Trust ETS and the College Board to Monitor Themselves?

"Elite Babies: The Weapon of the Future." So said the London *Times* headline to a 1981 article describing a forty-three nation conference held in Montreal the previous week. The topic of the conference: how to identify and educate an elite. "Our final hope is to develop the brain as a natural resource," said Venezuela's Dr. Luis Alberto Machado, minister for the development of intelligence. "Any country which develops its intelligence will become the most powerful in the world. Human intelligence will be the weapon of the future."[1]

The United States does not yet have a minister for the development of intelligence whose final hope is to develop the brain as a natural resource. But like most other countries the United States does have organizations and individuals to look after the nourishment of its intellectual resources: a national Department of Education, state and local educational bureaucracies, and hundreds of educational corporations, associations, lobbies, and research and survey agencies, as well as the local press and academic researchers.

This book is about two of these organizations, the College Entrance Examination Board and the Educational Testing Service. Ever since its founding in 1900, the College Board has issued reports on the state of America's intellect, especially its youth, and it has had tremendous influence on educational policy through its membership, which now numbers over 2,500 colleges, schools, and educational associations.

The Educational Testing Service (ETS), which the College Board helped found in 1947, is the nation's largest nonprofit educational research organization, with over 2,400 employees. Its headquarters are just outside Princeton, New Jersey, but it has field offices in seven other American cities, and it boasts that its international activities "extend to every continent, to nations ranging alphabetically from Argentina to Zaire."[2]

Nearly six million persons took ETS tests in 1983. In 1985 ETS conducted over 35,000 test administrations in 10,000 centers, and spent more than $2 million on mail and freight alone for 245,000 shipments of publications, test books, and other materials.

ETS gives tests that help determine where more than a million young Americans will go to college each year. ETS also gives tests that help decide who will enter the nation's most elite secondary schools, who will be a certified teacher, an attorney, or enter graduate school or business school. One may be required to take an ETS test to become a respiratory therapist, podiatrist, construction code inspector, shopping center administrator, real estate agent, insurance agent, or electrician, or to be selected as a policeman or fire fighter. ETS even has a test to select golf pros and a test to certify picture framers.

ETS's tests are sold to such diverse groups as the Central Intelligence Agency, the Defense Department, the National Security Council, the Institute for Nuclear Power Operations, the National Committee of Contact Lens Examiners, the Commission on Graduates of Foreign Nursing Schools, the Institute of International Container Lessors, the Malaysian Ministry of Education, and the Institute for the Advancement of Philosophy for Children. In some states you must pass an ETS test to become a certified beautician or barber, moving consultant, auto mechanic, business-form consultant, manicurist, or esthetician. If you want to become a paid worker at the 1988 Summer Olympics in Seoul, you will need to pass an ETS test.

ETS's worldwide research and activities, now in more than one hundred countries, expand the market for its tests. ETS recently carried out attitude studies in Italy and Poland; a cross-cultural study of children's learning styles in Italy, Mexico, and the Netherlands; a feasibility study for a measurement and training center for Central and South America; a survey of educational needs in Brazil; and an evaluation of instructional television in El Salvador. It even has an agreement with the People's Republic of China for test development, educational research, and organizational management.

ETS now administers tests outside the United States at more than 1,200 centers. In addition to testing foreign citizens, its ambitious international goals include "efforts to create a universal scale for all proficiency exams in English as a second language." This project, now in its developmental stages, will produce a "common yardstick for measuring levels of skill in conversation, listening comprehension, reading, and writing in English."[3]

ETS has come a long way since its founding in 1947. Its revenue in 1985 was only $163.2 million, which is small if compared with Du Pont or General Motors. Nonetheless, since 1948 ETS has usually doubled its revenues every six years. Its nonprofit status plus a persistent strategy of diversification and reinvestment of its tax-free revenues led *Forbes* to describe it in 1976 as "one of the hottest little growth companies in U.S. business."[4] But ETS's power and influence are not told by its revenues alone, but by its effect on the lives of those who take its tests. How ETS uses this power and influence is a central concern of this book.

Section 18 of ETS's bylaws establishes a Committee on Public Responsibility. "The Committee shall prepare for the Board of Trustees an annual report to the public regarding ETS's response to public concerns and adherence to the ETS Standards for Quality and Fairness."[5] These standards develop 140 principles, policies, and procedural guidelines covering ETS's accountability, confidentiality of data, product accuracy, research and development, technical quality of tests, test use, and public information. Along with the trustees' annual public accountability reports that assess ETS's adherence to them, these standards illustrate how "ETS and its Board of Trustees believe the organizaton must act with a clear sense of public responsibility in what it does."[6]

Says the *Trustees' 1984 Public Accountability Report*: "ETS has a special responsibility as a publicly chartered, tax-exempt organization to contribute to the public good—in our case to contribute to the research base of psychometrics, statistics, psychology, and education; to provide high quality tests; to promote the fair and appropriate use of these tests; and to expand the public's understanding of testing."[7] This is the sort of thing we would expect a publicly chartered, tax-exempt testing organization to say and try to do. Americans expect their nonprofit companies to serve the admittedly vague ideal of the public interest in some way, and to hold themselves to high standards.

However, no one realistically expects ETS to hold to these standards all the time regardless of cost. After all, ETS competes with a half-dozen or so other testing firms for a share of a growing market for tests and testing services. A decline in market performance is not good for anyone who works for ETS. ETS may not be able to afford a dispassionate search for answers without regard to what it will discover. Scholarship and dispassionate objectivity are time-consuming virtues, which understandably tend to get sacrificed to revenue in any company that depends on market advantage for survival.

Furthermore, ETS is an organization dedicated to the development and administration of tests. It should be no surprise that people who work for ETS believe testing to be valuable. Such people do not spend their time in endless self-questioning. They spend their time developing and promulgating tests. From their viewpoint this is appropriate.

Yet ETS has public trust for a high level of attention to *some* additional standards besides revenue, growth, and survival. This does not require ETS's innermost workings to be open constantly to its severest critics. No company could operate efficiently under those conditions. But serving the public interest outside of some areas of national security and a few other cases does imply a substantial level of openness and forthrightness. If the market does not create incentives to conform to these ideals, as we believe it does not, and the result is a violation of public confidence, as we think it is, then the public interest is served by showing how the company acts. That is part of what this book tries to do.

Inadequate Analysis of the SAT's Usefulness

ETS's largest and most controversial testing program is its Admissions Testing Program, which administers the SAT to college-bound students and accounts for a substantial part of ETS's revenues. Last year about 1.5 million high school juniors and seniors took the SAT, many of them for the second or third time. No one takes the SAT for fun. The test is three hours of nail-biting anxiety for many high school students. They take the test because they plan to apply to one of the more than 1,500 colleges that require or strongly recommend it for admissions. It would be surprising indeed if such a test were free from controversy.

Yet few people would detect any sign of controversy with the SAT or ETS's other tests if they read only what ETS says about them. For example, in 1983 ETS used about 125,000 different questions on its tests taken by nearly six million persons. They report astonishingly that "only 11 questions on all the different tests and test forms administered this year by ETS were found to be flawed in some way."[8] One wonders how any organization of ETS's size and complexity could do anything with near-perfect proficiency, let alone write test items that well.

ETS takes great pains to publicize popular support for its products. A pamphlet entitled *What the Polls Say* summarizes results from polls conducted by Gallup and other well-known pollsters since 1978. ETS's overall conclusions:

> Most parents support standardized tests.
> Most teachers favor standardized tests and use the results.
> Many high school students, including minorities, support standardized tests.
> Parents do not want governmental control of standardized testing.

The SAT in particular shines in the polls cited by ETS. According to a 1977 survey of three thousand high school seniors by the Response Analysis Corporation for the SAT Monitor Program, 79 percent believed that SAT scores should have "a great deal" or "a fair amount" of influence on college admissions officers' decisions. The students believed this even though only 30 percent expected their SAT scores to be one of their strong points in getting into college.[9]

Furthermore, under the heading *By 2 to 1*, ETS points out that students who favored the SAT in admissions outnumbered those who would eliminate it by a two to one margin. Why? Because according to ETS "it is an impartial and objective measure of student ability."[10] Four out of five students rated the math section as "very fair" or "pretty fair," and nearly three out of four students said the same about the verbal section.

However, majority opinion is not always a reliable guide to truth. Few of us have access to the information we would need to make up our own minds about the value of the SAT. The information published by ETS is couched in technical jargon and shrouded by controversy that takes a long time to understand. Since the College Board and ETS have a virtual monopoly on technical information about the SAT, and since their credibility is reinforced by colleges that require SAT scores for admissions (how could 1,500 colleges be misled?), most people believe what the College Board and ETS tell them. And the board and ETS have taken a rosy view of the SAT from its outset.

The SAT scores that ETS sends colleges are supposed to help colleges improve the accuracy of their admissions decisions over what they could achieve by relying solely on applicants' high school records and other information. How successful is the SAT at doing this? As George H. Hanford, president of the College Board, puts it: "Thousands of validity studies prove that the SAT increases predictive efficiency by 40 to 50 percent when it is used in helping to estimate first-year college grades."[11]

This conclusion is questionable. ETS has conducted over 3,000 validity studies of the SAT for American colleges and universities. But there is less to these studies than meets the eye. The vast majority of them compare the predictive validity of the high school record alone with the predictive validity of the high school record and SAT scores combined. For one thing, when ETS uses the term "high school record," it does not typically mean the high school record as most people understand it. High school records normally include grades, courses taken, and extracurricular activities. What ETS typically means by high school record is only grades or rank in class.

More important, however, are the comparisons ETS reports in its validity studies. Comparing the predictive validity of the high school record alone (rank or grades) to the predictive validity of the high school record and SAT scores combined is highly misleading. It is misleading because it does not show the actual people admitted and rejected if colleges were to select with the SAT and high school record combined instead of the high school record alone. This is a serious deficiency.

Admissions officials are interested in predicting freshman grades mainly as an aid to selecting a freshman class from their applicants. SAT scores can provide important information only when they lead admissions officers to make admission decisions they would not have made without SAT scores. This book compares the admissions decisions colleges would make using the SAT to those they would make without it. We try to find out which applicants to a national sample of American colleges would be admitted or rejected with and without the SAT. Our results show that for the vast majority of colleges, an admissions policy that ignores the SAT admits almost the same freshman class as an admissions policy that includes the SAT.

Acceptance or rejection of applicants is, however, not the main way most colleges increase the academic quality of their freshman class. Most selective colleges try to increase the academic quality of their entering freshman by attracting the kind of applicants they want, not by choosing among those who apply. Most selective colleges give all kinds of signals in their cataloges and a half dozen or so widely read college handbooks to let prospective applicants know what kind of students they hope to enroll.

Prospective applicants are also concerned with finding colleges where they can do the academic work. Few applicants want to apply to colleges where they stand a good chance of being rejected or to enter colleges where they are likely to get a lot of F's. Students seldom apply to Harvard, for example, unless they have good grades and high SAT scores. This kind of self-selection also takes place elsewhere, so that American colleges attract mostly students who can handle the academic work.

The College Board and ETS both claim that college-bound students can use their SAT scores to help select a college appropriate to their level of ability. The board says: "Students use the score reports they receive to help select colleges or universities suitable to their interests and abilities."[12] But the College Board and ETS have never tried to find out how prospective applicants use their score reports in deciding where to apply. Prospective college applicants know a lot about their own abilities and willingness to persist at academic work from their past grades and school experience. They may know even before they take the SAT that they have to work hard for their B's, and that they would have trouble in a demanding college. Or they may know that they have never cracked a book and have still gotten B's, and that they don't often meet people who seem better at learning than they are when they try. If the rationale for the SAT is that it helps applicants choose the "right" colleges, we must again ask how much SAT scores add to the information that prospective applicants have accumulated about themselves in school. The College Board and ETS have not tried to do this.

Throughout their history the College Board and ETS have also made broad statements about the social and economic virtues of the SAT and standardized testing. They have argued that tests like the SAT help create more equal opportunity and promote economic growth. We would expect the board and ETS to speak out carefully on matters as important as these. As its public accountability report proclaimed in 1984, "ETS has a special responsibility as a publicly chartered, tax-exempt organization to contribute to the public good," and one of the ways it stresses is "to expand the public's understanding of testing."[13] In our judgment ETS has frequently failed to do this.

ETS's approach to the SAT and equal opportunity provides a good illustration. Neither the College Board nor ETS gives colleges specific guidance about how to use the SAT with minority or poor white applicants.[14] Normally, neither ETS nor the board is shy about giving colleges advice. They urge colleges to combine the SAT with the high school record to predict applicants' freshman grades. They provide a service that calculates prediction equations for colleges, and they give colleges detailed instructions on how to compute their own equations. But they give colleges no guidance on predicting freshman grades for blacks and low-income students. With blacks, for instance, colleges must decide whether to develop a single prediction equation (based on the high school record and SAT) for blacks and whites combined, or whether to treat blacks and whites as separate groups and develop separate prediction equations for each group.

This is a critical decision because the choice of a combined or separate equation can lead to different predicted grades for a black student. Thus, one issue here is whether ETS and the board think colleges should treat blacks differently from whites when predicting freshman grades, and if so, how they should do it. Another issue is how colleges should decide. When we wrote to Gregory Anrig, president of ETS, and asked him these questions, he passed them on to Warren Willingham, ETS's assistant vice president for program research. "The simple answer," said Willingham, "is that ETS has no established position on the issue you raise."[15]

The questions we asked Anrig and Willingham's answer to them merely scratch the surface of ETS's failure to expand the public's understanding of SAT use and equal opportunity. It has been known for a long time that one can predict fairly well where young children will end up in the competition for college admissions by knowing their race, the quality of their schooling, and their family background. If we can predict where young people will end up merely by knowing their race or family background and the advantages these create for the development of college-related qualifications, then the competition may be unfair to some people. It may be unfair because some people may be given many more advantages than others in developing high SAT scores. Assessment of qualifications with the SAT or other tests may simply perpetuate this pattern of unequal opportunity.

Whether the competition for college qualifications is fair and what the SAT's role in this competition is are issues about which people will inevitably disagree. Yet ETS's public statements have given such questions only superficial analysis and have done little to expand the public's understanding of testing.

For example, ETS did not even accept at first that the competition might be unfair. In 1960 ETS took the view that "we believe that justice should be done each individual according to his merit." The objective test "is a common touchstone. . . . It gives all students who take it the same chance, asks them to run the same race—even though they have had different economic backgrounds, different educational, cultural, and social opportunities."[16]

Twenty years later, after overwhelming evidence had accumulated that ETS's "common touchstone" had a substantial relationship to students' race, family income, and parental education, ETS guardedly admitted that the competition might be unfair:

> While there is a correlation beween family income and test scores, other indicators of educational achievement, including school grades, have similar relationships to students' economic backgrounds. These are reflections of a [*sic*] fact that, in our society, students from higher income families enjoy educational advantages that many lower income students do not.[17]

By 1984 ETS acknowledged not only that the competition was unfair, but said that tests were part of the solution: "To attack testing because of unfavorable results is to attack a potential force for improving those results. Throwing away the thermometer does not cure a virus. So it is with the problem of unequal educational opportunities. . . . Such information [test results] helps to focus public attention on unequal opportunities and to keep public pressure on these inequities until they are corrected."[18]

ETS's public statements on these issues do not result from careful research. In 1979, after officers of ETS and the board were quoted publicly to the effect that admissions tests open gates to higher education as well as close them, and that they increase minority group access to higher education, Walter Haney, then staff director of the Huron Institute's National Consortium on Testing Project, wrote to these officers inquiring about their evidence.

Haney reports that one individual had an aide write back and the other called him personally to respond. "The written response explained that my correspondent knew of no published study to support the idea that tests open or close the doors to higher education. He said that he knew of only anecdotal evidence on both sides of the question."[19] Haney adds that the other response was similar. "No empirical evidence was cited—instead I was referred to several special programs, such as the Council for Legal Educational Opportunities, whose intention it is to use admissions tests and other information to enhance minority opportunities for higher education."[20]

We find it hard to imagine that the board and ETS are unaware of the importance of untangling the roles of the SAT and other tests in creating or eliminating inequality of opportunity. We suspect instead that they have chosen not to discuss these problems fully because doing so might heighten tensions that are now relatively muted within their heterogeneous constituency. To raise these issues could challenge both the internal solidarity of the board and ETS, and, ultimately, their legitimacy. No organization concerned with its own survival would want this to happen. Yet not to discuss them fully and carefully conflicts with ETS's responsibility to the public.

In our view, institutional self-interest too often wins out over the responsibility to "expand the public's understanding of testing" at ETS and the board. To see why, one has to understand how ETS reacts to individuals who try to assess what it does or to hold it accountable.

Unresponsiveness and Secrecy

"Maybe there's something in the air in Princeton that makes you think you know everything. I felt that way. It was a quite a humbling experience to leave Princeton and find I didn't have all the answers." These are the words of John Fremer, director of testing development at ETS from 1976 to 1983. Fremer considers himself a friend of ETS. He told Gerald Bracey, special assistant for policy and planning in the Virginia Department of Education, who was writing for the *Phi Delta Kappan*: "I tell my friends there [at ETS] all the time. It *is* ETS's greatest fault. That's my message to them, and I think it is a message that they need to hear over and over again."[21]

Like many organizations and people, ETS does not take criticism very well. Writing in 1984, Vice President Winton Manning and his colleague Rex Jackson, a former vice president, accused ETS's critics of having difficulty coping with the contrast between the American ideal that merit should count and the actuality of schooling that objectively appraises individual merit through tests: "It is therefore understandable that hostility towards testing would become, perhaps *irrationally*, one important means of dealing with this larger conflict of values, indeed, with the *guilt* and *frustration* that have arisen over the failures of education. A campaign to abolish testing in education thereby becomes an *escape* from persevering in the effort to understand the reasons that the fruits of our educational policies have fallen so short of our social expectations.''[22] In short: ''Modern day polemicists of the antitesting movement have sought to *displace* the responsibility for public miseducation onto educational tests.''[23]

Arguments like this reveal one way ETS dismisses its critics, but they do not show how far ETS will go to be unresponsive to criticism. A good example of ETS's unresponsiveness is its refusal to admit to bad SAT items. This is not to say that ETS *never* admits to faulty SAT items. Since 1980 ETS has acknowledged seven flawed SAT mathematics items, and these admissions attracted wide media coverage. But ETS has publicly acknowledged only one ambiguous verbal question among the more than six thousand it has used since 1980.[24]

ETS has always been hesitant to give SAT takers much information. Until 1958 ETS did not even tell SAT takers their scores. But New York State's 1979 truth-in-testing law—which ETS bitterly opposed—required ETS to disclose each person's SAT questions, the answers they selected, and the desired answers. As a result, New York applicants could at least scrutinize their own questions and answers. In March 1981 ETS extended disclosure to everyone. In 1982 ETS released old editions of the SAT for prospective college applicants.

But publishing questions and answers is not the same as getting ETS to admit that a question is faulty. ETS goes to great lengths to convey interest in the fairness and accuracy of test questions. In 1981, and again in 1983, it said in special flyers that explained test development to the public: ''At every stage of the process, ETS does all that is possible to assure the accuracy and fairness of individual test questions and the examinations as a whole. It's a demanding and time-consuming process. . . but it's worth the effort.''[25] ETS also tells every SAT candidate that any concerns about specific test questions should be put in writing and will receive a written response.[26] Further, ETS says: ''All complaints are responded to within ten working days.''[27]

ETS's actions do not meet this standard, however. In an article in *Harper's* in May 1983, for example, David Owen looked at forty-five verbal items in the first section of the first SAT presented in *6 SATs*, which the College Board had published in 1982 to show prospective test takers what the SAT was like. Owen concluded that four of these forty-five items had serious flaws. He argued in great detail that these items had several plausible "correct" answers, and that ETS's preferred answer was no more plausible than one or more of the alternatives.

Owen repeatedly asked ETS and the College Board to reply to his criticisms of these items. He took the trouble to gather additional criticism from five leading American intellectual and political analysts: Nicholas von Hoffman, a highly respected political writer; William F. Buckley, Jr., editor of the *National Review*; John Simons, associate professor of English at Colorado College, who has graded essay exams for ETS for a half-dozen years; Elizabeth Hardwick, a novelist and a critic and advisory editor of the *New York Review of Books*; and Andrew Hacker, professor of political science at Queens College in New York, and a distinguished political essayist. Owen's book *None of the Above* documents ETS's refusal to reply.[28]

Owen wrote to ETS's president, Gregory Anrig, about the four verbal SAT items he criticized in his *Harper's* article, accusing ETS of stonewalling on the criticisms. He also told Anrig that he was expanding his *Harper's* article into a book to be published by Houghton Mifflin.[29]

Anrig's reply to Owen fifteen days later said, "I must admit to being amazed that you accuse ETS of 'stonewalling.' " Anrig was also displeased that Owen was doing a book with Houghton Mifflin. "Surely you must be aware that Houghton Mifflin is a major publisher of standardized tests and a competitor of ETS. That is a strange definition of fairness (much less journalistic ethics)." His last paragraph concluded: "I'm sorry that your actions make clear that no constructive purpose can be served by further communication with you. I really very much regret this."[30]

That same day, Anrig sent a copy of his letter to Owen to each member of his executive advisory board with the instruction: "Please ask your staff to honor the position reflected at the end of my letter regarding any further communication with Mr. Owen. Let Joy McIntyre or me know if any inquiry is received from Mr. Owen." Anrig added in parentheses: "You should have seen my first draft!"[31]

More than two years later, Owen wrote: "Anrig's no-talk policy was carried out with great gusto, and it extends to this day. I was not included on the original mailing list for ETS's response to *None of the Above*, and Mr. Anrig did not return my two phone calls when I called to request a copy."[32]

Although ETS never replied to Owen's criticisms of these questions, it prepared a seven-page single-spaced criticism of his book less than a month after it was published.[33] George Hanford, president of the College Board, then distributed ETS's criticisms to all 2,500 College Board members, committees, and councils as a useful backgrounder, "which offers incisive and pithy rebuttals to the major points made in Mr. Owen's book."[34] Neither Hanford nor ETS made any mention of Owen's criticisms of faulty SAT verbal questions.

Four faulty questions out of forty-five would not ordinarily have much effect on applicants' chances of getting into the college of their choice. But ETS's response to criticism of these items does tell us a lot about its general response to criticism. As far back as the early 1970s, one ETS vice president confided to *New York* magazine's Steven Brill during an "off-campus" dinner conversation: "The general attitude of the executives is like the way the Nixon White House was described during its last days. It's a bunker mentality. We're in the bunker and everyone's out there trying to get us. So when someone from the outside asks for any kind of information at all, we first try to figure out why he wants it and if it can possibly hurt us."[35]

Since 1973 every broad look at either the College Board or ETS has mentioned this attitude. Warner Slack and Douglas Porter comment in the *Harvard Educational Review* in 1980, for example: "An aura of secrecy surrounds the SAT. Detailed information about the test is hard to come by. The data that can be tracked down and analyzed are often at variance with the numerous summary statements to be found in ETS's technical documents and promotional literature."[36] The Nairn/Nader report expresses this same theme.[37] So does Owen's book.

The critics do not say that the board and ETS give out *no* information. No close look at the board or ETS would ever get off the ground if it were not for information they supply. What the critics complain about is the kind of information they can get and the difficulty they have getting it.

During the spring of 1984 we requested some ETS-controlled data from the College Board. ETS says in its *Standards for Quality and Fairness* that it "will make ETS-controlled nonproprietary data available to other researchers."[38] The executive at ETS who controlled the data eventually gave us the data, but only after we sent him a letter promising to report our results only if he agreed with what we wrote, or he coauthored the report, or he published the analyses first.[39] In effect, he made us agree to publish the results only if we came to the right conclusion. He also made us write that this was his personal request and not the College Board's or ETS's request.[40]

Of course, ETS and the board bristle at accusations of secrecy and unresponsiveness: "We do not operate in secrecy, exist in a vacuum, or conspire behind closed doors—as has been charged. . . . Secrecy, and an accompanying sense of conspiracy, remain favorite shibboleths of the critics.''[41] ''ETS is on record as supporting more openness in testing. And our programs stand behind the record.''[42] ''If we find we are wrong on an issue, we will say so.''[43] Despite these protestations of openness, however, we believe that both the College Board and ETS exhibit arrogant and unresponsive attitudes that contribute to the failure of both organizations to analyze the usefulness of the SAT and testing issues in a forthright and objective manner.

Why Don't ETS and the Board Do a Better Job?

Our conclusion after six years of research is that the College Board and ETS have not competently appraised the usefulness of the SAT or provided a balanced response to criticism. In the course of our research, we have increasingly met with subtle and not-so-subtle resistance from both organizations and encountered individuals in their employ who have engaged in decidedly unscholarly behavior. At times, ETS and the board behave more like corporations bent on defending their principal products at all costs than like institutions working for the public good.

ETS presents itself as a company that develops its products according to the highest scientific standards. It prides itself, for example, on conforming to the standards for test development and test use of the American Psychological Association, American Educational Research Association, and National Council on Measurement in Education. But when we examined its record, we did not find a company that assessed the effects of its products openly or empirically, or that freely entered into debate with the scientific community over the adequacy of others' assessments.

Instead, as we will illustrate throughout this book, we find that ETS promotes claims for its products without trying very hard to gather serious evidence for these claims. It also tends to ignore or denounce, rather than answer, evidence that undermines its positions.

The root problem is that ETS has too much influence over what the public learns about it and its tests, and the market has not worked well to create the needed information for colleges and other consumers. Our argument showing this and our suggestions on what to do about it are developed in the remaining chapters. Since our argument is complex, and is filled with statistics, as well as diversions and qualifications, a brief overview of what is to come may be useful.

Chapter 2 discusses how the College Board and ETS grew to achieve their power and influence without having ever to justify their often extravagant claims about products like the SAT seriously. It tries to understand how so many of these two organizations' views about the SAT became accepted both by psychometricians and by the public. Chapters 3 through 7 statistically document the errors in claims the board and ETS have made about the SAT. Chapter 3 shows that the use of the SAT by colleges does not help improve the academic quality of their selection decisions. Chapter 4 shows that the SAT does not help prospective applicants improve their selection of an academically appropriate college. Chapters 5 and 6 show the adverse impact of colleges' use of the SAT on blacks and low-income applicants. Chapter 7 shows that our findings about the SAT have been true since at least 1960. Chapter 8 presents our conclusions and what we think should be done next.

TWO

Overselling the SAT since 1926

The founders of the College Board sought initially to standardize college admissions testing to overcome problems caused by colleges having different entrance requirements and examinations. The board grew in influence partly as a result of the leadership, political acumen, and power of the people behind it. But the board benefited mainly from its ability over the years to promote testing to fit important national trends and events.

The board's work profited early on from the enthusiasm for intelligence testing after World War I. Somewhat later, the growth of the board and ETS drew from the transformation in American society toward organizational planning by experts and administration by scientific management. Still later, the further spread of testing was accelerated by the Cold War and the Civil Rights movement.

Public statements by the board and ETS illustrate how both organizations have promoted the SAT by shifting their ideological statements to suit the times. The shifts show the adaptability of testing to ideas about merit, equality, efficiency, and national defense. They also illustrate how organizations can avoid examining the assumptions under which they operate and the claims they make if they can fit their goals to widely felt anxieties.

The shifting justifications for the SAT also illustrate ETS's development into an organization that acted to protect and expand its own size and power. Given this kind of self-protective behavior, it is not surprising that ETS has often been unwilling to examine its claims about the SAT and the limits and contradictions in its assumptions.

In the Beginning

A few colleges that used entrance examinations undertook important reforms beginning in the 1870s.[1] Harvard and Yale, for example, began in the 1870s to administer entrance examinations at some off-campus locations, and other colleges followed suit. Colleges increasingly permitted students to take certain examinations up to a year ahead of time, and some colleges began to offer examinations in June before faculty departed for the summer.[2]

Even so, colleges that relied on entrance examinations faced serious problems. Many colleges at the turn of the century still prescribed their own examinations, examination dates, and standards. Applicants usually had to leave their secondary school for more than a week to travel to their chosen college to sit for its examinations. Since entrance examinations varied from college to college, secondary schools often also had to provide somewhat different instructional programs for students.

The men who eventually created the College Board, and who were associated with examination colleges, were acutely aware of these problems nearly ten years before they founded the College Board.[3] Nicholas Murray Butler at Columbia, for example, who wanted America's future leaders to have suitable moral and intellectual training, hoped to increase the numbers of students attending college. He sought to widen Columbia's admissions requirements to accommodate the diversity of students seeking admission, many of whom had not studied the classics. He also hoped to establish uniform entrance requirements to reduce the necessity of secondary schools offering different curricula for students wanting admission to different examining colleges.

In 1893 Butler asked the Columbia faculty to establish a board to administer uniform entrance examinations. But it was not until 1899 that Butler and Charles Eliot at Harvard, who had made a proposal similar to Butler's in 1877, helped persuade the Middle States Association at its annual meeting to establish a board of examiners to administer uniform college entrance examinations. With appointment of the chief examiners on 17 November 1900, the College Board came into existence.[4]

The work of the board started slowly. Its initial offerings were essay examinations in chemistry, English, French, German, Greek, history, Latin, mathematics, and physics. Spanish, botany, geography, and drawing were added the second year. Both college and secondary school representatives wrote the examinations, which readers then graded seated around tables in the Columbia University library. The examinations were first administered to 973 students during the week of 17 June 1901, at sixty-seven centers in the United States and two in Europe; 758 of the candidates were seeking admission to either Columbia College or Barnard College.[5]

Only thirty-five colleges initially agreed to honor the board examinations as substitutes for their own. The number of applicants taking the board's examinations grew steadily over the first decade, but schoolmasters, especially on the high school level, frequently criticized the board for trying to dictate what they should teach. Colleges in turn did not want to relinquish control of what their applicants were expected to know by abandoning their own entrance examinations.

The board's early examinations were based mainly on memorization rather than on the ability to reason independently or to compare and contrast ideas within a broad field of study. In 1916 the board began to administer new comprehensive examinations along with the regular essay examinations. The new comprehensive examinations lessened the rigidity of requirements, and were broader in scope, but they did not gain widespread acceptance. Nor did they significantly improve the understanding between secondary schools and colleges about the virtues of uniform examinations. Because the comprehensive examinations were less tied to required content than the board's earlier exams, teachers and students "hounded" the board's secretary, Thomas Fiske, to use his own word, about the nature of the examinations. Teachers complained that it would be impossible to prepare for the tests, that it would be difficult to grade test papers accurately, and that they placed an emphasis on superficial cleverness instead of thorough preparation.[6]

In 1916 the board was a long way from having its examinations substitute for those of the various colleges and was hardly in a position to promote uniform entrance requirements and academic standards nationally. Even after twenty-five years of the board's existence, most colleges still admitted students by their own examinations, by certificate, or by other means. The ten thousand students who took board tests in 1925, for example, comprised only 5 percent of the two hundred thousand freshman who entered the nation's colleges, and only ten colleges used the board examinations to admit all their students.[7]

It is doubtful whether the board at this early stage in its development could successfully have promoted its comprehensive examinations, no matter how it might have modified them. The board would have needed to create widespread agreement among colleges and secondary schools about proper subject-matter content and academic standards for college preparation. Fortunately, from the board's point of view, the need to do this in order to promote its examinations receded in importance. With the rise of intelligence and aptitude testing in the United States, the board could develop a new, and as we will see, far more effective strategy for promoting new kinds of tests and organizing the meritocracy.

The Rise of Intelligence Tests

College enrollments in the United States increased nearly five times as rapidly as the general population between 1890 and 1924. Many colleges began to feel strained to accommodate all who sought admission. At Columbia University, the first college to use intelligence tests for admissions, administrators and faculty in the first two decades of the twentieth century began to fret over who these students were.

By 1910 about half the children attending New York City public high schools were first- or second-generation immigrants, many of whom were eastern European Jews. They often enrolled in City College, which charged no tuition, or New York University, which had a convenient location. But many found Columbia attractive after a change in 1908 permitted part of Columbia's entrance requirements to be met by Regents' work in secondary school. The percentage of students admitted by Regents' credential, which never varied by more than a few points from 1903 to 1908, jumped from 19.3 percent in 1908 to 34.5 percent in 1909, and climbed steadily to 73.2 percent in 1915. By 1915 a substantial portion of Columbia's undergraduates were immigrant eastern European Jews from New York City.[8]

The dean of Columbia College feared that the influx of Jewish students might drive away Columbia's natural constituency of students from "homes of refinement."[9] Many of Columbia's faculty and administration considered the eastern European Jews socially backward, clannish, and hostile to upper-middle-class values. They were scorned as achieving far beyond their native intelligence. Many at Columbia therefore worried about the academic caliber of the student body, its increasing parochialism, and a social environment increasingly antipathetic to Columbia's traditional clientele.[10]

Columbia was not, of course, the only elite American college to face challenges to its customary upper-middle-class white, Anglo-

Saxon, Protestant clientele after the turn of the century. Harvard, Yale, Princeton, and other colleges confronted similar challenges from upwardly mobile Jews, Catholics, and, later, blacks and women. But Columbia faced these ''problems'' earlier than the others, largely due to its location in New York City.[11]

Nicholas Murray Butler, Columbia's president at this time, described the ''quality'' of the 1917–18 freshman class as ''depressing in the extreme.'' ''It is largely made up of foreign born and children of those but recently arrived in this country. The boys of old American stock, even many of them under draft age, have sought opportunity for military or other public service and have no time to go to college.''[12]

At about the time Butler made this assessment, Columbia was preparing for its first Student Army Training Corps class, to be admitted in the fall of 1918. Columbia was deluged with applicants, largely because of the War Department's low qualifying standards. A. L. Jones, Columbia's admissions director, noted there were ''hundreds of applicants . . . wholly unsuited by personality to become army officers.'' Of those who passed the personality test, he said, many ''did not possess the necessary mental alertness and power.''[13]

''To measure the mental alertness of the candidates,'' Jones went on, ''we required them to take the Thorndike Tests for Mental Alertness.''[14] With this, Columbia became the first college to use an intelligence test for admissions. The experiment was judged a success. Only three of the fifty Student Army Training Corps students advised to withdraw after their freshman year had attained a B on the Thorndike tests. The following year Columbia permitted regular students whose secondary school records, health, character, and promise were satisfactory in all respects to substitute the Thorndike tests for its entrance examinations.

Butler hoped Columbia's use of intelligence tests would limit the number of Jewish students without a formal policy of restriction, while at the same time increasing Columbia's attractiveness to desirable students from areas where the appeal of the certificate system had discouraged them from taking Columbia's entrance examinations. This appeared to happen. Columbia's registration outside New York State in 1919 jumped 73 percent over 1918, while the total increase was only 28 percent.

Furthermore, Butler hoped to enroll the kind of student who ''will be able to enter college and by virtue of his native intelligence as indicated by the psychological tests, more than hold his own.''[15]

This also appeared to happen. Only two of the roughly sixty freshmen admitted who had high scores on the Thorndike tests did unsatisfactory work at midterm of their freshman year in 1919. A Columbia study in 1920 found higher correlations between college grades and the Thorndike tests than between college grades and Columbia's old entrance examinations, the secondary school record, or the New York State Regents' Examination.[16]

Why did Columbia introduce the Thorndike intelligence tests? Partly, as noted, the Columbia faculty and administration were motivated to use intelligence tests to retain their traditional clientele in the face of demographic changes that threatened Columbia's social and academic position. But their belief that the tests would select a desirable clientele was not independent of other important ideas that characterized intellectual and popular thought in the early twentieth century.

For instance, some of the testing movement's most influential spokesmen were associated with the eugenic and Social Darwinist idea that inherited intelligence was a source of superior moral character and fitness.[17] Although their precise views and influence are subject to intense debate,[18] they often held that superior moral character and fitness associated with higher intelligence were particularly common in the Nordic stock that populated northern and western Europe. Low intelligence was linked to negligence, shiftlessness, and imprudence, which supposedly characterized the Alpine (mainly eastern European Slavs) and Mediterranean stocks. When Columbia (and later other universities) used intelligence tests for selection, they did so no doubt partly because some faculty and administrators shared these ideas.

Use of intelligence tests in college admissions was also influenced by the apparent success of the nation's first mass intelligence testing during World War I. Most psychologists thought the Army's Alpha test had proved successful in the identification of "officer material." After the war, many of the psychologists and educators who had used the Army Alpha test became missionaries for the use of intelligence tests in education. Their enthusiasm derived largely from the tests' ability to predict academic success in college.

At Lafayette College in Pennsylvania, for example, a 1920 study showed that 56 percent of all freshman withdrawals came from the lowest quartile of the intelligence distribution. The same year, Carnegie Tech found 40–45 percent of freshman withdrawals from the lowest intelligence quartile. And published studies by Brown, Columbia, Cornell, Goucher, Rutgers, Smith, and Yale between 1919 and 1921 showed most correlations of intelligence tests and academic grades to be in the 0.35–0.60 range.[19]

The administration of intelligence tests by colleges spread very rapidly. The United States commissioner of education estimated that by the end of the 1920 academic year over two hundred colleges and universities had given intelligence tests. But intelligence testing had yet to have a major impact on admissions. In the early 1920s, much of the testing was for institutional study, with little use in actual admissions decisions.

The Board Discovers Intelligence Testing

The College Board first expressed an interest in intelligence tests for college admissions in 1919, and the following year set up a commission "to investigate and report on general intelligence examinations and other new types of examinations offered in secondary school subjects."[20] By 1922 the full board adopted resolutions declaring that it looked "with favorable interest" on the use of "general intelligence examinations" and stood ready to give them as soon as practicable. However, it was not until April 1925 that the board appointed a commission to prepare and score the board's new test.

The commission was headed by Carl Campbell Brigham, whose views must have been known to the board. Brigham was a professor of psychology at Princeton who, just two years earlier, had published *A Study of American Intelligence,* a massive analysis of the Army's intelligence test data from World War I recruits. Closely associated with the eugenics movement, Brigham concluded that Catholics, Greeks, Hungarians, Italians, Jews, Negroes, Poles, Russians, and Turks had all inherited less average intelligence than the Nordic stocks of western Europe. "The really important steps," wrote Brigham, "are those looking toward the prevention of the continued propagation of defective strains in the present population."[21] Widespread intelligence testing could identify and reward persons whose genetic endowment gave them the greatest moral character and fitness for human betterment.

Brigham's commission selected the name Scholastic Aptitude Test (SAT) for its new test, even though it bore a strong resemblance to the Army Alpha test that Brigham had helped administer to World War I recruits. The new test was specifically labeled an "aptitude" test to distinguish it from the more traditional College Board achievement exams. The commission explicitly tied the SAT to intelligence when it said that "the term 'scholastic aptitude test' has reference to examinations of a type now in current use and variously called 'psychological tests,' 'intelligence tests,' 'mental ability tests,' 'mental alertness tests,' et cetera."[22]

Even though the commission linked the SAT to intelligence tests, it seemed to back away from strong claims about how well the SAT measured general intelligence: "Any claims that aptitude tests now in use really *measure* 'general intelligence' or 'general mental ability' may or may not be substantiated."[23] Actually, it is not even clear that the commission felt obligated to say what the SAT did measure, since it added later in the same publication "nor is it necessary to prove before adoption exactly what the tests measure."[24] It is also not clear that the board's leadership would have wanted to be specific about how well the SAT measured intelligence. The board's secretary, Thomas Fiske, told a supervisors' meeting in January 1926 that "colleges would like to know the result of it; but we certainly do not want to do anything which will enable a candidate to be terribly offended."[25]

However, by saying the SAT was like an intelligence test, the commission encouraged colleges to think of it the way they thought about intelligence tests. In effect, the commission encouraged colleges to transfer their enthusiasm for intelligence testing to the SAT. It did this by making many of the same arguments for the SAT that colleges made for intelligence tests.

For example, the commission argued that the SAT predicted success in higher education: "It has . . . been very generally established that scores in such tests usually indicate ability to do a high order of scholastic work."[26] Even though the commission acknowledged that the "general positive relationship . . . between aptitude tests and subsequent academic standing carries with it no certainty of prediction," it argued that "boards of Admission to colleges, now forced to estimate the future worth of candidates, need all the information which is available and pertinent to reach wise decisions."[27]

Additionally the commission argued that the SAT would help colleges identify applicants who could be expected to overcome poor preparation and succeed if admitted. The "tests are so constructed that they put as little premium as possible on specific training, and more emphasis on potential promise as distinguished from prior accomplishment." The commission added that "a candidate whose educational opportunities have been limited has a much better chance to show his real capacity in a test which is not a measure of specific preparation, and which is devised so that any person may find increasingly harder and harder problems in which to demonstrate his ability.''[28]

The SAT accommodated diversity within and between high schools the same way that intelligence tests did. High schools could offer many different courses without worrying about preparing students for entrance examinations in specific subject areas because the SAT did not depend on specific preparation. The board was thus relieved from the strain of devising uniform admissions tests for colleges that valued their differing entrance requirements and for high schools that prepared students in a multitude of ways. The SAT, like intelligence tests, identified future promise independent of past opportunity.

The commission's views about the benefits of the SAT in predicting success in college also dovetailed neatly with popular views about the virtues of intelligence tests for occupational selection. The highest occupational strata required high ability that only a few had, and intelligence tests could help identify these few to everyone's benefit. The basic principle was that no person should be employed in work that was either above or below his or her ability. Any other allocation of talent was wasteful of ability. Lewis Terman, developer of the Stanford-Binet intelligence test and perhaps the most influential psychologist of the period in testing, said it very clearly:

> Preliminary investigation indicates that an IQ below 70 rarely permits anything better than unskilled labor; that the range from 70 to 80 is preeminently that of semi-skilled labor, from 80 to 100 that of skilled or ordinary clerical labor, from 100 to 110 or 115 that of semiprofessional pursuits; and that above all these are the grades of intelligence which permit one to enter the professions or the larger fields of business. Intelligence tests can tell us whether a child's native brightness corresponds more accurately to the median of (1) the professional classes, (2) those in semiprofessional pursuits, (3) ordinary skilled workers, (4) semi-skilled or (5) unskilled laborers.[29]

As we will see, these ideas find expression in the board's and ETS's justifications for the SAT throughout this century. Their logic is ''to each according to his or her predicted success.'' Entitlement based on expected success is justified by both fairness and efficiency. The individual's entitlement to college is fair because the test that measures whether he or she will succeed is not biased by the quality of the person's past schooling. The individual's place in a college is efficient because any allocation other than by predicted success is a waste of potential talent. For example, to accept unqualified students who failed would not only produce unnecessary psychological damage but would also deny places to qualified students and cripple the efficiency of the educational and occupational system.

By shifting and aligning these ideas to suit the changing circumstances brought about by a rising college-bound population, World War II, the Cold War, and the Civil Rights movement, the board and ETS were able to promote the SAT in a widely appealing way. Few people took the trouble to examine the validity of their messages because they reinforced widely held beliefs. The board's and ETS's messages would be warmly received and rarely questioned by colleges in an age when norms of economic rationality and efficiency characterized America. But this did not happen immediately.

The Rise of the SAT

At first, colleges showed no great enthusiasm for the SAT. Candidate volume and use of the SAT by colleges did not increase substantially until after World War II. The board administered its first SAT to 8,040 candidates on 23 June 1926. During the next decade, the number of candidates grew slowly. In 1937, for example, only 9,272 candidates took the SAT. The depression probably contributed to the slow growth in SAT takers over the test's first decade. The board's regular examinations declined in candidate volume from over 22,000 in 1925 to fewer than 14,000 in 1935.

Another reason for the slow success of the SAT is that it took some time for colleges to assess the test. SAT questions were not available, and the test and its scoring were often misunderstood because psychometric terminology was still relatively unfamiliar to colleges. Furthermore, although colleges and secondary schools still had many complaints about the board's other examinations, many were at least comfortable with subject matter and essay exams. They were therefore reluctant to drop those examinations for one that was new and that they did not fully understand.

Possibly another reason for the slow initial growth of the SAT is that although the College Board and its psychologists may have embraced the virtues of intelligence testing, enthusiasm over the tests in the 1920s and 1930s was not universal. Walter Lippmann, for example, had written seven influential essays for the *New Republic* in 1922 in which he criticized intelligence tests as crude and uncertain measures. He argued that they were not as generally useful as performance-based measures of achievement would be.[30] Also, some progressive educators feared that all admissions tests shackled any effort to orient secondary education toward students and their developmental needs. The Progressive Education Association's Eight Year Study, begun in 1932, secured agreements with over three hundred colleges to waive formal admissions requirements for graduates of the study's schools. And evidence by 1940 suggested that graduates from these schools did well in college.[31] Finally, a number of colleges including Harvard had by 1932 adopted the practice of admitting students from the top percentiles of high school classes without examinations.[32]

The College Board gave its older exams and newer SAT in June throughout the 1930s. College applicants traditionally were notified about college acceptance in July. Beginning in April 1937, however, the board included the SAT in a special one-day battery of tests for scholarship applicants. Two thousand and five scholarship applicants took these tests, and the April series caught the attention of a number of colleges that wanted to use it for regular admissions and to notify their applicants before July. Beginning in April 1939, the board made this possible, and 10,318 persons took the exams in 1940.

With the entry of the United States into World War II, Harvard, Yale, and Princeton announced wartime plans for year-round instruction. So that freshmen could begin in June or early July, each of these institutions agreed to notify candidates of admission in early May. The plan called for most applicants to take the one-day April series of board tests, which included the SAT in the morning and several short achievement tests in the afternoon. Other colleges soon followed suit.

Shortly after Harvard, Yale, and Princeton announced this wartime plan, the board voted to drop its older and longer essay examinations, already announced for June 1942. This moved the SAT to center stage. The executive secretary said in his 1942 report that "the passing of the June essay-type examination after continuous use for 41 years marks the end of an era so far as the history of the Board is concerned."[33]

And so it did. By 1942 the board examinations for undergraduate admissions had evolved to much the same basic form that remains today. Testing required only a single day. The SAT was the primary test and could be supplemented with shorter achievement tests in specified subject areas. All the tests were standardized, with no professional readers required. Content, construction, and many other aspects of the tests and their administration have undergone changes since 1942, but the essential nature of the board's program for admissions testing was in place by 1942 and remains today.

Faced with more applicants than ever after World War II, colleges wanted to select promising freshman classes and reduce attrition. They adopted the College Board's admissions examinations partly because they were highly respected and partly because they were convenient. But the quality of services offered almost certainly is not the whole story. Nor did the board and ETS expand simply because of increasing demand for their services. As we shall see, the board and ETS played a critical role in promoting demand for their services. College admissions officers seldom have either the resources or technical skills to make independent judgments about the merits of different kinds of tests. They therefore rely on what testing agencies tell them. And what the board and especially ETS told colleges was a tale of social efficiency and fairness in which its tests played a central role.

Enter ETS

ETS came into legal existence on 19 December 1947, when New York State granted it a charter. Carved out of assets from the College Board, the Carnegie Foundation for the Advancement of Teaching, and the American Council on Education, ETS was a nonprofit, nonstock corporation without members, administered by a board of trustees. By advance agreement, the College Board gave up most of its activities, including laboratories and research staff, to ETS, and limited itself to problems connected with the transition from high school to college and admissions testing. The board continued to set the admissions test dates and fees, as well as to appoint examining committees and specify the general procedures to be followed in administration, scoring, and reporting test data. But actual test preparation, distribution, scoring, and reporting was to be done by ETS under contract with the board.[34]

ETS's first board of trustees included some of the most influential educational spokesmen of the time,[35] and its standing committees and staff included many of the leading experts in tests, measurement, and research.[36] The ability of ETS through the years to maintain a wide constituency has been an important organizational accomplishment. With representatives of higher education, secondary education, the political sector, and the private sector regularly sitting on its committees, ETS is able both to make and receive requests routinely and quickly from its most important constituencies—an important administrative resource.[37]

It is hardly surprising that when ETS spoke, it was listened to in high places. The people listening often had connections with ETS. This network to some degree foreclosed acceptance of contrary opinions. ETS has, of course, at times tolerated views differing from its own, and some of its own researchers have even published pieces mildly slapping its wrist.[38] But the network of ties between ETS, secondary schools, institutions of higher education, other testing agencies, and specialists in measurement, testing, and educational research is so extensive that most criticisms seem to come from outside the fraternity, and thus to lack legitimacy.

These ties strengthened ETS's ability to promote its vision of fairness and efficiency in a society where testing plays a prominent role. The men and women who have passed in and out of ETS, who have served on its many committees and commissions, and who have been consultants comprise a network of personal friendships. They tend to share special sources of information and influence with one another, as well as trust and inside help in professional opportunities. They also occupy influential positions in universities, professional organizations, and secondary schools. Because they often share a common desire to promote testing, they have provided ETS with a broadly grounded voice and leadership.

Over the years ETS has in effect become the central administration of an invisible college of scholars and policy makers that influences how the public thinks about testing issues. This is not to imply conspiracy or deviousness, but merely to describe one aspect of how the testing movement developed in the years following the founding of ETS.[39] Nor should this view imply that everyone within ETS always agrees with ETS's positions, which are often compromises. But the end result has been amazingly consistent. ETS has been able to shift its public message throughout the postwar period to offer solutions to important national concerns.

The 1940s: Talent Must Be Measured

The most forceful spokesman for ETS during its first two decades was Henry Chauncey, former dean of Harvard College and ETS's first president. His annual reports to the board of trustees strikingly reveal ETS's interpretation of the widely shared concerns of the times, which ETS used early on to promote its tests. Chauncey, for example, raised the specter of "a dearth of talent" in America. Citing with approval a report from the Conference on Human Resources and the Fields of Higher Learning, which he said raised "one of the most arresting warnings in the recent history of our country," Chauncey quoted the report's conclusions for the trustees:

> It seems . . . evident that our society is rapidly developing more specialized activities, vocations, and professions, each one presupposing that a supply of personnel will be available of very high innate ability and with special training. The aggregate of these demands, when seen over against the character of the population, seems to make it clear that we do not possess the requisite number of highly competent personnel to satisfy these demands. We are paralleling in the field of human resources the phenomenon which is becoming more and more characteristic of America, that our demands for material resources outstrip our supply.[40]

Chauncey blamed the educational system: "A tremendous amount of talent waste, which proper use of tests could materially alleviate, takes place in the course of the educational process itself."[41] One type of talent waste occurred whenever "an individual fails to receive the training he needs to enter upon an adult career appropriate to his ability—as when he elects an unsuitable course of training or, having elected a suitable course, terminates it prematurely."[42] A second type occurred when schools provided inadequate opportunities for superior students.

"We must discover in detail the quality and quantity of our human resources," Chauncey told the trustees. To do this, he urged a census of human abilities. "Such a census would bring to light the aptitude areas in which our talent shortages are most critical and would provide a basis for realistic planning on a nationwide scale, in peace or war."[43]

The information gathered through such a census would have value beyond its relation to a national emergency. Chauncey pointed out that the data could be used advantageously in economic and industrial planning. However, the most immediate application was in educational planning, where data on the abilities of the school-going population could be used for planning of educational programs. Chauncey said the data would be of greatest value in the educational and vocational guidance of students whose abilities could be compared with reliable national norms.[44]

For Chauncey, the rising demand for talent and the fear that the supply was faltering justified ETS's plan to assess the national talent reservoir. Discovery and effective utilization of human resources was the goal. Chauncey thus expressed the concerns that would drive educational reform later in the 1950s when anxieties over the Cold War became more important. In the 1940s his ideas were an attractive alternative to controversial Progressive notions of proper education.

During the 1940s progressive school leaders increasingly saw their task as fitting children to the needs of the social order, in the spirit of the early *Cardinal Principles* published by the National Education Association in 1918. A series of reports from the Educational Policies Commission, founded in 1936 and sponsored by the National Education Association, called for greater curricular differentiation and practical training. To be useful, English courses would have to teach the skills of polite conversation as well as poetry. Science and mathematics would need to be reoriented to vocational life, and history and government to good citizenship. Education would prepare for home and family life, for better physical health, use of leisure time, effective personality, and cultivation of adult interests.

In 1944, building on the progressive urge to broaden the curriculum to meet "the imperative needs of youth," the Educational Policies Commission published *Education for All American Youth,* which was widely regarded as the consensus statement of progressive education. It stressed less rigid schools, less recitation, and more preparation to live effectively as a worker, homemaker, citizen, and well-adjusted person. "There is no aristocracy of 'subjects.' . . . Mathematics and mechanics, art and agriculture, history and homemaking are all peers."[45]

By the late 1940s, there was little that schools were not supposed to accomplish. But by this time, progressivism—or "life adjustment," as it came to be known after the war—was drawing more criticism. Progressivism had always had critics, but until the late 1940s they were generally drowned in a sea of enthusiasm.

Critics charged, for example, that the schools had diverted their energies from basic intellectual disciplines and had become everything to everyone. They complained about poor mastery of fundamentals, about a lack of common standards, about poor discipline and absence of values for sustained hard work in progressive schools, and about the tendency of progressives to adopt the latest fad from child development experts. Life-adjustment education was "the latest gimmick among U.S. educators," *Time* declared sarcastically in 1949. The teacher's job was "not so much to teach history or algebra, as to prepare students to live happily ever after."[46]

Chauncey put ETS squarely against the jargon, slogans, and anti-intellectualism of life-adjustment education when he expressed concern for "talent waste" and a more effective utilization of human resources. In so doing he aligned ETS with a rising tide of popular criticism against progressivism that grew through the early 1950s. But Chauncey did more than just criticize; he offered a solution to the problems he saw.

The solution ETS offered to the waste of talent was, as one might expect, "the assistance which tests can furnish in reducing its toll." The "use of tests, and application of the kind of thinking which is encouraged by the use of tests, can increase the efficiency of the educational process itself."[47] Chauncey asserted that "tests can help prevent dropouts and malassignments." Tests that had been available for many years could reliably indicate a student's potential for advanced training. Thus, with the use of tests, students who were able, and yet likely to need assistance because of limited family resources or to need encouragement because of unfavorable expectation and motivation, could be singled out for special attention and help.[48] Tests, continued Chauncey, could also help reduce the manpower shortage:

> If it is possible to place as many as one-third of the engineers who will be graduated during the next five years into active productive status *one* year earlier than would ordinarily be the case, let alone *three,* there will be some 30,000 engineer man-years at the disposal of the nation, the equivalent of almost one thousand engineer lifetimes. The comparable savings which might be made in the fields of chemistry, physics, medicine and other specialities in critically short supply add up to a very substantial amount of manpower.[49]

Efficiency, reduction of talent waste, and assignment of individuals to career tracks based on predicted performance are the main values expressed by these statements. The rising criticism of the soft pedagogy of life adjustment and the growing concern over talent waste, followed by the beginnings of international Cold War competition and its rhetoric, made virtually any amount of testing done in the name of these causes seem reasonable. And ETS responded with a vision of massive testing to help order the American meritocracy.

With tests, ETS said, by the time a student had reached eighth or ninth grade, schools could advise against clearly unsuitable programs of study and help direct students toward the general vocational areas likely to utilize their strongest capabilities. An extensive battery of aptitude tests should be administered at the end of the eighth or ninth grade, with retesting every year or two after that. The tests would help to define with increasing precision desirable vocational goals for students whose interests and abilities pointed toward termination of formal education upon completion of high school. In the case of high-level talent, the successive retesting would also provide progressively more accurate identification of the work for which each individual was particularly suited.[50]

Chauncey had little patience with critics who failed to see the societywide efficiency that would result from the widespread testing he proposed. Calling his critics the "new menace," he said:

> To many the prospect of measuring in quantitative terms what have previously been considered intangible qualities is frightening, if not downright objectionable. Yet I venture to predict that we will become accustomed to it and will find ourselves better off for it. In no instance that I can think of has the advance of accurate knowledge been detrimental to society, unless it was misused.[51]

Nor did Chauncey seem to have much sympathy for the way people would come to think and feel about themselves as their test results were increasingly used to guide them into their most productive educational slots. There is no problem when tests identify a talented person in high school who is then encouraged to attend college. The problem arises when tests identify a marginally talented person who refuses to accept that he or she lacks ability because a test score predicts low success. As Chauncey stated the problem of individual adjustment:

> With respect to knowledge of individuals, the possibilities of constructive use are far greater than those of misuse. Educational and vocational guidance, personal and social adjustment most certainly should be greatly benefited. Life may have less mystery, but it will also have less disillusionment and disappointment. Hope will not be a lost source of strength, but it will be kept within reasonable bounds.[52]

Chauncey's views reflect those of a leader at the top looking down with a clear idea of what is best for others. Keeping low scorers' hopes within "reasonable bounds" seems profoundly pessimistic about the capacities of many students, and antidemocratic in not giving them chances to get ahead. Yet no one can be against "reasonable" bounds for anything, including hope. The question is, what is "reasonable"? Is it reasonable to tell a high school senior in the bottom quartile of his or her high school SAT distribution that he or she is unlikely to get into a "good" college? Is this true for the bottom half? Although using tests to keep hope within reasonable bounds may from one point of view be pessimistic as regards some students' abilities, and antidemocratic in not giving them an equal chance to excel, from another point of view, it seems neither humane nor realistic to encourage aspirations that cannot be achieved.

But Chauncey's views do not grapple with these complexities. Like many reformers in education before him, Chauncey embraced his ideas with great optimism. Schools would achieve new efficiency in the use of human resources by adopting the methods of the new science of psychometrics. This efficiency would serve American democracy because testing and placement would prepare people equally well for work that matched their capability. Anything less might mismatch abilities with educational and occupational demands and result in failed preparation as well as talent waste.

The 1950s: Our Own Secret Weapon

During the years following the Korean War, as competition with communist countries shifted away from fighting, ETS became increasingly aroused by the challenge of Russia's educational system. Again Chauncey broadcasted ETS's view. In his 1957–58 report to the ETS trustees, he proclaimed: "There is in Russia a power drive with one admitted goal: to equal or surpass the United States, in every way. The Russians see education as basic to building up their scientific, military and industrial strength to surpass us, and it may well be that the Russian commitment to education will prove to be their most important 'secret weapon.'"[53]

But the United States could win this battle. It was necessary first to recognize that in today's world education must be a national concern, and then to make a strenuous effort to carry all students further in academic subjects. This meant schools had an additional responsibility to offer rigorous courses and to place students in them properly. "If scholastically able students are ducking the academic courses and gliding through those designed for students of different kinds of abilities and interests, our system has serious flaws," Chauncey said. "If students who could handle the rigorous academic courses never even try because they are unaware of their ability, they and our nation will suffer a real loss."[54]

Of course, Chauncey had a solution to discovering ability in students who might be unaware they had it. "Testing and guidance, as we know it, does not exist in Russia. I think that American testing and guidance techniques could be our own 'secret weapon' in education, if we develop and use them properly. They can help us make our educational system fit the needs of all our youth better than the Russian system meets the needs of Soviet youth.''[55] Chauncey then went on to propose more research on just what should be taught in each subject, improvements in testing and guidance programs, better large-scale testing programs, and resource materials to help classroom teachers encourage students to use their test results to examine their own abilities and interests.

When Chauncey expressed these enthusiasms for testing and guidance, his good friend James Conant, former president of Harvard and first chairman of ETS's board of trustees, was beginning his research and fieldwork for *The American High School Today,* which in a few years would become the most influential education book of the period. Conant and Chauncey had similar views about guidance and ability grouping. In November 1957, only two months into his fieldwork, Conant wrote a long ''First Thoughts'' memo offering a strong defense of grouping on the basis of aptitude.[56] *The American High School Today* would later stress ability grouping and guidance on the basis of aptitude as fundamental to high school reform.

Chauncey's and Conant's enthusiasm about the use of tests for ability grouping and guidance represents testing ideology and salesmanship at its strongest. Both men's public rhetoric stressed the predictive value of tests for placement. They justified placement of each according to predicted success by reason of efficiency and fairness. But their public cheerleading never addressed the limits of the predictive usefulness of tests that were known at the time. Furthermore, both men knew of these limits.

In a letter written in the spring of 1958, Conant asked Chauncey whether tests given in the eighth grade could certify that 80 percent of the top scorers would rank at the top of their high school class four years later. Chauncey replied that he could ''come close to meeting your standard of 8 out of 10, though that is a very rigorous standard.'' He told Conant: ''If you will reduce the standard to something like this: that 8 out of 10 of those in the top 15% on the basis of test score should be in the top 25% [of their high school graduating class], then I think tests can satisfy your purposes.''[57]

Chauncey must have known, however, that to make eighth grade tests this accurate required some highly questionable assumptions. ''We have to make a number of corrections to get an estimate of the correlation we're looking for,'' he wrote Conant, and then made corrections for unreliability of grading, industriousness, carefulness, accuracy, good health, and range of ability that increased the predictive relationship of the tests with later grades by 70 percent.[58]

In making these corrections, Chauncey completely disregarded a careful analysis given him just one day earlier by his associate Martin R. Katz, which showed that the tests had limited statistical usefulness. Katz suggested that Chauncey tell Conant: "I am afraid that, if you want to evaluate a school's guidance program in terms of the 4-year program choices of pupils who score high on 8th grade aptitude testing, we have to give you the 'wrong' answer."[59] Katz' advice is not, however, the kind of advice that furthers the growth of testing. And ETS was a growing business. Candidate volume on the SAT, just one of ETS's tests, increased tenfold from 1951 to 1961. Only 81,200 SATs were taken during 1951–52. Ten years later the number had increased to 802,500.[60]

By the mid 1950s, ETS had outgrown its Princeton headquarters and began moving its main operations to the new 400-acre Rosedale campus, which would eventually be complete with tennis courts, swimming pool, sauna, jogging trails, and picnic areas. As William Turnbull summarized it in his review of the history of ETS: "If the story of ETS in its first 25 years were reduced to a single word, that word would have to be *growth*."[61]

The 1960s: Opportunity for All . . . and Growth for ETS

The late 1960s marked the beginning of new efforts to increase opportunities for minorities in America. The Civil Rights Act of 1964 charged the U.S. commissioner of education to conduct a nationwide survey of educational opportunity. That survey resulted in publication of *Equality of Educational Opportunity* by James Coleman and his colleagues, which described the test results of school children from differing ethnic and economic groups. Shortly after the Civil Rights Act of 1964 came the Elementary and Secondary Education Act of 1965, which provided federal funds for educating the poor, but also required test results to measure success.

ETS again seized the opportunity to promote its tests. This time, ETS viewed its tests as a way to give all students an equal chance to demonstrate merit, even though their backgrounds differed. "We are dedicated to the principle of equal opportunity and we believe that justice should be done each individual according to his merit," Henry Chauncey declared in his 1961 report to the trustees, three years before the Civil Rights Act. "Unlike the personal interview, the classroom test, or the teacher's subjective evaluation, the objective test is a common touchstone. . . . It gives all students who take it the same chance, asks them to run the same race—even though they have had different economic backgrounds, different educational, cultural, and social opportunities."[62]

This view clearly portrays ETS's approach to equality of opportunity. Its commitment is to the principle of "to each according to his or her merit," with objective tests the measure of that merit.

In the 1960s ETS promoted the SAT somewhat differently from its achievement tests in relation to opportunity. By encouraging colleges to think of the SAT as an aptitude test that predicted success in college and saw through the veneer of poor preparation and social and economic circumstances, ETS promoted the SAT as an instrument relatively unblemished by the social ills of differing opportunity. Because the SAT is a uniform, color-blind test for predicting success, minority students and students from poor families would stand on an equal footing with white middle-class students.

In the case of its achievement tests, ETS acknowledged that impoverished backgrounds and different educational, cultural, and social opportunities will cause some groups to have lower average scores than others. But the achievement tests are merely the messengers that bring the bad news. Achievement tests cannot be expected to overcome the ills of society, though they can be a thermometer that measures them. ETS was therefore able to promote its achievement tests as useful tools for the standardized measurement of achievement as the first step in the diagnosis of unequal opportunities. When national concern about equal opportunity grew in the 1960s, ETS was ready with its achievement tests to help diagnose it.

These arguments skillfully blended promotion of ETS's tests and missions with the rising social concerns of the 1960s, which would last well into the 1970s. ETS therefore achieved the same outcome—use of its test products—with issues of opportunity in the 1960s as it had done with national security in the 1950s. ETS could argue that its achievement tests could help diagnose the evils of poor opportunity, which it condemned, and that its aptitude tests could efficiently allocate by merit, which was desirable. All of this was to the greater social good, since the efficiency and allocative fairness resulting from the use of tests would benefit the nation.

Government policy also aided ETS's ability to promote its tests. ETS grew in part because federal and state hiring, promotion, and firing policies created a demand for testing services. Government-mandated testing in education for selection, placement, diagnosis and remediation, guidance, program evaluation, and, more recently, certification of competence is another source of growing demand for tests. ETS's operating expenses grew 1,100 percent in constant dollars from 1948 through 1972. Its staff grew by 555 percent during this same period, and its revenues increased 25-fold.[63]

To the Present: Will the Synthesis Remain?

Looking back at the events of the past six or seven decades in admissions testing, one sees a gradual fusing of meritocratic ideology and aptitude testing. Merit reigns supreme as the central principle of efficient and fair selection, and the SAT has become the nation's main admissions exam. There are many qualifications and exceptions, of course. Some of the nation's colleges do not require any aptitude test score for admissions, and many colleges admit virtually anyone who applies. But none of this changes the fact that when colleges do try to be selective, they typically justify their selectivity by appeal to meritocratic ideology. This ideology is reinforced with some kind of aptitude test, which is more often than not the SAT. The SAT has become the symbol of meritocratic college admissions.[64] It also symbolizes how selective colleges are, or how "good" their freshman classes are.[65]

Meritocratic selection has wide appeal. Efforts by motivated individuals to get into our nation's most selective colleges and universities, and later into the most prestigious professional schools and jobs, are a crucial ingredient to economic growth. The amount of room at the top of American universities is fixed, since the best ones do not increase their enrollments to accommodate increased demand, but raise standards to become even more selective. Productivity may be increased when the top universities enroll the top talent and allocate it later to the top of the occupational scale. Competition created by the rewards of gaining one of these scarce positions may also be an incentive to acquire useful skills and knowledge even if one fails to get into as selective a college as one would like.

There is little serious challenge to the principle of meritocratic selection in the United States at present. Even advocates of affirmative action, who often argue that meritocratic selection should in some instances be set aside, rarely argue against meritocratic selection as a general principle. However, the past ten to fifteen years have seen a growing number of challenges to the idea that the goals of enhancing efficiency, productivity, and social welfare are well served by aptitude testing.

In employment testing, for example, the aftermath of Title VII of the 1964 Civil Rights Act brought massive confusion over employee selection procedures among the Equal Employment Opportunity Commission, the Department of Labor's Office of Federal Contract Compliance and Programs, the Civil Service Commission, and the Department of Justice. Judicial standards were also unclear. In educational testing, policy and standards were unclear for the testing and placement of handicapped children in special classes, for grade promotion and graduation, and for a host of other purposes.[66]

In college admissions testing, the attack mostly took the form of efforts to discredit the SAT. The most widely publicized report, written by Allan Nairn and associates in 1980 and sponsored by Ralph Nader, was a broadside attack entitled *The Reign of ETS: The Corporation That Makes Up Minds,* which charged that the SAT was a respectable fraud.[67] Both ETS and the College Board believed that a group of extreme critics had in effect declared war on testing and were assaulting the admissions process that the board and its members had developed. The Nairn/Nader report was followed by a number of criticisms of ETS and the SAT in academic journals and a spate of anti-testing articles in national magazines and newspapers. The criticisms of the SAT in the 1970s and early 1980s were so widespread that George Hanford, president of the College Board, could write that "these attacks present a serious challenge to both secondary schools and colleges . . . they directly threaten existing policies and practices of admissions officers and their institutions."[68]

Criticism of ETS and the SAT has not abated through the mid 1980s. In 1985 a group of educators, students, and civil rights leaders, many of them critics of standardized admissions testing and the testing industry during the 1970s, formed the National Center for Fair and Open Testing (FairTest) to monitor testing practices and defend the rights of "the 10 million Americans who take standardized exams each year."[69] FairTest, along with several public interest research groups and civil rights advocates, has actively backed legislation and litigation to safeguard the SAT and other tests against racial bias and to extend public disclosure of test information.[70]

The important question raised by criticism of the SAT, however, is the fate of the synthesis that fuses the desirable aspects of meritocracy with the practice of measuring merit with the SAT. As we have seen, the blending of meritocratic ideology—justified by appeals to efficiency, fairness, national security, economic growth, and equal opportunity—with aptitude and achievement testing has deepened over the past three-quarters of a century, even as the conditions that nurtured it have changed.

Many things could happen over the next decade to hold this synthesis together or cause it to fall apart. Perhaps the most important unknown is what people come to believe the SAT does and does not accomplish for American education and contemporary society. If a large number of Americans become dissatisfied with the SAT, it will almost certainly fall into disrepute.

What people believe the SAT does and does not accomplish depends partly on how it is promoted. But if the use of a test is having clearly undesirable outcomes, and a large number of people recognize this, the test will be difficult to promote, no matter how clever its promoters are. What people believe about a test depends ultimately on a continued deep-seated faith in the merit principle, and on evidence about the outcomes of its use. It is to the effects of using the SAT that we turn in the following chapters. We will see that they are not what the College Board and ETS say they are.

THREE

The SAT Does Not Help Colleges Make Better Selection Decisions

Many people believe what the College Board and ETS have claimed for decades about the SAT: that the test helps colleges make better academic selection decisions. This chapter shows that this view of the SAT is not supported by the facts. If the board and ETS are to continue encouraging colleges to require applicants to submit SAT scores, they must justify this with reasons other than the benefits to colleges of improving the accuracy of their admissions decisions or the academic performance and graduation rates of those they admit.

How ETS Assesses the SAT

The College Board says that SAT scores are "intended to supplement the secondary school record and other relevant information about the student in assessing competence for college work."[1] Why use SAT scores as a supplement to assess competence for college work? Because, ETS says, although "students' previous grades are the most important indicators . . . the addition of scores on good tests adds significantly to the prediction of success."[2]

The predictive effectiveness of the SAT has been the object of assessment by the College Board, ETS, and others almost from the outset of the test. Hunter Breland, a senior researcher at ETS, says the preferred method of assessing the SAT's validity is "based on the past performance of students in specific institutions. Usually, high school GPA (or rank) is combined with a test score (or scores) to predict college freshman GPA. A regression equation is developed from data on past students and is used to predict performance for applicants." Then "applicants who would be predicted to exceed a certain level of performance (FGPA) are eligible for admission."[3] Breland calls this the predicted performance model.

Breland's study reviews five separate admissions models and concludes that although colleges differ in their entering students' abilities, in their grading standards, and in minimum requirements for remaining in good standing, "the predicted performance model is the only one of the five examined that necessarily recognizes these institutional differences. And, it is the only model that customizes the weighting of various component indexes for specific institutions. As a result, student retention would be maximized through the use of the predicted performance model." Breland argues that "of the five admissions models examined, the predicted performance model is clearly preferable."[4]

ETS and the board do not just rely on scholarly articles and technical manuals to encourage colleges to base applicant eligibility on predicted performance. The College Board's Validity Study Service, run by ETS, gives colleges very practical advice on how to do it. The Validity Study Service tells colleges how to choose a criterion (usually freshman grades), how to choose predictors (usually high school record and SAT scores), and then computes equations for colleges that maximize linear prediction of freshman grades. The Validity Study Service even gives colleges computational aids to simplify calculation of their applicants' predicted grades.[5]

A surprising number of American colleges follow ETS's and the board's advice. The 1979 College Board/American Association of Collegiate Registrars and Admissions Officers survey found that 11 percent of the public and 3 percent of the private four-year colleges surveyed compute a predicted freshman GPA and use a minimum predicted grade cutoff for admissions. Another 14 percent of the public and 20 percent of the private colleges use forecasted grades as one factor in their admissions decisions. Still another 20 percent of public and 15 percent of private colleges forecast grades, but only for guidance.[6]

Nonetheless, if one talks to admission officers at highly selective or even moderately selective colleges, one finds that in addition to the high school record and any use of test scores, they use information from campus interviews, teacher recommendations, personal statements, essays, patterns of courses taken, special academic and nonacademic talents, race, and residence, among other things. How they use this information depends on the college.[7] At many institutions, a decision to admit or reject is simply the judgment of individual admissions officers or committees based on evaluations of information in applicants' folders. One must also remember that many American colleges are not selective and admit the great majority of applicants. Consequently, admissions officers may spend much time encouraging accepted applicants to attend or debating cases that are borderline or contain inconsistent information.

For purposes of assessing the predictive power of the SAT, it does not matter that American colleges have a plethora of admissions procedures. The fact that few colleges base admissions decisions on SAT scores alone or that colleges are concerned with other admissions criteria does not mean that the incremental effect of SAT scores on predictions of freshman grades cannot be determined. One can examine SAT scores and high school records in isolation from other admissions factors for the same reason the board does—to develop a sense of the SAT's unique contribution to admissions.

The College Board occasionally notes that not all colleges use SAT scores to predict their applicants' success. The board is, in effect, acknowledging that some colleges do not use SAT scores to maximize predictions of academic success. The number of these colleges is irrelevant, however. What we want to know is how much benefit colleges *could* get from using the SAT. Whether they actually do so is irrelevant. Since decisions based on predicted academic performance maximize the academic benefits colleges can get from the SAT, it is quite reasonable to limit our discussion to admissions based on predicted performance.[8] Thus, colleges that do not admit according to predicted performance are probably making even less efficient academic admissions from their applicants' high school records and SAT scores than we estimate below. They may be maximizing other institutional goals, but these do not affect assessment of the maximum academic benefits they could derive from using the SAT.

The Evidence for Prediction

Since 1964 the College Board Validity Study Service has encouraged colleges to conduct studies of the SAT's predictive effectiveness. Half the four-year public colleges and universities and about 40 percent of the private four-year colleges and universities who replied to a 1985 survey by the American Association of Collegiate Registrars and Admissions Officers (AACRAO) said they conducted or commissioned predictive validity studies.[9] The College Board periodically releases summary results from these studies, which now number over three thousand.[10] In addition, other organizations surveyed American high school students in 1960, 1972, 1980, and 1982 to assess the state of American education in general, and SAT scores are on these data files or can be added to them. Since each of these surveys followed up students after high school, the predictive effectiveness of the SAT for college and later life outcomes can be measured.[11]

The results of these studies show overwhelmingly that addition of the SAT to the high school record improves prediction of freshman grades. Precise estimates of the improvement due to the SAT are difficult to make, since range restriction, sampling error, differences in measuring high school and college records, and differences in colleges' standards, student populations, and curricula can all produce variations in the estimated increment. The safest generalization is that when predicting average freshman grades, the SAT and high school record together increase the multiple correlation typically 0.06–0.08 over the high school record alone.[12] Increments in the multiple correlation within this range can appear very dramatic, as we now show by looking at results from the National Longitudinal Study (NLS) of the high school class of 1972.

The NLS surveyed 19,144 seniors from 1,069 high schools in the spring of 1972, whom it followed up with mailed questionnaires, telephone interviews, and personal interviews in the fall of 1973 after one year of college. It was able to find SAT scores for 5,873 respondents, and our analyses are based on these students.

The NLS survey gives an increment of 0.063 in the multiple correlation between freshman grade point average predicted from the SAT and high school record together over the high school record alone. Table 3.1 presents in more detail what the NLS survey shows

Table 3.1 College Predictions for Students Whose SAT Scores and High School Class Ranks Differ

High School Class Rank (percentile)	SAT Total Score					
	500	700	900	1100	1300	1500
	1. Predicted FGPA					
10	1.711	1.908	2.104	2.300	2.497	2.693
30	1.903	2.099	2.296	2.492	2.689	2.885
50	2.095	2.291	2.488	2.684	2.880	3.077
70	2.287	2.483	2.679	2.876	3.072	3.269
90	2.479	2.675	2.871	3.068	3.264	3.460
	2. Predicted Freshman Percentile Rank in Class					
10	5	8	14	21	31	42
30	8	13	21	31	42	53
50	13	21	30	41	53	65
70	21	30	41	53	64	75
90	30	41	52	64	75	83

(*continued*)

Table 3.1 *(continued)*

High School Class Rank (percentile)	SAT Total Score 500	700	900	1100	1300	1500
	3. Probability of Average Grades Less Than B					
10	.99	.97	.94	.88	.81	.70
30	.97	.94	.89	.81	.70	.58
50	.94	.89	.81	.71	.58	.45
70	.89	.81	.71	.58	.45	.32
90	.82	.71	.59	.45	.33	.21
	4. Probability of Average Grades Less Than C					
10	.69	.56	.43	.30	.20	.12
30	.57	.43	.31	.20	.12	.06
50	.44	.31	.20	.12	.07	.03
70	.31	.20	.12	.07	.03	.01
90	.21	.12	.07	.03	.02	.01
	5. Probability of Graduation					
10	.42	.48	.53	.58	.64	.69
30	.49	.54	.59	.65	.70	.75
50	.55	.60	.66	.71	.76	.81
70	.61	.67	.72	.77	.82	.88
90	.68	.73	.78	.84	.89	.94

Notes: Same sample as tables 3.2 and 3.3. All values in table 3.1 were derived from equations 7 in tables 3.2 and 3.3 assuming a college of average selectivity (1041.584).

Panel 1. The predicted value of the dependent variable in equation 7 in table 3.2 with college selectivity fixed at 1041.584. We used the SAT and class rank values in the table for these computations. As a check, we computed the actual mean of the predicted FGPA distribution for all those cases actually in each combination of rank and SAT class interval. These observed means differed from the predicted means, but not by enough to make any substantive difference where there were a reasonable number of cases.

Panel 2. Freshman grade point averages have a mean of 2.829 and standard deviation of 0.660. Panel 2 is the area in the FGPA distribution to the left of the predicted FGPA in panel 1.

Panel 3. Area to the left of 3.0 in the distribution of freshman grades having a mean equal to panel 1 and a standard deviation equal to the standard error of estimate of 0.58159 from equation 7 in table 3.2.

Panel 4. Area to the left of 2.0 in the same distribution as panel 3.

Panel 5. The predicted value of the dependent variable from equation 7 in table 3.3 with college selectivity fixed at 1041.584.

about the predictive effectiveness of the SAT, demonstrating that students with the same high school rank whose SAT scores differ have varied prospects of college success. A student with a higher SAT score has a higher predicted freshman grade point average, freshman percentile rank in class, and probability of graduation. That student also has lower chances of earning grades below a B or a C.

These results appear initially to be dramatic evidence for the usefulness of the SAT. They seem to affirm what the College Board and ETS have claimed for many years about the test and to refute critics who charge that the SAT adds little to prediction of college success over the high school record alone.[13]

The predictions in table 3.1 are derived from the regression equations in tables 3.2 and 3.3. The equations in table 3.2 that predict freshman grade point average allow for the fact that grading standards vary among colleges differing in selectivity, so that a student with a given SAT score and high school rank who attends a very selective college will have lower average freshman grades than if he or she attended a less selective college. Selectivity is based on the average freshman SAT score reported by the college to the American Council on Education. Similarly, equations predicting bachelor's degree attainment in table 3.3 allow for the fact that the chances of obtaining a bachelor's degree from colleges differing in selectivity are not equivalent for students with a given SAT score and high school rank.[14] The main finding from these tables is that the SAT makes an independent contribution predicting both freshman grade point average and bachelor's degree completion, as can be seen from the significant SAT coefficients in equation 7 for each outcome and comparison of R^2 for equations 5 and 7 for each outcome.

How Accurate Are Predictions of Freshman Grade Point Averages?

The College Board and ETS use information like this to illustrate the predictive usefulness of the SAT in admissions. Even though these results seem impressive, great care should be exercised when using them. Colleges derive predictions of applicants' performance from regression equations based on the performance of students who actually enrolled and completed one year, since colleges cannot give freshman grades and bachelor's degrees to rejected applicants. However, there are substantial risks in using information from students who currently attend a college to make predictions for future pools of that college's applicants.

Table 3.2 Regressions of Freshman Grade Point Average on High School Rank, SAT Scores, College Selectivity, and Socioeconomic Background for 2,470 NLS Respondents

	Independent Variables									
Equation	High School Rank	SAT	College Selectivity	Father's Education	Mother's Education	Father's Occupation	Family Income[a]	Constant	$\bar{R}^2$	SEE
1. B	.012714*							1.875	.168	.60220
beta	.411									
2. B		.0012622*						1.5636	.142	.612
beta		.378								
3. B	.0092375*	.0007865*						1.347	.211	.58663
beta	.298	.235								
4. B			.00050035*					2.308	.009	.65734
beta			.096							
5. B	.0129504*		−.00013583					1.999	.168	.60209
beta	.418		−.026							
6. B		.00143391*	−.000561016*					1.976	.151	.60843
beta		.429	−.108							
7. B	.0095901*	.000981767*	−.00069745*					1.851	.224	.58159
beta	.310	.294	−.134							
8. B				.002795	.015677*	.0003231	.00706659*	2.4701	.010	.657
beta				.014	.061	.011	.050			
9. B			.00040378*	.0011568	.014715*	.00021055	.00618775	2.1029	.015	.655
beta			.078	.006	.057	.007	.044			
10. B	.0131696*		−.00027316*	.0020974	.012628*	.00061096	.0093530*	1.7684	.180	.598
beta	.425		−.053	.011	.049	.021	.066			
11. B		.0014288*	−.00056104	−.004814	.007646	.00010343	.00043688	1.9358	.150	.609
beta		.427	−.108	−.025	.030	.004	.003			
12. B	.0098826*	.00092640*	−.00072976*	−.0020086	.0085657	.0004416	.0048344	1.7436	.226	.581
beta	.319	.277	−.140	−.010	.033	.015	.034			

Notes: The National Longitudinal Study (NLS) of the high school class of 1972 surveyed 19,144 high school seniors during the 1971–72 school year from a target population of 1,200 public and private high schools in the United States. NLS administered an extensive questionnaire to students from

April through June of 1972, and also obtained students' SAT scores and information about their high school records from school administrators. The 19,144 seniors who participated in the base year were followed up during the fall of 1973, at which time NLS asked them questions about where they had applied to college, whether they were accepted, and their freshman grades at the college they attended. This sample consists of 2,470 NLS males and females who attended a four-year college in October 1972 for which we had college selectivity information, whose high schools reported SAT scores and class rank, and for whom we had data on FGPA and whether the respondent graduated from college. We constructed a missing data dummy for each socioeconomic background variable and then recoded missing data on each background variable to the sample mean. None of the dummies had a significant coefficient when added to the equations in the table. Variables are coded as follows for all our NLS analyses:

SAT is the sum of scores on the verbal and math sections of the Scholastic Aptitude Test. Students' SAT scores were reported by school administrators during the base-year survey (April–June 1972).

High school rank is the student's senior class standing expressed in percentiles. Our preliminary investigations of the data showed the NLS inadvertently coded many cases to missing data when, in fact, data were available to compute a high school rank. We used the following formula for percentile class rank:

HSR = (1 − [rank in class/class size]) * 100

College selectivity is the average SAT score (SATV and SATM summed) of the 1971 entering freshman class at the student's first-choice college. The college selectivity data were obtained from the American Council on Education's Institutional Characteristics File for 1971–72 and added to the NLS data file. We used the 1971–72 ACE file as this is the information that would have been available to high school seniors applying for fall 1972 college entrance.

B.A. degree is coded 1 if students reported (on the fourth NLS follow-up) that they had at least earned a bachelor's degree by October 1979; 0 otherwise.

Freshman GPA is the student's estimated grades in college coursework since leaving high school through October 1973. We coded the seven grade categories as follows: Mostly A (3.75–4.0) = 3.87; about half A and half B (3.25–3.74) = 3.5; mostly B (2.75–3.24) = 3.0; about half B and half C (2.25–2.74) = 2.5; mostly C (1.75–2.24) = 2.0; about half C and half D (1.25–1.74) = 1.5; mostly D or below (less than 1.25) = 1.0.

Father's occupation is the student's report on the first follow-up of father's occupation. NLS converted students' written responses to 1970 detailed census codes and then to Duncan scores. We employed the Duncan score coding.

Father's and mother's education is the student's report (on the first follow-up) in nine categories of his or her parents' education. Responses range from grade school only to Ph.D., M.D., or equivalent. We coded these categories into years from rough estimates of category means from the 1970 Census.

Family income is the student's estimate of his or her family's before tax income from all sources. Respondents could select one of ten categories with ranges of $0–2999, 3,000–5,999, 6,000–7499, 7,500–8,999, 9,000–10,499, 10,500–11,999, 12,000–13,499, 13,500–14,999, 15,000–18,000, or 18,000+. We coded each category to the midpoint except for the final category, which we coded 20,000.

[a]Coefficients multiplied by 1,000.

*Designates coefficients more than twice their standard error.

Table 3.3 Regressions of Bachelor's Degree Attainment on High School Rank, SAT Scores, College Selectivity, and Socioeconomic Background for 2,470 NLS Respondents

	Independent Variables									
Equation	High School Rank	SAT	College Selectivity	Father's Education	Mother's Education	Father's Occupation	Family Income[a]	Constant	$\bar{R}^2$	SEE
1. B	.0046421*							.414	.054	.4141
beta	.232									
2. B		.00048250*						.27852	.050	.415
beta		.224								
3. B	.00324909*	.000315165*						.202	.070	.4106
beta	.163	.146								
4. B			.00053226*					.208	.025	.4204
beta			.159							
5. B	.0040621*		.0003327125*					.111	.062	.4122
beta	.203		.099							
6. B		.000413202*	.000226413*					.112	.053	.4143
beta		.192	.068							
7. B	.00315734*	.00026434*	.000181494*					.0712	.072	.4101
beta	.158	.123	.054							
8. B				.0069945	.0078448	−.0003265	.0079380*	.4698	.019	.422
beta				.056	.047	−.017	.087			
9. B			.00045430*	.00515171	.0067622	−.00045306	.0069492*	.056713	.036	.418
beta			.136	.041	.041	−.024	.076			
10. B	.00421375*		.00023771*	.0054527	.0060945	−.00032494	.00796195*	−.05032	.076	.409
beta	.211		.071	.043	.037	−.017	.087			
11. B		.00037388*	.00020184*	.0035893	.00491245	−.00048109	.0054444*	.012990	.058	.413
beta		.173	.060	.029	.029	−.026	.060			
12. B	.0035226*	.00019479*	.000141697	.004589	.0052403	−.0003606	.007011812*	−.05554	.081	.408
beta	.176	.090	.042	.037	.031	−.019	.077			

Notes: Same sample as table 3.2. See notes to table 3.2 for variable descriptions. None of the missing data dummies were significant.
[a]Coefficients multiplied by 1,000.
*Designates coefficients more than twice their standard error.

The problems are caused by the selection of the sample used in making the predictions. To predict freshman grade point averages (FGPA) from SAT scores and high school rank (HSR), colleges use this unstandardized regression equation:[15]

$$\text{FGPA} = b_1\text{SAT} + b_2\text{HSR} + b_3 + e \tag{3.1}$$

But colleges do not base their estimates of SAT or HSR coefficients on their applicant population or a random sample from it. They could do so only if they admitted every applicant, or admitted a random sample of them. Also, none of the enrolled students should drop out before the end of the freshman year when grades are recorded. Since these conditions are virtually impossible to achieve, colleges instead predict freshman grades for applicants based on the SAT scores and HSRs of the previous year's enrolled freshmen. Consequently, the coefficients in equation 3.1 are potentially biased.[16]

The size and direction of bias depends on how the students completing their freshman year differ from the college's applicant pool. Losing all students from the applicant pool with freshman grades below some specified level, for example, would lower the coefficients for both SAT and high school rank. But as long as applicants' freshman grades, SAT scores, and high school ranks have multivariate normal distributions, conventional formulas designed to correct for restriction of range will correct adequately for the bias. Such formulas remain adequate even if truncation of these variables occurs because of explicit selection.

The problem is that the separation between accepted and rejected applicants at most colleges does not occur in such tidy ways. Consequently, conventional formulas for correcting the bias in coefficients may not be accurate. Many variables besides SAT scores and high school rank influence acceptance, enrollment, and completion of the freshman year, but these variables—letters of recommendation, family connections, athletic promise, extracurricular accomplishments—are either unknown or unmeasured.[17] No college tries to measure and quantify all these factors.[18]

The important question is whether estimates of FGPA are seriously distorted because they are based on the academic performance of the previous year's freshmen. If they are, one would want to warn colleges that their use of prediction equations computed from nonrandom samples of attending students could give inaccurate estimates of applicants' predicted success in college. Techniques exist to estimate the direction and extent of bias and to correct sample coefficients for it, but these techniques all require assumptions that are difficult to test.[19] Moreover, we are skeptical about whether the corrections they make are an improvement over the uncorrected predictions and estimates shown in tables 3.1–3.3.[20]

We will therefore assume, because there is no practical alternative, what all colleges assume, and what the College Board and ETS tell colleges to assume: that predictions of freshman performance based on nonrandom samples of students attending college are the firmest basis on which to make accurate predictions for applicants.[21] We will assume that equations like those in tables 3.2 and 3.3 and the predictions they generate in table 3.1 are accurate for college applicants. Acceptance of this view provides dramatic evidence for the predictive effectiveness of the SAT when added to the high school record. And, as we have seen, the results of the NLS merely illustrate the kind of evidence for the predictive effectiveness of the SAT that has accumulated over the years from validity studies numbering in the thousands. But there is more to the story.

Redundancy of the SAT

The board and ETS have used these kinds of results for decades to justify colleges' use of the SAT. Our impression is that the vast majority of educators, psychologists, admissions specialists, and testing and measurement experts in this country would share the board's and ETS's enthusiasm. But, in fact, ETS's and the board's justifications for colleges' use of the SAT tell us almost nothing about the usefulness of the test to colleges.

Why? The simple reason is that predicting freshman grades is not the ultimate goal of the admissions process. The raison d'être of a college admissions office is to make admissions decisions. For the SAT to be of academic benefit to colleges, the test must influence admissions decisions. The SAT can be useful to college admissions officers only if it helps them admit applicants they would reject using only high school records and reject applicants they would admit using only high school records. If colleges that used the high school record were to admit and reject the same students whether or not they also used the SAT, the test would add nothing to colleges' actual admissions decisions—though it might still be useful for counseling those admitted.

If colleges predict their applicants' freshman grades using high school rank alone, some of those predictions will differ from those made using high school rank and the SAT together. How different will these predictions be? Will the differences be large enough to influence any college's actual admissions decisions?

To find out, we need to look at the distribution of predicted freshman grades using high school rank alone to see how much it differs from the distribution of predicted freshman grades using both high school rank and SAT scores. We analyzed a sample of 2,781 high school seniors in the NLS survey who applied to a four-year college as their first choice and for whom SAT scores, high school rank, and selectivity data for the first-choice college were available. We predicted freshman grades for each of these 2,781 applicants at their first-choice college in two ways. First we used high school class rank alone (see equation 5 in table 3.2); second, we used their high school rank and SAT scores combined (see equation 7 in table 3.2). Table 3.4 presents these two distributions of predicted freshman grade point averages and their cross-tabulation.

Table 3.4 is typical of the distributions and cross-tabulations of predicted freshman grades one finds at many American colleges.[22] And the distributions of these predicted freshman grades have some important implications for understanding the usefulness of the SAT in college admissions decisions. Suppose that a college represented in the NLS decided to accept applicants whose predicted freshman grade point average was above 2.5 and to reject applicants whose predicted freshman grade point average was 2.5 or below. Now, comparing the predictions from high school rank alone and high school rank plus SAT, we can see that 74.2 percent of the applicants would be accepted and 16.6 percent rejected under either policy. Identical admissions decisions would be made for a total of 90.8 percent of the applicants. Only 9.2 percent of the applicants to college would be accepted under one policy but not under the other.

Note that this finding depends somewhat on where the college sets the cutoff point for admission. The percentage of cases classified identically by the two policies bears a systematic relationship to where the two distributions are split with the cutoff point and their correlation. The percentage is lowest when the two distributions are split exactly at their means, and rises as the distributions are split further toward the tails with more extreme selection ratios. But when the correlation of the distributions is 0.881, as here, the percentage of cases classified identically is always high, no matter where the cutoff or selection ratio is set.

Suppose we set the cutoff in table 3.4 at successively higher points from 2.0, 2.1, 2.2, . . . 3.3. The percentage of cases classified identically is 98.4, 97.5, 95.4, 94.0, 92.5, 90.8, 89.1, 86.8, 83.8, 84.1,

Table 3.4 Cross-Tabulation of Predicted Freshman Grade Point Averages of 2,781 NLS High School Seniors at the College They Applied to as Their First Choice

FGPA Predicted from High School Rank[b]		FGPA Predicted from High School Rank plus SAT[a]																						
		1.6	1.7	1.8	1.9	2.0	2.1	2.2	2.3	2.4	2.5	2.6	2.7	2.8	2.9	3.0	3.1	3.2	3.3	3.4	3.5	3.6		N
1.9			3	1	6	2	3	1																16
2.0		1	1	4	6	4	6	2																24
2.1				2	5	9	8	7	11	3			1											46
2.2					3	6	10	25	14	11	7	2	1											79
2.3	N = 463					4	11	18	19	17	9	4	1										N = 81	83
2.4	(16.6%)					2	5	21	22	40	27	7	2	2									(2.9)%	128
2.5					1		1	7	23	31	44	43	13	5										168
2.6	N = 175					1	2	6	12	26	37	46	40	13	5								N = 2,062	188
2.7	(6.3%)								6	19	21	54	58	42	21	8	1						(74.2%)	230
2.8									1	8	19	36	57	72	65	23	3	3						287
2.9										2	11	29	64	83	98	60	31	8	4					390
3.0										1	3	9	19	64	124	126	92	51	11	1				501
3.1													12	23	43	104	153	144	93	31	12			615
3.2														1	1	1	3	6	5	5	2	2		26
N		1	4	7	21	28	46	87	108	158	178	230	268	305	357	322	283	212	113	37	14	2		2,781

Notes: Sample consists of 2,781 NLS men and women who applied before October 1973 to a four-year college as their first choice, who reported whether or not they were accepted, and for whom we had college SAT selectivity data, high school class rank, and SAT scores.

[a]Computed using equation 7 in table 3.2.

[b]Computed using equation 5 in table 3.2.

86.0, 86.9, 94.0, and 98.1 respectively. Consequently, a college that sets its cutoff to accept applicants with forecasted grades above 2.8 will classify 83.8 percent of its applicants identically with the two policies. But this is a minimum. Any cutoff above or below this one will result in a higher percentage of identical classifications.

Colleges therefore make identical admissions decisions, either to admit or reject, on a great majority of their applicants whether they use the SAT along with the high school record, or the high school record alone. There is no mystery why colleges make these identical admissions decisions about so many of their applicants. The reason is that colleges' estimates of their applicants' predicted success from high school records and SAT scores combined differ very little from estimates from their high school records alone. The SAT therefore has very little impact on who is in colleges' freshman classes and who is not. It is, in effect, statistically redundant.

The SAT's Effects on Admissions Outcomes

The above observations suggest that, since the SAT has very little effect on who is in a college's freshman class, it can also have very little effect on any college outcome. College officials mean several different things when they say they want to maximize their correct admissions decisions. On the one hand, they want to admit students who will make satisfactory freshman grades and earn degrees and to deny admission to those who will not finish their programs. But admissions officers also care about the kinds of mistakes they may make; they do not want to admit potentially unsuccessful applicants and reject potentially successful ones. One should therefore use a variety of standards in evaluating the correctness of admissions decisions.[23] The high school rank and high school rank plus SAT admissions policies can be compared by simulating what would happen were colleges to admit applicants whose predicted freshman grades were above a certain cutoff point and reject applicants whose predicted freshman grades were below the cutoff. Any other method of admitting students makes less efficient use of high school rankings and SAT scores and will lower the academic benefits of selection.[24] This method of selection is therefore the most efficient use of information and estimates the greatest gains colleges could achieve by using the SAT for selecting students. Colleges that select applicants differently probably get smaller academic benefits from the SAT than we estimate below.

Estimates of selection effects on actual college outcomes must be calculated from students who attend college, because only admitted and attending students have college outcome data. Since everyone in our analyses entered college and completed at least the freshman year, we can determine every student's actual college success. But because they all attended college, we must worry—as we discussed earlier—that estimates computed from nonrandom samples of attending students may not be accurate estimates for applicants.

For one thing, the distributions of predicted freshman grades and their cross-tabulation for the 2,470 NLS respondents who actually attended college could differ in important ways from the ones in table 3.4 for applicants. But they do not.[25] Therefore, if the data presented in table 3.4 reasonably approximate the predicted grade point averages in the applicant pools of many U.S. colleges, the cross-tabulations of attending students are also representative.

However, there still exists the potential problem that distributions of college outcomes conditioned upon predicted freshman grades for nonrandom samples of attending students may not be the same as the ones for applicants. This means that we must assume that applicants with any given predicted grade will have the same college outcomes as those we observe for attending students with the same predicted grades. The board and ETS both make this assumption when they tell colleges that inferences based on attending students are the best way to make predictions for applicants, and colleges make the same assumption implicitly when they follow the board's and ETS's advice. We must assume, in other words, that sample selection bias is not a serious problem.

Table 3.5 summarizes our results of treating the 2,470 NLS attending students as applicants to a college and making admissions decisions on them.[26]

PERCENTAGE OF CORRECT ADMISSIONS FORECASTS

Admissions officials make correct admissions forecasts when they accept applicants who earn satisfactory freshman grades and eventually graduate. They also make correct forecasts when they reject applicants who would earn unsatisfactory freshman grades and eventually drop out or flunk out.

Assume now that a college seeks students who will earn grades above a 2.5 average during their freshman year. The criterion of success is thus freshman grades above 2.5. If the college predicts the freshman grades of its applicants from their high school ranks and admits only those applicants whose predicted freshman grades are above 2.5, they would make 62.2 correct forecasts per 100 (table 3.5, line 1*a*). This is 9.2 correct forecasts per 100 better than the forecasts made if high school rank had no relation to freshman grades (table 3.5, line 1*b*).

If the college added SAT scores to the high school rank prediction equation, and continued to admit only those applicants whose predicted freshman grades were above 2.5, they would now make 64.6 percent correct forecasts; 11.9 correct forecasts per 100 above what would be expected if high school rank and SAT had no relation to actual freshman grades (table 3.5, line 1*b*).

This means that when a college uses high school rank plus SAT, it will make 11.9 − 9.2 = 2.7 more correct admissions forecasts out of each 100 than it would using rank alone. This is a proportional increase of 29.3 percent. Nonetheless, we doubt that most colleges would notice such a small increase in the number of correct forecasts, no matter what the proportional improvement.[27]

One might ask, why not simplify matters and say the added value of the SAT plus rank over rank alone is 64.6 − 62.2 = 2.4 additional correct admissions forecasts out of each 100? One answer is that this makes it look as though 62.2 percent correct admissions forecasts result from using high school rank, with the SAT adding only another 2.4 percent. In fact, if high school rank had no relation to actual freshman grades, one would expect 53.0 percent correct admissions decisions. The improvement from using rank is therefore only 9.2 additional correct forecasts per 100 over the zero predictor validity base rate, not 62.2. We therefore chose to present all our calculations as gains relative to a base success rate.[28]

The results are similar when a 3.0 predicted FGPA is required for admission. With this higher admission standard, basing the prediction on both the SAT and high school rank improves correct admissions forecasts from 14.0 per hundred to 16.2 (see table 3.5, columns 3 and 4, line 1*b*). While this is a proportional improvement of 15.7 percent, again, we do not think that most colleges would notice the impact of an additional 2.2 correct forecasts per 100.

The results are much the same regardless of where the admissions cutoff point is set. We explored each cutoff between 2.2, 2.3, . . . 3.2, for this and all the remaining analyses, and none of the results we report below change appreciably when differing cutoffs are used.

Table 3.5 Outcomes of High School Rank and High School Rank plus SAT Admissions Policies at Two Admissions Standards (%)

		Standard for Admissions and Admissions Policy			
		Above 2.5		Above 3.0	
		High School Rank	High School Rank plus SAT	High School Rank	High School Rank plus SAT
FGPA:					
1. Correct admissions forecasts	*a.*	62.2 (53.0)	64.6 (52.7)	61.7 (47.7)	64.0 (47.8)
	b.	9.2	11.9	14.0	16.2
2. False negatives	*a.*	4.6 (9.2)	4.7 (10.6)	34.0 (41.0)	32.3 (40.4)
	b.	−4.6	−5.9	−7.0	−8.1
3. False positives	*a.*	33.2 (37.8)	30.7 (36.6)	4.2 (11.2)	3.7 (11.8)
	b.	−4.6	−5.9	−7.0	−8.1
4. Conditional acceptances	*a.*	91.6 (83.1)	91.4 (80.5)	37.4 (24.7)	40.7 (25.9)
	b.	8.5	10.9	12.7	14.8
5. Conditional successes	*a.*	60.1 (54.5)	61.9 (54.5)	82.6 (54.5)	85.7 (54.5)
	b.	5.6	7.4	28.1	31.2

Bachelor's degree:					
1. Correct admissions forecasts	*a*.	73.4 (67.3)	72.2 (66.0)	42.6 (36.7)	43.4 (37.3)
	b.	6.1	6.2	5.9	6.1
2. False negatives	*a*.	9.9 (12.9)	11.8 (14.9)	54.5 (57.4)	53.4 (56.5)
	b.	−3.0	−3.1	−2.9	−3.1
3. False positives	*a*.	16.7 (19.7)	16.1 (19.2)	2.9 (5.8)	3.1 (6.2)
	b.	−3.0	−3.1	−2.9	−3.1
4. Conditional acceptances	*a*.	87.0 (83.1)	84.5 (80.5)	28.5 (24.7)	29.9 (25.9)
	b.	3.9	4.0	3.8	4.0
5. Conditional successes	*a*.	79.9 (76.2)	80.0 (76.2)	88.2 (76.2)	88.0 (76.2)
	b.	3.7	3.8	12.0	11.8

Note: a = Observed percentages (and expected percentages given random admissions); *b* = Observed minus expected percentages from (a). Same sample as table 3.2.

Line 1. Let decisions and outcomes be labeled as follows: A = applicants accepted and successful (true positives); B = applicants rejected and unsuccessful (true negatives); C = applicants rejected and successful (false negatives); D = applicants accepted and unsuccessful (false positives). Let all values be proportions of the total sample. The first value in Line 1*a* is then $A + B$ and the second value is $((B + D) * (B + C)) + ((C + A) * (D + A))$. Line 1*b* is the first value minus the second value from line 1*a*.

Line 2. The first value in line 2*a* is C. The second is $(C + A) * (B + C)$. Line 2*b* is the first value minus the second value.

Line 3. The first value in line 3*a* is D. The second is $(B + D) * (D + A)$. Line 3*b* is the first value minus the second value.

Line 4. The first value in line 4*a* is $A/(C + A)$. The second is $D + A$. Line 4*b* is the first value minus the second value.

Line 5. The first value in line 5*a* is $A/(D + A)$. The second is $C + A$. Line 5*b* is the first value minus the second value.

Consequently, we report most of our analyses for cutoffs above 2.5 and 3.0, and do not comment on results at other cutoffs.

While all colleges are concerned with the grades their freshman earn, most try to avoid flunking out freshmen, because freshmen with poor grades often do better during their sophomore year and eventually graduate. Neither the College Board nor ETS has tried to estimate the effect on college completion of different admissions policies, nor have they encouraged colleges to do so themselves.

When we use bachelor's degree attainment as the yardstick, the results are even less impressive than when freshman grade success is the criterion. Indeed, correct forecasts increase only 0.1 per 100 by using the SAT with the 2.5 predicted GPA admissions standard, and by 0.2 per 100 using the 3.0 predicted GPA admissions standard (table 3.5, panel 2, line 1*b*).

FALSE POSITIVES AND FALSE NEGATIVES

Rank alone and rank plus SAT policies decrease the number of false positives (acceptances of students who will fail) and false negatives (rejections of students who would succeed) below what would be expected if high school rank and SAT scores had no relation to FGPA or bachelor degree attainment. But the added prediction value of the SAT over high school rank alone is never more than 1.3 fewer errors per 100 admissions decisions (table 3.5, lines 2 and 3) for either FGPA or bachelor's degree outcomes.

CONDITIONAL PERCENTAGES

Conditional acceptances estimate the percentage of successful applicants who will be accepted, and conditional successes estimate the percent of accepted students who will be successful (table 3.5, lines 4 and 5). The largest gain from using the SAT with rank for either of these conditional percentages is only 3.1 persons per 100 with the higher admissions standard and grade point average criterion for success (table 3.5, line 5).

In all, the additional correct decisions and reductions in errors from using both the SAT and high school rank rarely exceed 2 to 3 decisions per 100. This is because the SAT has little effect on who is in a college's freshman class. The major difference between the two policies therefore depends on the relatively few applicants for whom the two policies lead to different admissions decisions. Tables 3.6 and 3.7 show that there are never large differences between the two policies for these few applicants.

Table 3.6 Freshman Grade Point Average for Applicants Admitted and Rejected by High School Rank and High School Rank plus SAT Admissions Policies at Two Admissions Standards

	Decision Made by High School Rank plus SAT					
	Reject			Admit		
Decision Made by High School Rank	Observed Freshman Grades 2.5 or below	Observed Freshman Grades above 2.5	Total	Observed Freshman Grades 2.5 or below	Observed Freshman Grades above 2.5	Total
	Admissions Standard: Predicted FGPA above 2.5					
Reject	265 (10.7)	82 (3.3)	347 (14.0)	40 (1.6)	31 (1.3)	71 (2.9)
Admit	100 (4.0)	34 (1.4)	134 (5.4)	719 (29.1)	1199 (48.5)	1918 (77.7)
Total	365 (14.8)	116 (4.7)	481 (19.5)	759 (30.7)	1230 (49.8)	1989 (80.5)
	Admissions Standard: Predicted FGPA above 3.0					
Reject	975 (39.5)	685 (27.7)	1660 (67.2)	45 (1.8)	156 (6.3)	201 (8.1)
Admit	57 (2.3)	113 (4.6)	170 (6.9)	47 (1.9)	392 (15.9)	439 (17.8)
Total	1032 (41.8)	798 (32.3)	1830 (74.1)	92 (3.7)	548 (22.2)	640 (25.9)

Note: Same sample as table 3.2.

With a 2.5 predicted freshman grade point average requirement, the two admissions policies lead to the same admissions decision for 91.7 percent of the applicants. The only difference between the two policies is that the rank plus SAT policy admits an additional 1.3 percent of the applicants who would be successful, while the high school rank policy admits an additional 1.4 percent who would be successful. The comparable values are 6.3 percent and 4.6 percent with the higher 3.0 admissions standard (see table 3.6, panel 2). The results are similar for completion of the bachelor's degree (see table 3.7). With the 2.5 admissions standard, the high school rank plus SAT policy admits an additional 1.8 percent of the applicants who will complete a bachelor's degree program, while the high school rank policy admits an additional 3.7 percent who will complete their bachelor's programs. The comparable values are 6.7 and 5.6 with the 3.0 admissions standard.[29]

Table 3.7 Bachelor's Degree Attainment for Applicants Admitted and Rejected by High School Rank and High School Rank plus SAT Admissions Policies at Two Admissions Standards

Decision Made by High School Rank	Decision Made by High School Rank plus SAT					
	Reject			Admit		
	No Bachelor's Degree	Bachelor's Degree	Total	No Bachelor's Degree	Bachelor's Degree	Total
	Admissions Standard: Predicted FGPA above 2.5					
Reject	147 (6.0)	200 (8.1)	347 (14.1)	27 (1.1)	44 (1.8)	71 (2.9)
Admit	43 (1.7)	91 (3.7)	134 (5.4)	370 (15.0)	1548 (62.7)	1918 (77.7)
Total	190 (7.7)	291 (11.8)	481 (19.5)	397 (16.1)	1,592 (64.5)	1,989 (80.5)
	Admissions Standard: Predicted FGPA above 3.0					
Reject	479 (19.4)	1181 (47.8)	1660 (67.2)	36 (1.5)	165 (6.7)	201 (8.1)
Admit	31 (1.3)	139 (5.6)	170 (6.9)	41 (1.7)	398 (16.1)	439 (17.8)
Total	510 (20.6)	1320 (53.4)	1830 (74.1)	77 (3.1)	563 (22.8)	640 (25.9)

Note: Same sample as table 3.2.

Overall Excellence

Administrators are concerned with improving the grade point average of their student body and increasing the number of years of higher education their students complete. But they cannot expect much improvement in these characteristics to result from using the SAT rather than high school rank alone. Our findings are presented in table 3.8.

For example, if a college had an applicant pool with SAT scores and high school ranks comparable to those in the NLS survey, and it admitted applicants randomly or admitted them all, freshman grades would average 2.83, and years of education would average 15.82. Using a high school rank admissions policy with a predicted FGPA of 2.5 as an admission standard increases the freshman grades to an average of 2.91 and the years of education completed to 15.92; a rank plus SAT policy increases them to 2.93 and 15.93. The gain from adding the SAT is therefore only an increase in average freshman grades of 0.02 on a four-point scale, while educational attainment increases by just 0.01 years.[30]

Table 3.8 Average Freshman Grade Point Average and Years of Education Attained by Students Accepted and Rejected by High School Rank and High School Rank plus SAT Admissions Policies at Two Admissions Standards

Decision Made by High School Rank	Decision Made by High School Rank plus SAT			
	Reject	Accept	Overall	
	Admissions Standard: Predicted FGPA above 2.5			
Average FGPA:				
Reject	2.40	2.60	2.43	
(*N* cases)	(347)	(71)	(418)	
Accept	2.46	2.94	2.91	
(*N* cases)	(134)	(1,918)	(2,052)	
Overall	2.42	2.93	2.83	= Random
(*N* cases)	(481)	(1,989)	(2,470)	Admissions
Average Years of Education:				
Reject	15.35	15.48	15.37	
(*N* cases)	(347)	(71)	(418)	
Accept	15.55	15.94	15.92	
(*N* cases)	(134)	(1,918)	(2,052)	
Overall	15.40	15.93	15.82	= Random
(*N* cases)	(481)	(1,989)	(2,470)	Admissions
	Admissions Standard: Predicted FGPA above 3.0			
Average FGPA:				
Reject	2.64	3.10	2.69	
(*N* cases)	(1,660)	(201)	(1,861)	
Accept	2.97	3.37	3.26	
(*N* cases)	(170)	(439)	(609)	
Overall	2.67	3.29	2.83	= Random
(*N* cases)	(1,830)	(640)	(2,470)	Admissions
Average Years of Education:				
Reject	15.66	16.10	15.71	
(*N* cases)	(1,660)	(201)	(1,861)	
Accept	15.89	16.29	16.18	
(*N* cases)	(170)	(439)	(609)	
Overall	15.68	16.23	15.82	= Random
(*N* cases)	(1,830)	(640)	(2,470)	Admissions

Note: Same sample as table 3.2.

The advantages of using the SAT are slightly greater with a 3.0 admissions standard. Average freshman grades increase by 0.03 and average years of education by 0.05 (table 3.8, panel 2). While the proportional gains are 7.0 and 13.9 percent respectively, the absolute gains of 0.03 and 0.05 are still small.[31]

The Preceding Results Hold For Hundreds of American Colleges

In 1964 the College Board established the Validity Study Service (VSS) to help member colleges perform their own validity studies. In addition to national data like those from NLS, summaries of VSS studies done for individual colleges are a valuable source of recent validity information about the SAT.

The College Board does not release data on individual students from VSS. But it does make available recent summary information from all participating colleges or subsamples of individual colleges.

If our argument about the predictive usefulness of the SAT is correct, the VSS data should also demonstrate that an admissions policy based on high school rank plus SAT will predict freshman grade point averages that correlate highly with those predicted from rank alone. In fact, these correlations are quite high: 0.868 for the average college that participated in the VSS between 1976 and 1980; 0.801 for the most selective colleges; and 0.840 for the least selective colleges.[32] The correlations drawn from the VSS data are not significantly different from the correlation of 0.867 for the attending students in NLS, nor do they differ much from the correlation of 0.881 for applicants in NLS.[33]

These figures strongly support the general conclusion that when admissions are based on predicted freshman grades, a policy using high school rank and SAT scores will make predictions that are very similar to a policy using high school rank alone. Thus, as we argue above, the SAT can have little impact on who is in a college's freshman class, and it is, therefore, statistically redundant. The main consequence of its redundancy is that it will have almost no impact on any college outcome.

Using the VSS data, the average college, for example, could expect to increase its mean freshman grades by 0.16 standard deviations above the mean for random admissions if it rejected the bottom fifth of its applicants on the basis of high school rank alone. With a rank plus SAT policy, rejecting the bottom fifth would produce a freshman grade point average 0.19 standard deviations above the mean for random admissions (table 3.9, columns 1 and 2). The difference between the two policies is 0.03 standard deviations (table 3.9, column 3).

The VSS data indicate that using the SAT never raises the freshman grade point average by more than about one-eighth of a standard deviation of applicants' freshman grade point averages in the applicant pool. If the actual standard deviation for applicants' freshman grade point averages is large, however, the improvement in predictive accuracy could be great. Assumptions about the standard deviation of freshman grade point average in the applicant pool are therefore very important.

But colleges cannot determine the standard deviation of freshman grades in their applicant population, because the applicants they reject never earn freshman grades. The most that can be done is to make assumptions about the size of the standard deviation, and then estimate the gains made by using the SAT given these assumptions. Even when a very large standard deviation is chosen, the gains from using the SAT are never large enough to be substantively significant (table 3.9, column 5).

The average college represented in the VSS data had a freshman grade point average standard deviation of 0.703. This is somewhat truncated compared to what would be observed if all applicants were admitted and earned freshman grades with no change in grading standards. If it is true that a school's rejected applicants would really do poorly, even a college that accepts the great majority of its applicants could have an observed freshman grade standard deviation that is smaller than that of its applicant pool. If it is assumed that the distribution of enrolled students is a 25 percent truncation of the applicant distribution, then the standard deviation of the application distribution is 0.961 (table 3.9, column 4).

Most colleges probably have a freshman grade distribution with a truncation of no more than 25 percent of their applicant pool. This is because most applicants try to apply to colleges where they think they will be accepted and do adequate work. Therefore, the 50 percent truncation in table 3.9 represents a somewhat unrealistic maximum.

Even when the standardized gains are multiplied by the largest possible applicant FGPA standard deviation (assuming 50 percent truncation), the largest mean gain in freshman grade point average that results from the SAT plus rank rather than rank alone is only 0.15 points on a four-point grade scale (table 3.9, column 5). And, in order to get this 0.15 gain, the college must reject 80 percent of its applicants. Fewer than one dozen colleges and universities in America are in a position to be this selective. Under a more realistic

Table 3.9 Effects of Admissions Policies on Admitted Students' Average Freshman Grades (from 1976 to 1980 Validity Study Service)

		Mean Standard Score of Admitted Group above Random Admissions[a]			Mean FGPA Gains above Random Admissions with Two Estimated Applicant Population FGPA Standard Deviations[b]	
Type of College	Selection Ratio	(1) Selection by High School Rank	(2) Selection by High School Rank plus SAT	(3) Gain with SAT (col. 2 - col. 1)	(4) 25% Truncation SD = (1.3676) * (.703) = .9614228	(5) 50% Truncation SD = (1.658898) * (.703) = 1.1662053
Average	.80	.1623	.1872	.0249	.024	.029
(N = 412)	.20	.6482	.7476	.0994	.096	.116
Most	.80	.1342	.1671	.0329	.032	.038
Selective	.20	.5360	.6675	.1315	.126	.153
(N = 45)						
Least	.80	.1447	.1718	.0271	.026	.032
Selective	.20	.5781	.6863	.1082	.104	.126
(N = 46)						

[a]The values in columns 1 and 2 are $(\overline{FGPA}_S - M_{FGPA})/SD_{FGPA}$ where $\overline{FGPA}$ is the mean freshman grade point average for admitted applicants, M_{FGPA} is the mean freshman grade point average of randomly selected applicants, and SD_{FGPA} is the standard deviation of freshman grades in the applicant

pool. Both M_{FGPA} and SD_{FGPA} are unknown and therefore cannot be directly measured. But the entire quantity $(\overline{FGPA}_S - M_{FGPA})/SD_{FGPA}$ is equal to $(R)(\phi/p)$ where R is the correlation between predicted freshman grades and actual grades, p is the selection ratio, and ϕ is the ordinate in $N(0,1)$ at the point corresponding to p. For further discussion, see J. E. Hunter and F. L. Schmidt, "Fitting People to Jobs: The Impact of Personnel Selection on National Productivity," in *Human Performance and Productivity: Human Capability Assessment*, ed. M. D. Dunnette and E. A. Fleishman (Hillsdale, N.J.: Lawrence Erlbaum Associates, 1982).

Column 1 is $(R)(\phi/p)$ with R taken for each subsample of colleges. Column 3 is column 2 minus column 1.

[b]Columns 4–5 are the values in column 3 multiplied by the estimated applicant standard deviations in columns 4–5. Thus (0.0249) (0.9614228) = 0.024 points gain in mean freshman grade point average on a 4-point scale using the SAT and rank over rank alone in the Validity Study Service's average college using a 0.80 selection ratio.

We estimated the standard deviations in columns 4–5 as follows. Assume the full applicant population is normally distributed with variance σ^2, and the observed distribution is truncated at $Z\alpha$ where α is the lower truncated area. The observed distribution has a known variance of σ_τ^2. We estimated the standard deviation of the full applicant population, σ, as

$$\sigma = \left(\frac{1}{B}\right)^{1/2} \sigma_\tau$$

where

$$B = 1 + \frac{Z_\alpha}{(1-\alpha)(\sqrt{2\pi})} e^{-\frac{Z_\alpha^2}{2}} - A^2$$

and

$$A = \left(\frac{1}{1-\alpha}\right) \frac{1}{(\sqrt{2\pi})} e^{-\frac{Z_\alpha^2}{2}}$$

using $Z_\alpha = 0.67$ in column 4, and $Z_\alpha = 0$ in column 5.

truncation of 25 percent, and a more realistic selection ratio of 0.80, the mean gain in freshman grade point average is in the 0.02–0.03 range (table 3.9, column 4), virtually identical to the range we estimated using NLS data.

Three Red Herrings

Occasionally a report will surface that shows an SAT coefficient larger than we estimate or an increment in the multiple correlation due to the SAT larger than we estimate above. ETS on several occasions has used these larger estimates to impugn the slightly smaller estimates of its critics.[34] However, occasional larger estimates of the predictive effectiveness of the SAT do not provide prima facie evidence against our view, because they do not translate automatically into improved selection decisions, as ETS and the board have assumed.

Recently, for example, ETS has reported an SAT coefficient from the VSS that is 25 percent larger than the one we report from the NLS survey.[35] It comes from 191 colleges that used SAT scores and high school grade point averages in validity studies for entering classes between 1977 and 1981. Despite this larger effect of the SAT, these new data from ETS confirm every aspect of our analysis.

The new ETS data demonstrate that an admissions policy based on high school grades plus SAT generates predicted freshman grade point averages that correlate highly with those based on high school grades alone. The correlation in the new ETS data is 0.881, virtually identical to the values we present above for NLS and ETS's other Validity Study Service data. Consequently, the SAT is also statistically redundant in the new ETS validity data.

Moreover, the estimated increment in average freshman grades of the accepted applicants at colleges using the SAT is also small. The new ETS data show that among these 191 colleges, the typical college improves the average freshman grades of its accepted students only 0.022 on a four-point scale if it uses the SAT plus high school grades rather than high school grades alone. This value is also within the 0.02–0.03 range we estimate from other Validity Study Service data and the NLS.

ETS often points out that the relationship between SAT scores and freshman grades may be dramatically underestimated when the range of SAT scores is restricted.[36] In the extreme case, for example, if a college enrolls students whose SAT scores are all the same, SAT scores can show no relationship to freshman grades. To get around this problem, ETS will make corrections for restricted range to estimate the validity of the SAT. This has the effect of making the validity of the SAT seem more impressive.[37]

Our results do not, however, arise because of restricted ranges. Recently, ETS searched its Validity Study Service records for the College Board and found twenty-one colleges where the distributions of SAT scores and high school records are virtually identical to those for the overall SAT-taking population. In these carefully chosen colleges with unrestricted range for high school records and SAT scores, the optimal equation for predicting freshman grades using high school records and SAT scores is among the best we have seen. The multiple correlation is 0.65, and the unstandardized coefficient for the SAT is 10 percent larger than the one for the recent ETS data reported above. If any data should show large benefits of the SAT, it should be these.

Yet they do not. The correlations between predicted freshman grades based on an admissions policy based on the high school record alone and one based on the high school record plus SAT scores is 0.889, which is nearly identical to the 0.881 for the ETS data reported above. Furthermore, the gains in freshman grades for the students selected with the SAT only average 0.03 on a four-point scale, again almost identical to the gains we report above.

A third criticism of our findings argues that while our conclusions may hold in general, many colleges admit students by curricular area or major, and our results will not hold for all majors. The usual development of this position points out that the verbal and math sections of the SAT have different optimal weightings when predicting freshman grades in different college curricular areas, and that using weights calculated over all areas reduces the predictive power of the test.

The verbal and math sections of the SAT do have differing optimal weights for predicting freshman grades in different subject areas.[38] But it does not automatically follow that these differences translate into substantial benefits in selection decisions or outcomes. The conclusions we report above appear to be robust over all major college curricular areas.

The University of Delaware has about 9,500 applicants each year to eight colleges in nine curricular areas. The admissions office uses applicants' high school grades and SAT scores to forecast freshman grades. The regression formulas used for these forecasts differ in each curricular area. If the SAT is to affect who gets admitted to Delaware, the predicted grades for Delaware's applicants based on high school grades plus SAT scores must differ from those based on high school grades alone. They do differ, but never enough to have much effect on who is offered admission and who is not.

The two sets of freshman grades correlate very highly for applicants at each college in the university (table 3.10, column 2). As a result, a freshman grade admissions policy based on high school grades alone will result in the same admission decision for more than 85 percent of the applicants in each curricular area (columns 3 and 4).

The SAT can only make a difference for the handful of applicants where it can lead to a different admissions decision. But even in the few cases where the SAT would lead Delaware's admissions office to make different decisions, they are not appreciably better ones. We estimate that the grades of freshmen admitted using the SAT never average more than 0.04 higher than those of the class that would be admitted using just high school grades. The number of admitted students earning freshman grades above 2.0 and 3.0 is also never improved by more than 2.2 cases per 100.

Note that these are estimates derived from basing admissions on forecasted grades. At Delaware, differences in forecasted grades explain only 25–40 percent of the variance of the decisions to admit or reject, depending on the college. This is primarily because Delaware admits about 90 percent of all applicants who are state residents, and admits applicants to some majors whose forecasted grades would lead to rejection in other majors. The SAT cannot help admissions in these cases. Table 3.10 therefore overestimates the actual benefits Delaware could get from the SAT, since it assumes admissions based solely on predicted grades.

For any practical purpose, then, all these data confirm our conclusions. An admissions policy based on applicants' high school records and SAT scores combined admits and rejects nearly the same people as one based on high school records alone. Both policies lead to highly correlated estimates of college success. The result is that colleges that admit applicants according to their academic eligibility now benefit little from use of the SAT over high school record alone.

Can the SAT Be Defended?

Our argument, in summary, is that from a practical viewpoint, most colleges could ignore their applicants' SAT score reports when they make selection decisions without appreciably altering the academic performance and graduation rates of the students they admit. None-

Table 3.10 Percentage of Fall 1983 Applicants to the University of Delaware for Whom Both Admissions Policies Make the Same Admissions Decision

College	Number of Applicants	Correlation Between Predicted Grade Indexes for the Two Policies	Predicted Grade Index Standard for Admission	
			Above 2.0	Above 2.5
Agriculture	210	.869	85.8	87.7
Arts and Sciences: Liberal Arts	3,445	.938	90.0	91.3
Arts and Sciences: Natural Sciences	1,700	.961	91.9	93.9
Business and Economics	1,746	.931	89.3	87.4
Education	207	.845	85.1	89.9
Engineering	1,257	.912	87.7	88.0
Human Resources	335	.975	93.1	96.4
Nursing	389	.893	85.9	87.2
Physical Education	177	.891	91.0	85.3

Note: Sample consists of all fall 1983 first-time, full-time freshman applicants at their first-choice college within the University of Delaware. Forecasted grade indexes for each college based on equations for first-time, full-time freshmen in that college in fall 1981.

theless, the College Board and ETS advise colleges that applicants' score reports will allow them to make better admissions decisions.

One defense of such advice is that even small improvements in FGPA may be important to some colleges. If there were no costs of using the SAT, then one might reasonably argue that a massive admissions testing program is a good thing, since it helps colleges make slightly better admissions decisions. But the SAT has substantial costs. Most of the nation's 1.5 million Admissions Testing Program candidates each year spend at least $30 taking the PSAT and SAT one or more times during high school. Many students also pay up to $600 for commercial coaching classes hoping to improve their test scores. Commercial coaching also costs time and effort as well as money. Stanley Kaplan Educational Centers, which has over half this market, has had a fivefold increase in its number of centers since 1970, and grossed over $22 million in 1981.[39]

Moreover, many high schools use valuable instructional time on SAT prep courses in which students memorize long lists of SAT words and practice taking SAT-type items from sample tests. This time and effort might be better spent on academic subjects. No one knows how much the high school curriculum shrinks because of the

SAT, but many teachers and others worry a lot about this. Sheila Fitzgerald, president of the National Council of Teachers of English, captures their sentiment when she says that educators "should be appalled" by recent increases in SAT scores, since they raise the question of "what has been sacrificed to achieve that."[40]

Then there is the anxiety of high school students (and their parents), who nervously await the day the test is given and the day the scores arrive. A 1977 survey designed to monitor the attitudes and reactions of students who take the SAT found that nearly a fifth of the students said they were "very nervous" about taking the SAT, and an additional 56 percent said they were "a little nervous."[41]

We think, however, that efforts to assess the usefulness of the SAT by setting its benefits to *colleges* against its many costs may be myopic. The SAT may have wider benefits than those that accrue to colleges alone, and the test's costs are also greater than thus far indicated. Assessment of the SAT also depends on the alternatives one assesses it against. What are some of the other possible benefits of the SAT?

1. Defenders of the SAT often argue that all college-bound students can use their SAT scores to help select a college that matches their ability. ETS encourages prospective applicants to use their score reports to choose a college where they are likely to be accepted and do satisfactory academic work. Potentially, this saves colleges both time and money because the SAT gives colleges a number that signals their relative standard of academic excellence, so they can attract the applicants they want and discourage the ones they do not want. Efficient signaling of colleges' relative standards also saves prospective applicants the time, effort, and costs of unsuccessful applications.

2. Defenders of the SAT also claim that the SAT has helped bring about gains in equal opportunity. According to ETS, "selective admissions to higher education was *[sic]* far more a matter of class and economic status prior to the use of national admissions tests than it has been since. . . . The introduction of tests resulted in a substantial increase in opportunities for educational advancement of low-income students by providing a credible demonstration that many such students from schools without reputations for educational excellence could succeed in the demanding academic programs of the most selective institutions."[42]

3. Proponents of the SAT often compare its benefits with the obvious alternatives. Eliminating all external standardized testing in favor of high school grades may, for example, appreciably increase

high schools' incentives to lower their grading standards. If a high school is under pressure from parents to get its graduates into selective colleges, and if the high school knows that admissions depend on the grades it gives students, the temptation to give more A's is strong. And if one school lowers standards, others may feel they have to follow suit to maintain their graduates' competitive advantage. Colleges can get around this problem to some extent by demanding that high schools supply grade distributions for their entire graduating class, or by paying more attention to rank in class, thereby allowing a college to see where an applicant stood relative to others. But an external examining system allows colleges to compensate more fully for differences in high school grading standards. It does not follow, however, that this external examining system ought to include the SAT.

4. Defenders of the SAT also say that replacing it with conventional achievement tests in the subject areas of the secondary school curriculum would lead eventually to a system not unlike the British 0-level and A-level examinations and a relatively higher degree of curricular uniformity than at present. These persons have great difficulty seeing how this kind of system could encourage the ideals of flexibility in student curriculum choice and of greater access to higher education for poor and minority students traditionally underrepresented in higher education.

We take up these arguments and others in the following chapters. Each needs to be evaluated carefully before one can decide whether the SAT is on balance a good thing. At this point, our argument is not about a general assessment of the SAT. Our argument is only that most colleges' use of their applicants' SAT score reports does not now help them improve either the accuracy of their admissions decisions or the academic performance and graduation rates of the students they admit. If the College Board is to keep urging its member colleges to require applicants to submit SAT scores, it should do so for other reasons. However, the board owes it to all concerned to do more than tell us what these other reasons are. It should show us why the reasons are valid.

FOUR

The SAT Does Not Help Applicants Select Colleges Where They Can Be Successful

One purpose of SAT scores, according to ETS, is to help prospective college applicants choose an academically appropriate college. ETS claims SAT scores give prospective applicants an objective and impartial assessment of their developed abilities that they can use to assess their chances of success at different colleges. ETS encourages applicants to use this information to select colleges that make academic demands that do not exceed their ability.[1] All our evidence strongly suggests, however, that applicants cannot effectively use their SAT scores this way. Nor, as far as we know, has ETS tried to verify the claim that they can.

The first part of this chapter describes the information prospective applicants use to self-select a college. The second part of the chapter estimates to what extent prospective applicants actually screen themselves into colleges where they are likely to be successful and out of colleges where they are likely to be unsuccessful. The third part of the chapter assesses the SAT's contribution to this process of self-selection. We argue that the SAT could be dropped without affecting the benefits to colleges and applicants from self-selection.

Self-Selection in College Admissions

Almost all American two-year colleges and many four-year colleges are relatively unselective. The 1985 American Association of Collegiate Registrars and Admissions Officers study of admissions policies showed that 90 percent of the two-year public colleges and 15 percent of the four-year public colleges surveyed either did not review applicants' academic qualifications or admitted any high school graduate.[2] Furthermore, every state in the nation except Maine has at least one public two-year college that admits anyone from within the state, or anyone with a high school diploma or an acceptable pattern of high school courses. At least fifteen states also have four-year colleges with no admissions requirements aside from these.[3]

Most four-year colleges are somewhat more selective, however. In addition to a high school diploma and minimum requirements in high school subjects, selective colleges stress candidates' academic performance in high school and admissions test scores.[4] And the most selective colleges have higher academic admissions requirements.[5] Private colleges may also consider their applicants' personal qualities when making admissions decisions.[6]

Sometimes selective colleges use their catalogs and other publications to tell the public quite explicitly what kind of students they want. At the nine campuses of the University of California, for example, state residents may be admitted if they meet one of three criteria: complete a prescribed pattern of high school course work with a minimum GPA of 3.3 or higher; have a GPA between 2.78 and 3.29 and qualify on the university's SAT/GPA Eligibility Index; or score 1100 or higher on the SAT, plus 1650 on three College Board Achievement Tests with a minimum score of 500 on each of the three. (The Eligibility Index requires SATs of 1600 for a student with a GPA of 2.78, but only 400 with a GPA of 3.29.)[7]

But anyone who has browsed through many college catalogs or the commercial guides to college selection knows that explicit descriptions of colleges' admissions requirements are the exception, not the rule. There is a lot that prospective applicants do not know. For one thing, prospective applicants do not know exactly how selective colleges forecast applicants' academic success. Prediction of academic performance in many colleges is a judgment made by an admissions staff and is based on considered, but informal, observations of how past applicants from known high schools have done.

Nor do prospective applicants know exactly how characteristics other than predicted academic success will count in a college's admissions decision. They do not know, for example, what exceptions a college might make to its own requirements. Nearly 40 percent of the four-year colleges told the 1979 AACRAO/College Board study that their published requirements were mainly recommendations. Only 6 percent of the colleges said their published statements were rigid requirements.[8]

Prospective applicants also do not know how colleges may weight extracurricular activities, athletic accomplishments, recommendations, community service, ability to pay for college, ethnic or racial status, and being a child of an alumnus. Each of these nonacademic personal qualities was thought to have a great deal or fair amount of importance for admissions by between 22 and 69 percent of the high school seniors in a 1977 survey done for the College Board's SAT monitor program.[9]

The available evidence suggests, however, that nonacademic factors may not be of very much importance. Warren Willingham and Hunter Breland, two ETS researchers, studied admissions decisions made by nine selective colleges.[10] They found that a college's academic rating of applicants, based largely on high school rank and test scores, received about three times more weight in predicting admissions decisions than nonacademic personal qualities. Furthermore, when the 1985 AACRAO study asked colleges about the importance of leadership ability, community and church involvement, work experience related to intended field of study, compatibility between institutional qualities and student needs, good citizenship and moral character, and special skills and abilities, a majority of colleges, even four-year private ones, did not report that these personal qualities were often important in admissions decisions.[11]

Selective colleges have good reasons for not fully describing their admissions requirements. They often want to convey the importance of high school grades and test scores, but want to make it clear that other things count too. They do not say what their standards are, or exactly how they will judge their applicants' probable academic performance, or what other things will count, however, because both the prediction of academic performance and building a freshman class with the right nonacademic composition are still largely exercises in subjective judgment.[12] Furthermore, some colleges may not want to say exactly whom they will admit, because they do not know in advance, or because they would thus increase the risk of appearing less selective than their competitors. As a result, applicants to many selective colleges may guess their chances of acceptance reasonably well, but the outcome is often far from certain.[13]

The College Board encourages high school students to begin refining their college choices even before they take the SAT. Most high school seniors who take the SAT take the Preliminary Scholastic Aptitude Test (PSAT) as high school sophomores or juniors. The PSAT is a shortened version of the SAT designed to estimate students' SAT scores. The College Board tells them how to make these estimates and then says:

> You can use your estimated SAT scores as you begin selecting colleges you will apply to during your senior year. Among the questions you may want to ask are: Do students with my estimated SAT scores typically apply to the college that I am considering? Are these students admitted? Do they enroll? You can answer these questions by looking at the directories and guides mentioned . . . some of which include information on the range of SAT scores for students the colleges admit. Compare your estimated SAT scores with these ranges to see what your standing might be among students at the college you are considering.[14]

As one might expect, applicants do try to narrow their college choices to ones that somewhat match their own characteristics. But the available evidence supports only a modest influence of the SAT on college applications, which seems about what one would expect given that many colleges do not depend greatly on the test and that many applicants know where they want to go before they even take the test.

For example, Leonard Baird surveyed a random sample of students who took the SAT in 1981. One year after their high school graduation 72 percent said that the SAT had no influence on their choice of colleges. Another 10 percent said they had already applied to colleges before receiving their scores. But 10 percent said they decided to apply to less selective colleges because of their scores and 7 percent said they decided to apply to more selective colleges because of them.[15] Charles Manski and David Wise in *College Choice in America* estimate that if two individuals' SAT verbal plus math scores differ by 400 points, they will typically apply to colleges with average SAT scores that differ by 120 points, even when both have the same high school rank, parental income, and parental education.[16]

Since completing college applications takes time and effort, submitting them costs money, and rejection can be painful, most high school students make some effort to apply to colleges where they have a reasonable chance of being admitted. Baird found that SAT takers applied on average to 2.4 colleges and were accepted at 1.9 of them. Overall, only 5 percent were not accepted at any college, and this figure typically varied only 1–3 percentage points by the applicant's family income and SAT score.[17]

Many parents and students imagine that selective colleges have far more applicants than places, and that colleges rely heavily on high school grades and admissions tests to choose among their applicants. But this is not the case. Because prospective applicants apply mostly to colleges where they are accepted, the vast majority of colleges accept a high proportion of their applicants.

In a random sample of the 1,700-odd four-year institutions in the 1979 College Board *College Handbook*, for example, 32 percent admitted more than 90 percent of their applicants, 54 percent admitted more than 80 percent, and 78 percent admitted more than 70 percent.[18] Richard Moll, former director of admissions at Bowdoin, estimates that no more than forty private colleges enjoy the luxury of rejecting 50 percent of their applicants, and no more than a half-dozen reject as many as 80 percent.[19]

Self-selection therefore implies that American colleges admit different freshman classes primarily because of application patterns, not because most competitive colleges reject a lot of applicants with low grades and test scores. One must be careful, however, not to overstate either the amount of differentiation among colleges in their average high school grades and SAT scores, or how much this differentiation arises from application patterns.

First, the differentiation is far from complete. Suppose we rank American colleges in terms of the average high school grade point average of their freshman class and again by the average SAT score of their freshman class, and then compare the top fifth of colleges in these two rankings with the bottom fifth. The top and bottom fifths will differ by 0.56 points on a four-point high school grade point average scale and by 140 points on the 200–800 SAT scale.[20] But the variation in high school grade point averages and SAT scores within most colleges is nearly as great as within the entire college-going population. The standard deviation of high school grade point averages within the average college is only 6 percent smaller than the standard deviation of high school grade point average overall, and the standard deviation of SAT scores within colleges is only 13 percent smaller than overall.[21]

Second, the differentiation among American colleges in their average high school grades and SAT scores does not arise entirely because of application patterns. Colleges' acceptance decisions account for some of the differentiation, but our analyses of the NLS data show that after controlling for differences in the SAT selectivity of the college applied to, differences in applicants' high school class ranks and SAT scores have only a small relationship to whether they are accepted for admission by that college. Applicants whose class ranks differ by 15 percentile points have admissions probabilities to their first-choice college that differ by an expected 4.1 percent. Applicants whose SAT verbal plus math totals differ by 200 points have admissions probabilities that differ by an expected 5.4 percent (see table 4.1, equation 7).[22]

Taken together, these results suggest that selection of colleges by prospective applicants is an important part of the transition from high school to college, although one must be careful not to overstate the extent to which colleges' freshman class SAT averages and high school grade averages are differentiated in this way. One must also be very careful not to assume that the mere existence of self-selection that differentiates the applicant pools of American colleges in high school grades, SAT scores, and other applicant characteristics proves that it is a good thing.

Suppose, for example, that some American colleges suddenly were to let all applicants know through their catalogs, directories, and other public information that "only whites need apply." If these colleges could stick to this racial admissions requirement over time, no doubt one would find a decline in the number of their nonwhite applicants. But only racists would argue that the discriminatory "whites only" admissions policy and the self-selection it caused were a good thing.

In principle, one also should not assume that self-selection that differentiates American colleges by their freshmen's average high school grades, SAT scores, and other characteristics is a good thing until someone demonstrates the benefits this has for colleges, applicants, or both. One important question raised by the existence of self-selection, therefore, is whether the students guided into each college's applicant pool by their SAT scores, high school record, and other factors are the ones most suited academically to each college.[23]

Do Colleges and Applicants Benefit Academically from Self-Selection?

Colleges usually have multiple admissions objectives, and they are nearly always willing to make trade-offs among them. Nonetheless, virtually all colleges want applicants who are likely to do successful academic work, and many colleges look for those applicants who will do the best academic work. Consequently, a good index of the potential academic utility of each prospective applicant from the college's viewpoint is the expected grade point average the applicant would have if he or she attended the college. We will assume that self-selection benefits a college academically if it increases the col-

Table 4.1 Regressions of College Acceptance on High School Rank, SAT Scores, College SAT Selectivity, and Socioeconomic Background for 2,781 NLS Respondents

	Independent Variables									
Equation	High School Rank	SAT	College SAT Selectivity	Father's Education	Mother's Education	Father's Occupation	Family Income[a]	Constant	$\overline{R}^2$	SEE
1. B	.00269*							.679	.033	.323
beta	.183									
2. B		.00016						.716	.010	.327
beta		.100								
3. B	.00260*	.00002						.668	.033	.323
beta	.177	.011								
4. B			−.00051*					1.418	.045	.321
beta			−.212							
5. B	.00373*		−.00067*					1.310	.105	.311
beta	.254		−.277							
6. B		.00042*	−.00081*					1.317	.097	.312
beta		.260	−.336							
7. B	.00271*	.00027*	−.00082*					1.274	.122	.308
beta	.185	.169	−.340							
8. B				.00155	.00162	−.00041	−.00193	.883	.000	.328
beta				.016	.013	−.028	−.028			
9. B			−.00054*	.00464	.00363	−.00019	−.00082	1.364	.045	.321
beta			−.223	.042	.028	−.013	−.012			
10. B	.00372*		−.00069*	.00284	.00297	−.00009	−.00029	1.261	.105	.311
beta	.253		−.288	.030	.023	−.006	−.004			
11. B		.00043*	−.00080*	.00172	.00076	−.00023	−.00023	1.316	.097	.312
beta		.264	−.334	.018	.006	−.016	−.035			
12. B	.00270*	.00027*	−.00082*	.00169	.00133	−.00015	−.00101	1.259	.121	.308
beta	.184	.168	−.341	.018	.018	−.010	−.015			

Notes: The National Longitudinal Study of the high school class of 1972 (NLS) surveyed 19,144 high school seniors during the 1971–72 school year from a target population of 1,200 public and private high schools in the United States. NLS administered an extensive questionnaire to students from April through June of 1972, and also obtained students' SAT scores and information about their high school records from school administrators. The 19,144 seniors who participated in the base year were followed up during the fall of 1973, at which time NLS asked them questions about where they had applied to college, whether they were accepted, and their freshman grades at the college they attended. This sample consists of 2,781 NLS males and females who applied before October 1973 to a four-year college as their first choice, who reported whether or not they were accepted, and for whom we had college SAT selectivity information, high school class rank, and SAT scores. We constructed a missing data dummy for each socioeconomic background variable and then recoded missing data on each background variable to the sample mean. None of the dummies had a significant coefficient when added to the equation in the table. Variables are coded as follows for all our analyses of NLS:

College acceptance is coded 1 if the student reported (on the first follow-up) having been accepted for admission to the college of their first choice; 0 otherwise.

SAT is the sum of scores on the verbal and math sections of the Scholastic Aptitude Test. Students' SAT scores were reported by school administrators during the base-year survey (April–June 1972).

High school rank is the student's senior class standing expressed in percentiles. Our preliminary investigations of the data showed that NLS inadvertently coded many cases to missing data when, in fact, data were available to compute a high school rank. We used the following formula for percentile class rank:

$$\text{HSR} = (1 - (\text{rank in class/class size})) * 100$$

College SAT selectivity is the average SAT score (SATV and SATM summed) of the 1971 entering freshman class at the student's first-choice college. The college SAT selectivity data were obtained from the American Council on Education's Institutional Characteristics File for 1971–72 and added to the NLS data file. We used the 1971–72 ACE file as this is the information that would have been available to high school seniors applying for fall 1972 college entrance.

Father's occupation is the student's report on the first follow-up of father's occupation. NLS converted students' written responses to 1970 detailed census codes and then to Duncan scores. We employed the Duncan score coding.

Father's and mother's education is the student's report (on the first follow-up) in nine categories of his or her parents' education. Responses range from grade school only to Ph.D., M.D., or equivalent. We coded these categories into years from rough estimates of category means from the 1970 Census.

Family income is the student's estimate of his or her family's before tax income from all sources. Respondents could select one of ten categories with ranges of $0–2,999, 3,000–5,999, 6,000–7,499, 7,500–8,999, 9,000–10,499, 10,500–11,999, 12,000–13,499, 13,500–14,999, 15,000–18,000, or 18,000+. We coded each category to the midpoint except for the final category, which we coded 20,000.

[a]Unstandardized coefficients multiplied by 1,000.

*Designates coefficients more than twice their standard error.

lege's expected freshman grade point average or reduces its expected academic failure rate.

Prospective applicants also have multiple objectives in selecting a college, and they, too, will often give up a little of one objective to get a little more of another from their college choice. For example, some applicants may settle for a C average at a prestigious college, but want higher grades in a less prestigious one. But again, virtually all students want to attend a college where they will do at least well enough to graduate. We will therefore assume that self-selection benefits applicants academically if it screens in applicants to a college with expected freshman grade averages of C or better and screens out applicants with expected freshman grades below a C average.

To estimate these academic benefits to colleges and applicants, one has to calculate the expected freshman grades of prospective applicants to colleges. We discussed the problems of doing this in chapter 3. The major problem is that the predictions colleges make must be derived from regression equations for students who actually attend college. This is the problem of sample selection bias.

Since we know of no analyses, including our own in chapter 3, that convincingly estimate the direction and extent of the bias, and since our attempts to correct the problem in chapter 3 were inconclusive, we will assume what colleges assume, and what the College Board and ETS tell colleges to assume: that equations based on nonrandom samples of students attending college are the firmest basis on which to make accurate predictions about applicants. Our assessment of the academic benefits to colleges from self-selection will therefore use expected freshman grades for applicants derived from equations based on samples of attending students.

We predicted the freshman grades of the NLS applicants with the same regression equations used in chapter 3, which were calculated on the basis of the 2,470 NLS respondents who attended four-year colleges and finished their freshman year (table 3.2, equations 5 and 7). Because college selectivity is controlled in these equations, the predictions allow for differing grading standards at colleges differing in selectivity. Thus, a student with a given SAT score and high school rank who applies to a very selective college will have lower expected freshman grades than if he or she applied to a less selective college.[24]

Our results show that self-selection screens in prospective applicants to selective colleges who are likely to be successful, and screens out prospective applicants who are likely to do poorly. For example, if a highly selective college whose freshmen average 1200 on the SAT accepted all the applicants who applied to similarly selective colleges, this college would have a freshman class whose predicted grades averaged 2.89 (see table 4.2, column 1, line 1, p. 82). The failure rate would be 9.0 percent (line 7). If this college accepted the applicants who applied to any four-year college regardless of its selectivity, then the average freshman grades would fall to 2.72, and the failure rate would increase to 14.7 percent (column 2, lines 1 and 7). And if it accepted the prospective applicants to any college, the freshman grade point average would fall to 2.61 and the failure rate would increase to 18.9 percent (column 3, lines 1 and 7). Self-selection therefore raises predicted freshman grades from an average of 2.61 to 2.89 and lowers the expected failure rate from 18.9 to 9.0 percent.

These results show how self-selection can offer some protection to the quality of very selective colleges' applicant pools. But self-selection also protects less selective colleges' applicant pools. In fact, all but the least selective colleges would find the average quality of their applicant pools lowered if for some reason self-selection broke down and they started to receive applications from persons who now typically apply to the least selective colleges.

Table 4.2 Distribution of Predicted Freshman Grade Point Averages at a College of 1200 Selectivity (NLS Survey)

	Number (and Percent) of Cases					
Predicted FGPA[a]	(1) Applicants at Selective Colleges[b]		(2) Applicants at All 4-Year Colleges[c]		(3) Prospective Applicants to Any College[d]	
1.6					5	(.1)
1.7	1	(.1)	7	(.3)	30	(.5)
1.8			16	(.6)	74	(1.3)
1.9	1	(.1)	30	(1.1)	133	(2.4)
2.0	5	(.5)	41	(1.5)	193	(3.5)
2.1	12	(1.2)	77	(2.8)	268	(4.9)
2.2	16	(1.7)	102	(3.7)	335	(6.1)
2.3	25	(2.6)	155	(5.6)	416	(7.5)
2.4	42	(4.3)	211	(7.6)	465	(8.4)
2.5	37	(3.8)	206	(7.4)	490	(8.9)
2.6	61	(6.3)	246	(8.8)	495	(9.0)
2.7	94	(9.7)	299	(10.8)	517	(9.4)
2.8	108	(11.2)	312	(11.2)	550	(10.0)
2.9	111	(11.5)	320	(11.5)	506	(9.2)
3.0	120	(12.4)	245	(8.8)	358	(6.5)
3.1	127	(13.1)	217	(7.8)	305	(5.5)
3.2	109	(11.3)	160	(5.8)	202	(3.7)
3.3	65	(6.7)	89	(3.2)	117	(2.1)

(*continued*)

Table 4.2 *(continued)*

	Number (and Percent) of Cases					
	(1)		(2)		(3)	
Predicted FGPA[a]	Applicants at Selective Colleges[b]		Applicants at All 4-Year Colleges[c]		Prospective Applicants to Any College[d]	
3.4	27	(2.8)	40	(1.4)	48	(.9)
3.5	7	(.7)	8	(.3)	10	(.2)
3.6					1	(.0)
1. Mean of predicted GPAs	2.89		2.72		2.61	
2. *SD* of predicted GPAs	.308		.345		.372	
3. *N* cases	968		2781		5518	
4. Mean (and *SD*) SAT	1092	(192)	993	(203)	993	(209)
5. Mean (and *SD*) high school rank	80.9	(18.9)	73.5	(22.3)	67.0	(25.0)
6. Estimated *SD* of actual GPAs[e]	.665		.683		.697	
7. Estimated percentage of cases below C average[f]	9.0		14.7		18.9	

[a]Predicted FGPA computed from the following equation for the 706 NLS respondents attending colleges with 1100–1600 selectivity:

$$\text{Pred. FGPA} = (-.0005124*\text{SEL}) + (.00795*\text{HSR}) + (.00108*\text{SAT}) + 1.67991$$

$$R^2 = .167$$

$$SEE = .589$$

College selectivity (SEL) was fixed at 1200 for the computation.

[b]968 respondents who applied before October 1973 to first-choice four-year colleges that had freshman SAT scores averaging between 1100–1600, and whose own SAT scores and high school class ranks were reported to NLS.

[c]2,781 respondents who applied before October 1973 to first-choice four-year colleges of any selectivity, and whose own SAT scores and high school class ranks were reported to NLS.

[d]5,518 respondents whose SAT scores and high school class ranks were reported to NLS.

[e]Predicted FGPAs in a college of 1200 selectivity have the standard deviation shown in line 2 for each sample. We estimate (see note a) that errors in predicting individual grade point averages in a college of 1200 selectivity have a standard deviation of 0.589. If errors are homoskedastic, the expected standard deviation of observed freshman grade point averages in a college of 1200 selectivity in each sample is:

$$[\text{SD}^2 \text{ errors} + \text{SD}^2 \text{ predicted GPAs}]^{1/2}$$

[f]The percentage of cases in N (0,1) with Z values smaller than

$$Z = \frac{(2.0 - \text{mean of predicted GPAs})}{(\text{estimated SD of actual GPAs})}$$

For example, table 4.3 shows that when a college whose freshmen have average SAT scores of 1200 attracts and admits applicants who apply to colleges in the 1150–1249 range, its predicted freshman grade mean is 2.88. If for some reason self-selection broke down and this college started to receive applications from persons who typically apply to less selective colleges, its freshman grade point average would fall. If it started to receive applications from persons who typically apply to colleges in the 1050–1149 range, their expected freshman grades would average 2.78, compared to its former applicants' average of 2.88. Table 4.4 shows this same situation exists for a less selective college whose freshman SAT average is 900.

Tables 4.3 and 4.4 show that while self-selection can affect the average quality of a college's applicant pool, it gives no college a monopoly on the students with the highest predicted freshman grades. Both the 1200 college in table 4.3 and the 900 college in table 4.4 could increase their average freshman grades by recruiting applicants with higher predicted freshman grade averages who apply to less selective colleges.

These results illustrate how self-selection can help colleges' applicant pools by screening in applicants who are likely to be academically successful and screening out those who are likely to lower the average quality of their freshman class or do failing work. Self-selection therefore benefits both colleges and applicants.

However, our results do not show that high school ranks and SAT scores are responsible for these benefits. Information that applicants

Table 4.3 Predicted Freshman Grade Point Averages at a College of 1200 Selectivity for Persons Who Apply to Colleges of Differing Selectivity

Selectivity of College Applied To	Mean Predicted FGPA	*N*
450–549	2.20	3
550–649	2.33	8
650–749	2.31	63
750–849	2.53	68
850–949	2.58	258
950–1049	2.64	1,094
1050–1149	2.78	636
1150–1249	2.88	376
1250–1349	2.95	205
1350–1449	3.15	70
Overall	2.73	2,781

Note: GPA means computed from equation in note a, table 4.2.

Table 4.4 Predicted Freshman Grade Point Averages at a College of 900 Selectivity for Persons Who Apply to Colleges of Differing Selectivity

Selectivity of College Applied to	Mean Predicted FGPA	*N*
450–549	2.40	3
550–649	2.54	8
650–749	2.53	63
750–849	2.75	68
850–949	2.79	258
950–1049	2.84	1,094
1050–1149	2.98	636
1150–1249	3.09	376
1250–1349	3.15	205
1350–1449	3.35	70
Overall	2.93	2,781

Note: FGPA means computed from equation in note a, table 4.2, but coefficients estimated for 756 NLS respondents attending colleges with 400–999 selectivity, and with selectivity fixed at 900.

receive from colleges, prospective applicants' own academic records, test scores, family influences, and a variety of other causes may all be somewhat redundant. We argue in the next section that information from the SAT is essentially redundant.

Can SAT Scores Help?

The question here is not whether SAT scores do help prospective applicants decide where to apply. We have already seen that to a modest extent they do. The issue is whether SAT scores can contribute to self-selection decisions that have academic benefits to colleges or applicants. We argue that they cannot. The reason they cannot is because the judgments applicants could make about their academic performance in college if they did use their SAT scores is essentially identical to the judgments they could make without knowing their SAT scores.

Suppose that applicants to a college used information about the college and about their own high school record to predict their freshman grade average. We can then ask about the respective accuracy of applicants' predictions if they were to use their SAT scores and if they were not use them. It does not matter that some applicants may not try to predict their own success. What is important is what would happen if they did.

ETS and the College Board have not tried to find out how well applicants can predict their academic success. Let us suppose that applicants can predict their freshman grade average as well as linear regression equations. It is unlikely that applicants can actually predict their freshman grades that well. A large amount of research shows that people's intuitive inferences, predictions, and probability assessments are often appreciably poorer than statistical predictions.[25]

However, it is useful to assume that applicants can predict as well as linear regression equations, because these predictions minimize prediction error. Applicants that cannot predict as well as regression equations will make predictions of their freshman grades that are less accurate than we estimate. Consequently, they are even less likely than we estimate to get useful information about their future freshman grades from their high school records and SAT scores.

Suppose first that applicants did not use their SAT scores. The most obvious information they could use to estimate their academic success at any college would be information about that college along with what they know about themselves from their high school performance and other sources. Obviously, those who did well in high school would probably estimate higher grades in any given college than those who did poorly in high school. Among persons with the same high school grades, those who apply to a highly selective college would probably estimate lower college grades than those who apply to a less selective college.

For our analysis, we turn to the same sample of 2,781 NLS applicants used in table 4.1. The best prediction of freshman grades for each applicant would be generated by the following equation:

$$\text{FGPA} = (-.00013583 \times \text{SEL}) + (.01295 \times \text{HSR}) + 1.99868 \qquad (4.1)$$

This is the same regression equation of freshman grade point average (FGPA) on college selectivity (SEL) and high school rank (HSR) as equation 5 in table 3.2. Ignoring minor nonlinearities, this equation gives predicted freshman grade point averages with smaller errors of prediction than any other prediction based on college selectivity and high school rank.

Now suppose each applicant also knew his or her own SAT score, and predicted his or her freshman grade average using high school rank in class, SAT score, and the selectivity of the college being considered. The best prediction each applicant could now make would be

$$\text{FGPA} = (-.00069745 \times \text{SEL}) + (.00959 \times \text{HSR}) + (.00098177 \times \text{SAT}) + 1.85142 \quad (4.2)$$

which is the same regression equation of freshman grade point average on college selectivity, high school rank, and SAT scores as equation 7 in table 3.2. Again ignoring minor nonlinearities, it gives predicted freshman grade point averages with smaller errors of prediction than any other prediction using college selectivity, high school rank, and SAT scores.

We can next ask about the freshman grades applicants would predict if they used the ideal prediction schemes in equations 4.1 and 4.2. Suppose, for example, that all 2,781 NLS applicants to four-year colleges are considering application to a college of 1200 selectivity. Table 4.5 shows the 2,781 NLS applicants' predicted freshman grade averages at this highly selective college using both equation 4.1 and 4.2. Using equation 4.2, applicants seldom have a predicted grade point average that differs by more than 0.3 from the one they would predict from equation 4.1, which ignores SAT scores.[26] The two distributions correlate 0.877.

The relationship between the two distributions of predicted freshman grade averages illustrated in table 4.5 for a highly selective college is general and holds for a college of any selectivity. Thus when one calculates the correlation between predicted freshman grade point averages from equation 4.1 and equation 4.2, the value will always be 0.877, no matter what level of college selectivity is chosen.[27]

Equation 4.1 explains only 16.8 percent of the variance in actual freshman grade point averages. Equation 4.2 explains only 22.4 percent of the variance. This means that neither prediction scheme gives a very accurate prediction of freshman grade point averages for individuals. There is almost as much variation in actual freshman grade point averages for people with the same predicted freshman grades as there is for the entire group.[28] The low accuracy of predicted freshman grades in both equations makes it unlikely that any applicant would notice the small difference in predicted freshman grades brought about by using equation 4.2 instead of equation 4.1.

These results suggest that even under ideal conditions in which high school students could use SAT information as efficiently as

Table 4.5 Cross-Tabulation of Predicted Freshman Grade Point Averages of 2,781 NLS College Applicants at a College of 1200 Selectivity

FGPA Predicted from High School Rank	FGPA Predicted from High School Rank plus SAT																				
	1.6	1.7	1.8	1.9	2.0	2.1	2.2	2.3	2.4	2.5	2.6	2.7	2.8	2.9	3.0	3.1	3.2	3.3	3.4	3.5	*N*
1.8	1			1																	2
1.9	1	4	5	3	4	1															18
2.0	2	7	6	5	3	4															27
2.1	1		8	7	8	14	8	2	1		1										50
2.2			8	5	24	11	11	14	4	2	1										80
2.3				8	11	17	21	27	10	1	2										97
2.4				1	17	13	28	39	22	11	3	2									136
2.5				1	2	10	34	32	42	31	24	6	2								184
2.6						6	17	23	40	31	29	21	11	1							179
2.7						2	5	17	31	43	56	57	22	13		3					249
2.8							2	10	24	42	53	75	62	31	6	2	1				308
2.9								1	18	30	44	87	81	68	43	20	8	1			401
3.0									4	9	19	39	92	117	86	67	22	8	2		465
3.1										1	9	10	34	74	113	125	114	81	23	1	585
N	5	11	27	31	69	78	126	165	196	201	241	297	304	304	248	217	145	90	25	1	2,781

Note: Sample consists of 2,781 NLS respondents who applied before October 1973 to their first-choice four-year college of any selectivity, and whose own SAT scores and high school class ranks were reported to NLS. Predicted freshman grades were computed with equations 4.1 and 4.2 in the text with college selectivity fixed at 1200.

linear regression equations do, they will get little or no useful additional information about their likely freshman grades from SAT scores beyond the information they already have with rank and the selectivity of the college under consideration. This conclusion also coincides with students' opinions about the test, since most high school students have little faith that SAT scores predict their college success in any event. Fifty-six percent of the respondents surveyed by the Response Analysis Corporation for the College Board's SAT Monitor Program said they thought low SAT scores did not make much difference in an individual's ability to do college work.[29]

But while SAT scores cannot give applicants much help in forecasting their freshman grades, the scores may still affect where high school seniors apply. When prospective applicants believe or are told that "low scorers need not apply," lower scorers probably will not apply, no matter how weak the relationship of SAT scores to freshman success.

Our results therefore raise the possibility that the SAT's effect on students' college choices arises for reasons that are independent of their forecasts or future success. Applicants' opinions of their SAT results can easily represent a hodgepodge of guidance counselor or high school teacher interpretations, parental judgements, peer mythology, and admissions officers' viewpoints. The SAT may therefore give some college applicants a signal to apply when they should not and thus raise false expectations. Just as troubling, the SAT may signal some applicants not to apply when they could be admitted and succeed in a demanding academic program.

ETS has never investigated how many potentially successful applicants to selective American colleges never apply because they are scared away by their low SAT scores. Nor has it tried to find out how many applicants to selective colleges apply because their SAT scores are high when they have little chance of being admitted. Nonetheless, the specter that SAT scores contribute to "inefficiencies" in high school seniors' applications to colleges is a very different message from the one ETS presents about the virtues of the SAT in self-selection.

FIVE

The SAT Has an Adverse Impact on Black Applicants

ETS's main justification for colleges' using the SAT to help assess blacks' competence for academic work is that the test predicts blacks' success in college: "There would appear to be no ambiguity with respect to the advantage of predictions based upon a combination of high school record and test scores. Whether black males, black females, or combined sex groups are considered, the median predictive correlation using a combination of high school record and test scores is substantially higher than that obtained when either test scores or high school record alone is used."[1]

Experts in testing outside ETS point to additional benefits from colleges' use of the SAT with blacks. For example, Arthur Jensen says:

> The SAT gives academically talented blacks a better chance of showing their strength than does high school GPA. . . . A bright student who, for whatever reason, made poor grades in high school would have virtually no chance of getting into many selective colleges if it were not for his SAT score. The SAT helps many students prove their abilities. . . . Unlike teachers' marks, letters of recommendation, and interviews, test scores have been found to be essentially colorblind as predictors of academic performance in college. They "read through" the veneer of social class background, as well.[2]

Not everyone agrees about these virtues of the SAT, of course. For years critics have questioned the SAT's impact on blacks. These criticisms culminated in 1980 with the widely publicized Nader report, which charged that "when ETS aptitude tests are used for regulating access to higher education, the systematic distribution of low scores creates formidable barriers to minorities trying to go on to college."[3]

Unfortunately, neither supporters nor critics of the SAT have offered much evidence for their sweeping claims. Until recently, ETS has even appeared reluctant to tell the public how blacks perform on the SAT. For example, although ETS has compiled summary data on all students who took the SAT since 1971, it was not until 1981 that ETS publicly released such data by race.[4]

Another problem in assessing claims about the effects of the SAT on blacks is that many colleges ignore or discount black applicants' SAT scores to some degree. SAT scores therefore do not enter into colleges' admissions decisions for these applicants. To assess the effects of the SAT, we must look at cases where the SAT is used. But the fact that some colleges place little or no weight on blacks' SAT scores does not lessen the importance of knowing the effects of the SAT on blacks when it is used. To evaluate the effects of the SAT on blacks, we look at a number of uses of the test and assess their consequences.

We look first at the impact of the SAT when selective colleges admit only blacks whose SAT scores at least equal those of their white applicants. We then look at admissions policies that do not require blacks and whites to have equal SAT scores or high school grades, but do require them to have equal forecasts of college success. Finally, we look at admissions policies that do not require blacks and whites to have equal forecasts of college success and admit blacks when they have lower forecasts of success than do whites. We summarize our conclusions in the last section of the chapter.

The Effects of Requiring Equal Credentials from Whites and Blacks

College-bound whites and blacks in the United States have dramatically different SAT scores. The differences, which favor whites, create a very large credential gap. This remains a most important fact about whites' and blacks' comparative credentials for college today, despite some evidence that the gap may be declining slightly.[5]

Few blacks could attend the nation's most selective and prestigious colleges if these colleges required blacks' credentials to equal whites'. Table 5.1 shows the SAT averages of freshmen attending some of the nation's elite colleges. One can compare them with columns 1 and 2 in table 5.2, which show the distributions for black

Table 5.1 SAT Verbal and Math Averages for Freshmen in Most Selective Colleges

College	SATV	SATM
Yale	660	680
Princeton	649	695
Brown	630	670
Columbia	630	660
Dartmouth	620	670
Stanford	620	670
U. of Chicago	620	645
Duke	606	657
U. of Pennsylvania	600	670

Source: Profiles of American Colleges (Woodsbury, N.Y.: Barron's Educational Series, 1985).

and white college-bound seniors in 1984. Only 283 of the 71,177 blacks who took the SAT in 1984 got 650 or above on the verbal section. Thus, only a handful of blacks got verbal scores higher than the average Yale or Princeton freshman.

When we drop down a little to the 600 and above range in table 5.2, which includes all the selective colleges listed in table 5.1, we see that whites' credentials as a group still vastly exceed blacks' as a group. Whites outnumber blacks greatly, as one would expect, since nearly ten times as many whites as blacks took the SAT. But the percentage of white SAT takers with scores of 600 and above is also 6–8 times greater than the percentage of black SAT takers.[6]

Of greater interest than the average SAT credential in our nation's selective colleges is the range of credentials within them. If we take 500 as a lower bound of SATV and SATM scores of most students in highly selective colleges,[7] the percentage of white college-bound seniors scoring above this lower bound is more than four times the percentage of blacks (31.1 percent versus 7.6 percent on the SATV and 46.1 percent versus 11.9 percent on the SATM). Nearly 75 percent of all blacks got verbal scores below 400, which on some forms of the test is fewer than thirty correct answers out of eighty-five questions. More than one out of five blacks got math scores below 300, which on some forms of the test is fewer than three correct answers out of sixty questions.[8]

At all except the least selective colleges, the number of blacks who can qualify for admissions with credentials matching whites is likely to be far smaller than colleges would like. Suppose, for example, that colleges want the ratio of blacks to whites in their fresh-

Table 5.2 SAT Verbal and Math Distributions for 1984 College-Bound Seniors

SAT Scores	SAT Verbal (1) *N* (and %) of Whites	SAT Verbal (2) *N* (and %) of Blacks	SAT Verbal (3) [(.104967) × *N* of Whites] (and %)[a]	SAT Math (1) *N* (and %) of Whites	SAT Math (2) *N* (and %) of Blacks	SAT Math (3) [(.104967) × *N* of Whites] (and %)[a]
750–800	1,236 (.2)	17 (.02)	130 (.2)	5,172 (.8)	20 (.02)	543 (.8)
700–749	6,136 (.9)	69 (.09)	644 (.9)	19,736 (2.9)	154 (.2)	2,072 (2.9)
650–699	15,597 (2.3)	197 (.3)	1,637 (2.3)	40,310 (5.9)	521 (.7)	4,231 (5.9)
600–649	34,025 (5.0)	649 (.9)	3,571 (5.0)	61,886 (9.1)	1,191 (1.7)	6,496 (9.1)
550–599	61,491 (9.1)	1,462 (2.1)	6,455 (9.1)	82,751 (12.2)	2,343 (3.3)	8,686 (12.2)
500–549	92,144 (13.6)	2,996 (4.2)	9,672 (13.6)	103,215 (15.2)	4,269 (6.0)	10,834 (15.2)
450–499	118,281 (17.4)	5,158 (7.3)	12,416 (17.4)	112,075 (16.5)	7,121 (10.0)	11,764 (16.5)
400–449	127,484 (18.8)	8,495 (11.9)	13,382 (18.8)	96,360 (14.2)	9,676 (13.6)	10,114 (14.2)
350–399	105,975 (15.6)	12,010 (16.9)	11,124 (15.6)	80,281 (11.8)	13,726 (19.3)	8,427 (11.8)
300–349	69,914 (10.3)	14,312 (20.1)	7,339 (10.3)	51,228 (7.6)	15,993 (22.5)	5,377 (7.6)
250–299	34,719 (5.1)	14,543 (20.4)	3,644 (5.1)	22,031 (3.2)	12,928 (18.2)	2,312 (3.2)
200–249	11,085 (1.6)	11,242 (15.8)	1,164 (1.6)	3,041 (.4)	3,232 (4.5)	319 (.4)
Total	678,087 (99.9)	71,177 (100.0)	71,178 (99.9)	678,086 (99.8)	71,174 (100.0)	71,175 (99.8)

Source: Solomon Arbeiter, *Profiles, College-bound Seniors, 1984* (New York: College Entrance Examination Board, 1984), table 10.

[a]Totals differ slightly from column 2 because of rounding.

man class to equal the ratio of blacks to whites in the college-bound SAT-taking population. The ratio of blacks to whites in the 1984 SAT college-bound population is 0.105 (table 5.2). If American colleges want to admit blacks numbering 10.5 percent of the whites at each SAT range, they will look for the numbers of blacks shown in columns 3 in table 5.2. But the number of blacks who could qualify for admissions with SAT scores equal to those of whites (column 2) falls short of the 10.5 percent colleges would want (column 3) at SAT verbal and math scores down to 350. Below these SAT scores, blacks exceed the numbers colleges would want.

These results suggest that if colleges insist on blacks having SAT credentials equal to those of whites, most blacks will be rejected from selective colleges because their SAT scores are too low, not because colleges do not want them. The requirement that blacks have credentials equal to whites' will crowd blacks into the least selective colleges and underrepresent them as a percentage of the white college-bound population at all except the least selective colleges.

These results show what happens to black admissions if colleges insist on blacks having SAT scores equal to whites'. Since selective colleges also look at their black applicants' high school records, it is instructive to look at the consequences of selective colleges admitting blacks when only their high school grades or class ranks equal whites'.

Blacks face a credential gap with their high school records, just as they do with their SAT scores. Blacks overall were numerically equivalent to 11.1 percent of the white 1984 college-bound population reporting high school grades and class rank to ETS (table 5.3). But blacks with grades averaging B or higher and in the top two-fifths of their graduating class were fewer than 11.1 percent of the white college-bound population. Only when high school grades fall below a B average and rank falls into the second quintile do blacks have credentials equal to whites' in numbers equal to 11.1 percent of the whites (table 5.3, column 3). This suggests that the number of blacks who can qualify for admission into the nation's selective colleges will be fewer than these colleges are likely to want if they insist on admitting *either* blacks whose high school grades match their white students' *or* blacks whose SAT scores match those of the whites.

Another use of SAT scores and high school records by colleges does not require blacks to have SAT scores or high school grades equal to those of their white applicants, but rather some equivalent combination of them. For example, some colleges calculate an eli-

Table 5.3 High School Grade Point Average and High School Rank Distributions for 1984 College-Bound Seniors

	N (and %) of Whites	*N* (and %) of Blacks	[(.111495) × *N* of Whites] (and %)
High school grade point average:[a]			
3.75–4.00	112,681 (16.0)	3,777 (4.8)	12,563 (16.0)
3.50–3.74	85,215 (12.1)	5,114 (6.5)	9,501 (12.1)
3.25–3.49	92,962 (13.2)	7,002 (8.9)	10,365 (13.2)
3.00–3.24	123,245 (17.5)	12,510 (15.9)	13,741 (17.5)
2.75–2.99	85,919 (12.2)	10,858 (13.8)	9,580 (12.2)
2.50–2.74	84,511 (12.0)	13,611 (17.3)	9,423 (12.0)
2.25–2.49	55,636 (7.9)	10,307 (13.1)	6,203 (7.9)
2.00–2.24	40,143 (5.7)	8,969 (11.4)	4,476 (5.7)
Under 2.00	24,649 (3.5)	6,452 (8.2)	2,748 (3.5)
Total[b]	704,961 (100.1)	78,600 (99.9)	78,600 (100.1)
Mean	3.07	2.74	
High school rank:			
Top Tenth	152,673 (22.5)	9,025 (12.0)	16,939 (22.5)
Second Tenth	143,852 (21.2)	13,913 (18.5)	15,960 (21.2)
Second Fifth	178,458 (26.3)	19,855 (26.4)	19,799 (26.3)
Third Fifth	177,780 (26.2)	27,225 (36.2)	19,724 (26.2)
Fourth Fifth	21,714 (3.2)	4,362 (5.8)	2,409 (3.2)
Lowest Fifth	3,393 (.5)	827 (1.1)	376 (.5)
Total[b]	677,870 (99.9)	75,207 (100.0)	75,207 (99.9)
Median percentile rank	75.1	65.1	

Source: Solomon Arbeiter, *Profiles, College-bound Seniors, 1984* (New York: College Entrance Examination Board, 1984), table 7.

[a]Calculated by weighting the latest self-reported grade on the Student Descriptive Questionnaire in English, mathematics, foreign language, biological sciences, physical sciences, and social studies by the number of years of study in the subject and dividing by the total years of study in all six subjects. If a grade was not reported in a subject, that subject was excluded in calculating the overall grade average.

[b]Totals differ slightly from the College Board's because of rounding.

gibility score for every applicant that combines both high school grades and test scores, and require blacks to have the same eligibility scores for admissions as whites. One method sets a minimum required high school grade average and a minimum SAT score. Another method uses high school grades or rank combined with SAT scores on a sliding scale. An applicant in the top tenth of his or her class, for example, might be admitted with any SAT score. But if the class rank is below the top tenth, a minimum SAT score is imposed.[9]

Selective colleges that base admissions on eligibility scores formulated these ways, and that require blacks to have the same eligibility scores as whites, will find fewer eligible blacks than they would like for the same reasons as colleges that insist on either equal SAT scores or equal high school grades. The reason is that SAT scores correlate positively with both high school grades and class rank, and a shortage of highly credentialed blacks exists both for SAT scores (table 5.2) and high school grades and class rank (table 5.3). Thus, it is not surprising that when Hunter Breland at ETS studied colleges' admissions policies using national data from the College Board's Admissions Testing Program, he found that at all except the lowest admissions standards, all admissions policies that used SAT scores and high school grades or class rank resulted in a lower percentage of blacks being eligible for admission than whites.[10] Blacks will therefore be sorted out of selective colleges by these admissions policies and crowded into the least selective colleges.

At some colleges, SAT use may dramatically affect blacks. In Connecticut, for example, three of the state's five technical colleges recommend a minimum combined SAT score of 900 for admissions.[11] This SAT minimum would exclude approximately 80 percent of the blacks who took the SAT in 1984. Similarly, the University of Colorado requires "a specified course-work pattern, a minimum composite SAT score of 1,000 . . . and class rank in the upper 40th to 50th percentiles.[12] The SAT minimum in Colorado would exclude 90 percent of the 1984 black SAT takers.

So far our assessment of the effects of the SAT on blacks has dwelt only on blacks' access to selective colleges if colleges require them to have credentials at least equal to those of whites. While colleges worry that many blacks have admissions credentials lower than whites', most do not believe that every applicant should be accepted. Colleges want the students they admit to perform satisfactorily regardless of their race. None of the admissions policies combining high school information and SAT scores that we have discussed so far in this chapter are designed to maximize the academic performance of the students they admit.

Colleges that assess applicants' eligibility by combining high school grades or rank with SAT scores use this information most efficiently only when they weight test scores and high school record to predict college success maximally. This is the predicted performance model of admissions that customizes weightings of the high school record and test scores to maximize college academic performance for selected students at each college.[13] Consequently, if we are to assess selection with the SAT and high school record to maximize black and white students' college performance, we must also weight the SAT and high school record to maximize predictions of college grades.

Effects of Requiring Equal Predicted Freshman Grades

When colleges derive prediction equations from a combined sample of blacks and whites, the procedures they follow may not give accurate predictions of blacks' freshman grades. Colleges' prediction equations from a combined sample of blacks and whites typically *overestimate* the freshman grades of blacks.

ETS is aware of this overprediction and has studied it extensively, but has never developed its implications for colleges. Hunter Breland, a senior researcher at ETS, published a College Board Research and Development Report in 1978 that even now is a good summary of the most important studies. Breland found that predictions based on the high school record alone overpredicted blacks' grades in twenty-five of twenty-six comparisons, with the median overprediction being 0.28 points when grades are measured on a four-point scale. Predictions based on the high school record plus SAT scores overpredicted blacks' grades in twenty-five of thirty-three comparisons, with the median overprediction being only 0.05. "The overpredictions for minorities occur whether the prediction is made from the high school record alone . . . or from combinations of grades and test scores," Breland concludes. "However, the overpredictions for minorities appear to be substantially reduced, on the average, when the high school record and test scores are used in combination as predictors."[14]

The National Longitudinal Study (NLS) of the high school class of 1972 gives results very similar to Breland's. The NLS reports on 1,987 whites and 201 blacks with high school ranks and SAT scores who attended four-year colleges whose selectivity we could determine, completed at least the freshman year and reported grades, and later reported whether or not they had earned a bachelor's degree or more.

We first combined blacks and whites into a single sample and computed prediction equations by regressing students' freshman grade point averages on their high school rank and the selectivity of the college they attended, and then on high school rank, selectivity, and SAT scores (table 5.4, equations 1 and 2). We then used these

Table 5.4 Regression Equations Used to Compute Predicted Freshman Grade Point Average in the NLS

	Independent Variables						
Equation	High School Rank	SAT	College Selectivity	Race	Constant	$\overline{R}^2$	SEE
1. B	.0129268*		−.000112026		1.976649	.167	.5989
beta	.416		−.022				
2. B	.0095624*	.00100584*	−.000717253*		1.849612	.225	.5779
beta	.308	.301	−.140				
3. B	.0128392*		−.000264169*	−.2604938*	2.165252	.179	.5947
beta	.413		−.051	−.115			
4. B	.0097022*	.00095488*	−.000739680*	−.0908962*	1.921859	.226	.5776
beta	.312	.286	−.144	−.040			

Note: Sample includes 2,188 blacks and whites who attended a four-year college or university with complete data on college grade point average, bachelor's degree attainment, high school rank in class, SAT, college selectivity, and race.

*Designates coefficients more than twice their standard error.

equations to predict freshman grades separately for whites and blacks.[15]

The mean black freshman grade point average predicted from high school rank is 2.76 (equation 1). Using both high school rank and the SAT (equation 2), it falls to 2.60. The observed black mean is only 2.54. High school rank therefore overpredicts the freshman grades of blacks by 0.21, while high school rank plus SAT overpredicts black grades by only 0.06. These results are quite close to the median values of 0.28 and 0.05 reported by Breland. The NLS findings therefore affirm Breland's and ETS's conclusion that overprediction occurs for blacks whether prediction is made from the high school record alone or from the high school record plus SAT scores, but that it is reduced with the SAT.[16] These findings may come as a surprise to some people, since a popular belief among blacks and critics of the SAT is that high school records and SAT scores underestimate blacks' college performance. But there really is little mystery to Breland's or our own results. Overprediction of blacks' freshman grades from a common regression equation occurs whenever black-white differences in high school records and SAT scores are not large enough to explain the entire black-white difference in freshman grades. This suggests that compared to whites, blacks may have some disadvantage in doing college work that is unrelated to their high school records and SAT scores and that lowers their actual freshman grades below those predicted by their lower high school records and SAT scores.[17] Speculations abound as to what these disadvantages might be, but no one really knows.[18]

Effects on Admissions

The NLS reports on 2,200 whites and 232 blacks who applied to a four-year college as their first choice and had complete data on high school rank, SAT, and the selectivity of the college. Table 5.5 shows cross-tabulations for these applicants of freshman grades predicted by high school rank alone and high school rank plus the SAT. The top panel is for the 2,220 white applicants and the bottom panel is for the 232 black applicants. These cross-tabulations are much like the ones we have seen before (see table 3.4, for example) and are probably typical of those at many American colleges.

Suppose a college with predicted grades like those of NLS applicants admitted students whose predicted grades were above 2.5, and rejected students whose predicted grades were 2.5 or below (table 5.5, dashed lines). Now let us compare the effects of using high school rank alone to the effects of using both rank and SAT scores. For 76.4 percent of the whites and 53.4 percent of the blacks, the verdict would be positive under either policy. For 15.4 percent of the whites and 26.3 percent of the blacks, it would be negative under either policy. Both admissions policies would therefore make identical decisions for 76.4 + 15.4 = 91.8 percent of the white applicants and 53.4 + 26.3 = 79.7 percent of the black applicants.

Even though both policies agree on the great majority of decisions, the level of agreement is higher for whites (91.8 percent) than for blacks (79.7 percent). This is because the rank plus SAT policy rejects a higher percentage of black applicants than rank alone. As a result, a higher percentage of blacks than whites are rejected by both policies (26.3 versus 15.4 percent). And, a higher percentage of blacks than whites are admitted by rank but rejected by rank plus SAT (19 versus 4.8 percent).

The increased rejection of blacks by adding the SAT to class rank is not a function of the cutoff point. Addition of the SAT to prediction lowers the mean of blacks' predicted freshman grades at almost every cutoff.[19] Addition of the SAT to high school rank lowers the overall predicted grade mean for blacks from 2.73 to 2.57 (table 5.5). Consequently, addition of the SAT shifts the predicted grade distribution downward so that more applicants fall below the cutoff point (compare the cumulative *N* for the two policies at any cutoff in table 5.5).

The finding that the SAT lowers blacks' predicted freshman grades but not whites' virtually guarantees that color-blind use of the SAT will lower blacks' admissions. For example, one admissions strategy used by colleges is to accept all applicants who meet the college's minimum standards on a first-come, first-served basis, until all places in the freshman class have been filled. This method is equivalent to a college determining the minimally acceptable cutoff for predicted freshman grades and admitting all applicants above that score without regard to their race. Qualitative distinctions are typically not made among candidates so long as they have predicted grades above the cutoff score. Another method of selection is to rank applicants without regard to race in descending order by predicted grades and select from the top down until all places in the class have been filled.[20]

Both of these selection strategies reduce black acceptances when the SAT is added to high school rank. Adding the SAT to the high school rank prediction equation lowers the black predicted grade point average mean, so that with the first method fewer blacks lie

Table 5.5 Cross-Tabulation of Predicted Grade Point Averages for Four-Year College Applicants in the NLS

66

Grades Predicted by HSR Alone	Grades Predicted by HSR plus SAT — Whites																						
	1.7	1.8	1.9	2.0	2.1	2.2	2.3	2.4	2.5	2.6	2.7	2.8	2.9	3.0	3.1	3.2	3.3	3.4	3.5	3.6	*N*	tive *N*	Mean
1.9	1		4																		5	2,220	1.9
2.0		2	3	4	5	1															15	2,215	2.0
2.1		1	3	8	6	6	11	2			1										38	2,200	2.2
2.2			3	4	9	14	12	10	6	1	1										60	2,162	2.3
2.3				3	5	14	15	16	8	4	1										66	2,102	2.3
2.4				1	4	15	19	33	18	8	2	2									102	2,036	2.4
2.5					1	4	18	25	29	38	14	3									132	1,934	2.5
2.6						3	8	17	28	33	33	14	2	2							140	1,802	2.6
2.7							3	12	13	46	49	36	22	6	2						189	1,662	2.7
2.8								4	12	24	49	62	59	23	2	3					238	1,473	2.8
2.9									4	16	45	69	80	50	30	10	2				306	1,235	2.9
3.0							1		2	4	16	48	109	98	80	44	12	1			415	929	3.0
3.1											4	12	22	89	124	127	82	25	12		497	514	3.1
3.2												1		1	1	4	3	3	2	2	17	17	3.3
N	1	3	13	20	30	57	87	119	120	174	215	247	294	269	239	188	99	29	14	2	2,220		
Cumulative *N*	2,220	2,219	2,216	2,203	2,183	2,153	2,096	2,009	1,890	1,770	1,596	1,381	1,134	840	571	332	144	45	16	2			
Mean	1.9	2.0	2.0	2.1	2.2	2.3	2.4	2.5	2.6	2.7	2.8	2.9	2.9	3.0	3.0	3.0	3.1	3.1	3.1	3.2			

N = 343 (15.4%)

N = 75 (3.4)%

N = 107 (4.8%)

N = 1,695 (76.4%)

Grades Predicted by HSR Alone	Grades Predicted by HSR plus SAT
Mean = 2.82	Mean = 2.82
SD = .278	*SD* = .322

	Blacks																				
	1.6	1.7	1.8	1.9	2.0	2.1	2.2	2.3	2.4	2.5	2.6	2.7	2.8	2.9	3.0	3.1	3.2	3.3	*N*	Cumulative *N*	Mean
1.9		1			1	1	1												4	232	2.0
2.0	1		2	1	1		1												6	228	1.9
2.1			1			1													2	222	2.0
2.2					2	2	6												10	220	2.1
2.3	*N* = 61				1	6	2	2	2								*N* = 3		13	210	2.2
2.4	(26.3%)					1	4	3	2	1	1						(1.3%)		12	197	2.4
2.5							3	4	3	5	1	1							17	185	2.3
2.6						1	2	6	2	6	3	1							21	168	2.4
2.7	*N* = 44						1	2	4	5	4	3	1	1			*N* = 124		21	147	2.5
2.8	(19.0%)							1	4	4	2	7	2	2		1	(53.4%)		23	126	2.6
2.9									1	4	12	10	7	2					36	103	2.7
3.0									1		3	3	3	9	3	1			23	67	2.8
3.1											1	6	8	9	7	8	2	1	42	44	2.9
3.2																1		1	2	2	3.2
N	1	1	3	1	5	12	20	18	19	25	27	31	21	23	10	11	2	2	232		
Cumulative *N*	232	231	230	227	226	221	209	189	171	152	127	100	69	48	25	15	4	2			
Mean	2.0	1.9	2.0	2.0	2.1	2.3	2.3	2.5	2.6	2.7	2.8	2.9	3.0	3.0	3.1	3.1	3.1	3.2			

Grades Predicted by HSR Alone

Mean = 2.73
SD = .319

Grades Predicted by HSR plus SAT

Mean = 2.57
SD = .322

Note: Sample includes 2,220 whites and 232 blacks in NLS who applied to a four-year college, had complete data on high school rank, SAT, the selectivity of the college applied to, and told NLS whether they were accepted by the college.

above the minimal cutoff (table 5.6), and with the second method fewer blacks have sufficiently high rank order positions to be admitted (table 5.7).

These results show only the expected decline in the percentage of blacks in colleges' freshman classes from adding the SAT to high school rank. The results do not assess whether the SAT also improves colleges' admissions decisions with respect to black students. If it does, colleges might conclude that the gains in predictive accuracy justify the exclusion of black applicants.

To assess how much the SAT improves colleges' admissions decisions with black students, it is necessary to turn to samples of students attending college, since only these students can actually earn freshman grades and graduate. This means that we must also make assumptions, just as ETS and colleges do, about how students attending college and earning freshman grades resemble applicants.

Table 5.6 Expected Racial Composition of Freshman Class When Selection Is above Various Cutoffs

	Number and Percentages Selected					
	High School Rank			High School Rank plus SAT		
Selection	White	Black	Total	White	Black	Total
≥3.1	514 (92.1)	44 (7.9)	558	571 (97.4)	15 (2.6)	586
≥3.0	929 (93.3)	67 (6.7)	996	840 (97.1)	25 (2.9)	865
≥2.8	1,473 (92.1)	126 (7.9)	1,599	1,381 (95.2)	69 (4.8)	1,450
≥2.5	1,934 (91.3)	185 (8.7)	2,119	1,890 (92.6)	152 (7.4)	2,042

Note: Same sample as in table 5.5.

Table 5.7 Expected Racial Composition of a Freshman Class When Candidates are Rank-ordered on Grades Predicted from High School Rank and High School Rank plus SAT (%)

	High School Rank		High School Rank plus SAT	
	White	Black	White	Black
Top 10%, or 245	90.6	9.4	98.8	1.2
Top 15%, or 368	91.6	8.4	98.6	1.4
Top 30%, or 736	92.8	7.2	97.0	3.0
Top 50%, or 1,226	92.7	7.3	96.0	4.0
Top 75%, or 1,839	91.8	8.2	93.4	6.6

Note: Same sample as in table 5.5.

We must assume, as we have throughout this study, that the cross-tabulations of predicted freshman grades for attending students are similar to the ones for applicants.[21] We must also assume that the distributions of observed grades for students with differing predicted grades who attend college are the same for applicants with these same predicted grades.[22] These two assumptions enable us to treat attending students as though they were applicants and to assess the impact of selection with the SAT on distributions of college outcomes.

Effects on Admissions Outcomes

Suppose a college whose applicants resemble NLS freshmen seeks to admit students who will earn at least a 2.5 grade point average during their freshman year and who will later graduate. If this college admits all applicants whose predicted grades are above 2.5 without regard to their race and rejects all the rest, its admissions outcomes would be those summarized in table 5.8. Admissions personnel typically distinguish among the four admissions outcomes table 5.8 presents. Correct outcomes admit students who prove to be successful in college (true positives) and reject students who would be unsuccessful (true negatives). Incorrect admissions outcomes admit students who are later unsuccessful in college (false positives) or reject students who would, in fact, be successful (false negatives). The unparenthesized numbers in the cells of each subtable give the percentages of these outcomes. The parenthesized values give the percentages expected if the admissions policy predictors had no relationship to the outcomes, but the admission/rejection rates and success/failure rates were those in the marginals.[23]

Adding the SAT to predictions based on high school rank lowers blacks' predicted grades and thereby lowers black acceptances. Supplementing high school rank with the SAT decreases black admissions from 74.6 percent to 57.7 percent. This substantially changes colleges' admissions outcomes for blacks.

True positives and false positives. The SAT actually reduces the percentage of black applicants who are admitted and will be successful (true positives) from 25.3 to 22.3 percent when freshman grades are the criterion. It reduces the percentage from 52.7 to 43.3 percent when earning a bachelor's degree is the criterion. But the SAT also reduces the percentage of black applicants who are admitted and will be unsuccessful (false positives) from 49.3 to 35.3 percent using freshman grades as a criterion and from 21.9 to 14.4 percent when earning a bachelor's degree is the criterion.

Table 5.8 Freshman Grade Point Average and B.A. Outcomes for High School Rank and High School Rank plus SAT Admissions Policies

	FGPA ≤ 2.5 or > 2.5					
	White (N = 1,987)			Black (N = 201)		
	≤ 2.5	> 2.5	Total	≤ 2.5	> 2.5	Total
High school rank:						
Reject	11.8 (7.0)	4.4 (9.2)	16.2	18.9 (17.3)	6.5 (8.1)	25.4
Admit	31.5 (36.3)	52.3 (47.5)	83.8	49.3 (50.9)	25.3 (23.7)	74.6
Total	43.3	56.7	100.00	68.2	31.8	100.00
High school rank plus SAT:						
Reject	12.8 (7.5)	4.4 (9.8)	17.2	32.8 (28.8)	9.5 (13.5)	42.3
Admit	30.5 (35.9)	52.3 (46.9)	82.8	35.3 (39.3)	22.3 (18.3)	57.7
Total	43.3	56.7	100.00	68.2	31.8	100.00
	Bachelor's Degree					
	No B.A.	B.A.	Total	No B.A.	B.A.	Total
High school rank:						
Reject	6.4 (3.7)	9.8 (12.5)	16.2	12.4 (8.7)	12.9 (16.7)	25.4
Admit	16.2 (18.9)	67.6 (64.9)	83.8	21.9 (25.6)	52.7 (49.0)	74.6
Total	22.6	77.4	100.00	34.3	65.7	100.00
High school rank plus SAT:						
Reject	6.4 (3.9)	10.8 (13.3)	17.2	19.9 (14.5)	22.4 (27.8)	42.3
Admit	16.2 (18.7)	66.6 (64.0)	82.8	14.4 (19.8)	43.3 (37.9)	57.7
Total	22.6	77.4	100.00	34.3	65.7	100.00

(*continued*)

Notes: Same sample as in table 5.4. Predicted FGPA was computed from equations 1 and 2 in table 5.4. The selection cutoff is a predicted grade point average less than or equal to 2.5. The actual number of cases in each cell may be found by multiplying cell proportions by the appropriate *N*. Some cell percentages do not add to marginals because of rounding.

The base rates (in parentheses) are computed as follows. Let decisions and outcomes be labeled as follows: *A* = applicants accepted and successful (true positives); *B* = applicants rejected and unsuccessful (true negatives); *C* = applicants rejected and successful (false negatives); *D* = applicants accepted and unsuccessful (false positives). Let all values be proportions of the total sample. The true positive base rate is 100 * [(*D* + A) * (*C* + *A*)].The true negative base rate is 100 * [(*B* + *C*) * (*B* + *D*)]. The false negative base rate is 100 * [(*B* + *C*) * (*C* + *A*)]. The false positive rate is 100 * [(*D* + *A*) * (*B* + *D*)].

Virtually all these declines occur because adding the SAT to predictions based on high school rank lowers black acceptances. This, in turn, decreases the percentages of both true and false positives. Consequently, supplementing rank with the SAT has virtually no impact on colleges' percentages of true positives or false positives once the base rate for these outcomes is controlled. For example, using freshman grades as a criterion, the rank plus SAT policy increases a college's true positive forecasts only (22.3 − 18.3) − (25.3 − 23.7) = 2.4 out of each 100 above the decline in base rate from reduced black admissions. The SAT decreases a college's false positives only (35.3 − 39.3) − (49.3 − 50.9) = −2.4 out of each 100 beyond the change in base rate. The changes are even smaller using graduation as the criterion.

True negatives and false negatives. The SAT increases the percentage of black applicants who are rejected and who would be unsuccessful (true negatives) from 18.9 to 32.8 percent using freshman grades as the criterion and from 12.4 to 19.9 percent using bachelor's degree attainment as the criterion. But the SAT also increases the percentage of black applicants who are rejected and who would be successful (false negatives) from 6.5 to 9.5 percent using freshman grades as the criterion and from 12.9 to 22.4 percent using bachelor's degree as the criterion.

Again, these increases occur largely because the SAT increases black rejections, so that the percentage of true and false negatives increases. Consequently, supplementing rank with the SAT has virtually no impact on colleges' true negative or false negative decisions once the base rate for these outcomes is controlled. Using freshman grades as the criterion, the rank plus SAT policy increases a college's true negative forecasts only (32.8 − 28.8) − (18.9 − 17.3) = 2.4 out of each 100 above the increase in base rate from additional black rejections. The SAT decreases a college's false negative forecasts only (9.5 − 13.5) − (6.5 − 8.1) = −2.4 beyond the increase in base rate. The changes are again smaller using graduation as the criterion.

We also studied all these admissions outcomes using selection cutoffs from 2.3 to 3.0, but do not present the results because the conclusions we reach from table 5.8 with a 2.5 selection cutoff also hold for the other cutoffs.

All in all, these results suggest that color-blind admissions with the SAT increase colleges' black true negative admissions decisions and decrease their false positive decisions. Both results seem desirable. However, colleges will also decrease their true positive admissions decisions and increase their false negative decisions. Both of these results seem undesirable.

Those who place substantial utility on the SAT's increasing colleges' true negative decisions and reducing false positive decisions for blacks will conclude that supplementing high school rank with the SAT brings an overall improvement in admissions outcomes. Some colleges may come to this conclusion because false positive errors impose substantial costs on colleges when students fail courses, get on probation, and drop out. Colleges' false positive decisions also impose substantial costs on students because students suffer the consequences of failure.

However, we doubt whether colleges want to decrease the percentage of true positive decisions and increase their percentage of false negative decisions for blacks, which the SAT also does. Some colleges might argue that both of these outcomes have minimal costs to the college because the rejected blacks go elsewhere and the college never sees them. But colleges normally do not choose an admissions policy to get these outcomes.

Certainly the College Board and ETS have never explicitly encouraged colleges to use the SAT because it helps them reject a higher percentage of potentially successful and potentially unsuccessful blacks or, alternatively, because it helps them admit a lower percentage of potentially successful and unsuccessful blacks. The College Board and ETS do implicitly encourage these outcomes, however, since they result from adding the SAT to colleges' prediction formulas.

Furthermore, we must consider why the SAT has these effects. The SAT has very little effect on admissions outcomes over high school rank alone except insofar as the test lowers black acceptances. Thus, when the admissions rate is controlled, the SAT cannot admit successful blacks or reject unsuccessful ones with substantively greater accuracy than high school rank. It is important to see what this means.

Suppose a college whose applicants resemble our NLS sample decides to reduce the black applicants it admits from 74.6 percent to 57.7 percent, but *not* by adding the SAT to high school rank and admitting students whose predicted freshman grades exceed 2.5. Instead, the college simply decides to identify all black applicants admitted with high school rank alone and reject an additional (74.6 − 57.7)/74.6 = 22.7 percent of them randomly.

This college would then find admissions outcomes that are very close to the ones in table 5.8 when the SAT is used. That is, compared to outcomes using rank alone, the college would decrease the percent of unsuccessful and successful blacks it admitted. And it would increase the percentage of successful and unsuccessful blacks it rejected.

For example, randomly rejecting 22.7 percent of the blacks admitted in table 5.8 using high school rank alone would decrease the true positives for freshman grades from 25.3 percent to 25.3 × (1 − 0.227) = 19.6 percent, which is very close to the 22.3 percent of true positives in the table the college would expect with SAT plus rank. The false positives would decrease from 49.3 percent to 49.3 × (1 − 0.227) = 38.1 percent, also very close to the 35.3 percent with SAT plus rank. The true negatives would increase from 18.9 percent to 18.9 × (1 + 0.665) = 31.5 percent and the false negatives from 6.5 percent to 6.5 × (1 + 0.665) = 10.8 percent. These values are all close to the ones the college would expect using the SAT in addition to high school rank.

Randomly rejecting the same additional percentage of blacks that the SAT rejects when added to the forecasted grade formula therefore produces admissions outcomes much like adding the SAT itself. The SAT thus acts much like a supplement to high school rank with zero validity that rejects additional blacks. The results are similar to these when bachelor's degree attainment is the criterion.[24]

Consequently, while the addition of the SAT to prediction rejects blacks by forecasted grades that are correlated with observed grades, the rejection of more blacks does not translate into improved admissions outcomes. The SAT does not improve colleges' ability to admit successful blacks and reject potentially unsuccessful ones. Instead, the SAT changes colleges admissions outcomes only if it changes colleges' base rates for these outcomes. The SAT affects colleges' admissions outcomes much like the random rejection of additional blacks. It therefore acts with respect to actual admissions outcomes very much like a supplement to high school rank with zero validity that increases rejections of blacks. This is exactly the meaning of the test having an adverse impact on blacks when used to supplement high school rank.

These findings are not limited to colleges in the NLS. Unfortunately, ETS does not collect data from colleges on race, so we cannot replicate our findings for a large number of individual colleges in the Validity Study Service. However, the University of Delaware enrolled 106 blacks in its 1983 freshman class, and these data confirm every essential aspect of our conclusions. Table 5.9 presents the results.

Adding the SAT to Delaware's equation predicting freshman grades from high school grades reduces overprediction of freshman grades for blacks. Adding the SAT therefore reduces the percentage of blacks whose predicted freshman grades are above the admissions cutoff. Table 5.9 estimates that adding the SAT reduces black admissions 69.8 − 62.3 = 7.5 per 100 using a 2.0 grade cutoff, and 51.9 − 42.5 = 9.4 per 100 using a 2.2 cutoff.

Furthermore, the SAT decreases Delaware's true positive and false positive admissions outcomes for blacks and increases its true negative and false negative outcomes, just as it does in the NLS. Adding the SAT has little effect on Delaware's black admissions outcomes beyond its impact on the base rate. Were Delaware to admit blacks on the basis of their high school grades, and then randomly reject the added percentage that the SAT rejects when added to the forecasted grade formula, the resulting admissions outcomes would closely duplicate the effects of adding the SAT.[25] Consequently, the SAT at the University of Delaware also acts with respect to admissions outcomes much like a zero-validity supplement to high school grades that increases rejections of blacks, and therefore has an adverse impact on them.[26]

The Effects of Colleges Lowering Admissions Standards for Blacks

Colleges usually do not discuss publicly how they admit or reject blacks. But with a desire to achieve integrated classes coupled with

Table 5.9 Freshman Grade Point Average Outcomes (and Base Rates) for High School GPA and High School GPA plus SAT Admissions Policies for University of Delaware Blacks (N = 106)

	Admissions Standard					
	> 2.0 Freshman Grades			> 2.2 Freshman Grades		
	≤ 2.0	> 2.0	Total	≤ 2.0	> 2.0	Total
	High School GPA					
Reject	22.6 (16.5)	7.6 (13.7)	30.2	33.9 (26.3)	14.2 (21.8)	48.1
Admit	32.1 (38.2)	37.7 (31.6)	69.8	20.8 (28.4)	31.1 (23.5)	51.9
Total	54.7	45.3	100.0	54.7	45.3	100.0
	High School GPA plus SAT					
Reject	25.4 (20.6)	12.3 (17.1)	37.7	38.7 (31.5)	18.8 (26.0)	57.5
Admit	29.3 (34.1)	33.0 (28.2)	62.3	16.0 (23.2)	26.5 (19.3)	42.5
Total	54.7	45.3	100.0	54.7	45.3	100.0

Notes: Sample consists of 106 black and 2,569 white first-time, full-time freshman who entered the University of Delaware in the fall of 1983 and completed at least one semester. We averaged freshman grades for the first semester for students who did not finish their freshman year, and for the full year for those who did finish at least their freshman year. We calculated prediction equations on the full sample of 2,675 whites and blacks combined and used predicted values from these equations along with observed grades for the 106 blacks in the table.

strong external pressures to admit blacks, few American colleges follow totally color-blind admissions policies.

Most selective colleges approach admissions of blacks much as they approach admissions of whites. Just as they want talented whites, they also want talented blacks. The major difference, as we have seen, is that if colleges use the same fixed predicted grade cutoff for whites and blacks, they may not admit as many blacks as they would like. Many colleges are therefore willing to lower their predicted grade cutoff if this is necessary to admit a sufficiently large number of black freshmen.

When colleges do this, they treat blacks no differently than any other identifiable group whose admission is important to them. Suppose, for example, that a college encountered a declining number of female applicants, or applicants from an important geographical area. To boost enrollment, it might lower its predicted grade cutoff for these groups, just as it would for blacks, to keep the class size and mixture it wanted. If necessary, colleges lower academic admissions standards for blacks and other groups because they have important objectives that are met by planning the composition of their student bodies. Some colleges admit only men, and others favor one religious preference or geographical region. Others plan diversity for generally the same reasons some colleges plan homogeneity. They do it for educational reasons, to meet institutional responsibilities, because of outside pressure, because they have always done so, and for other reasons.

Of course, colleges may not announce to the world that they operate this way. And American colleges obviously differ in how much they will lower their admissions criteria to maintain the black enrollments they want. Some may not have to lower them at all. Others, under pressure to increase black enrollments, may quietly have to admit nearly every black who applies.

Data are sparse on how much different kinds of colleges lower their admissions standards to provide opportunities for blacks. Charles Manski and David Wise found that in 1972, black applicants in both the South and the rest of the country were more likely to be admitted than white applicants with the same SAT scores, grades, and other characteristics, but the difference was very small.[27]

In 1979, 46 percent of the four-year public colleges and universities and 41 percent of the private ones surveyed by the College Board/AACRAO said that racial and ethnic minorities might be offered admission even though their grades and test scores were significantly lower than those of other applicants. Racial and ethnic minorities received more exceptions than any other group to the formal admissions requirements of these universities.[28]

Also in 1979 Warren Willingham and Hunter Breland at ETS asked admissions officers at nine private colleges to indicate how much weight their institution placed on various selection factors.[29] Seven of the nine colleges said they gave substantial weight to minorities, one said it gave moderate weight, and one said some weight. Willingham and Breland also found that minority status was the most important personal quality affecting admission into these colleges after controlling for high school rank and test scores.[30]

In 1985, 41 percent of the public colleges and universities surveyed by AACRAO and 26 percent of the private colleges reported making exceptions to formal academic requirements for racial and ethnic minorities. Furthermore, of all the applicants admitted as exceptions for any reason in these institutions, 23 percent in the public colleges were minorities and 15 percent in the private colleges were minorities.[31]

The reasons for a paucity of data on exactly how much colleges lower their admissions standards to admit the number of blacks they want are easy to understand. The decision is a trade-off between more admitted blacks and lower academic qualifications. Colleges do not quantify this trade-off for whites, so why should they for blacks? Colleges that have to lower their academic standards also differ in how they make the trade-off. Saying what they do puts them in the public spotlight where they are vulnerable to political and social pressures. The result is that most colleges publicize their policies on black admissions as little as possible.

This section takes as given that colleges may lower admissions standards for black applicants. We ask how colleges can best select the number of blacks they want from an applicant pool. Table 5.10 repeats the cross-tabulations for NLS applicants from table 5.5 in a slightly different way to investigate this question.

Suppose a college with distributions of predicted grades for blacks and whites like those in table 5.10 decides to admit 1,800 of its 2,220 white applicants and 170 of its 232 black applicants. This would give it a black to white admissions ratio of 170/1,800 = 9.4 percent, or one black for every 9.4 whites. The college could come very close to this number of white admissions by setting a predicted freshman grade cutoff above 2.5 for both the high school rank only and rank plus SAT admission policies (see cumulative *N*s in table 5.10 for whites). For blacks, the cutoff for the high school rank only policy would also need to be above 2.5, but the rank plus SAT cutoff would need to be above 2.3 (table 5.10, cumulative *N*s for blacks).

The two policies for blacks have a different predicted grade cutoff because the high school rank only policy gives higher predicted grades for blacks than rank plus the SAT. Consequently, the rank plus SAT policy must have a lower selection cutoff to admit the same number of blacks as the rank only policy.

When the admissions cutoffs are set to admit the desired number of blacks and whites, 76.4 percent of the whites and 66.8 percent of the blacks are accepted by both the rank only and rank plus SAT policies (table 5.10); 15.4 percent of the whites and 20.7 percent of the blacks are rejected by both policies. Both admissions policies therefore make

Table 5.10 Cross-Tabulation of Predicted Grade Point Averages for Four-Year College Applicants in the NLS

Grades Predicted by HSR Alone	Grades Predicted by HSR plus SAT																						
	Whites																						
	1.7	1.8	1.9	2.0	2.1	2.2	2.3	2.4	2.5	2.6	2.7	2.8	2.9	3.0	3.1	3.2	3.3	3.4	3.5	3.6	*N*	Cumulative *N*	Mean
1.9	1		4																		5	2,220	1.9
2.0		2	3	4	5	1															15	2,215	2.0
2.1		1	3	8	6	6	11	2			1										38	2,200	2.2
2.2			3	4	9	14	12	10	6	1	1										60	2,162	2.3
2.3	*N* = 343			3	5	14	15	16	8	4	1								*N* = 75		66	2,102	2.3
2.4	(15.4%)			1	4	15	19	33	18	8	2	2							(3.4)%		102	2,036	2.4
2.5					1	4	18	25	29	38	14	3									132	1,934	2.5
2.6	*N* = 107					3	8	17	28	33	33	14	2	2					*N* = 1,695		140	1,802	2.6
2.7	(4.8%)						3	12	13	46	49	36	22	6	2				(76.4%)		189	1,662	2.7
2.8								4	12	12	49	62	59	23	2	3					238	1,473	2.8
2.9									4	16	45	69	80	50	30	10	2				306	1,235	2.9
3.0							1		2	4	16	48	109	98	80	44	12	1			415	929	3.0
3.1											4	12	22	89	124	127	82	25	12		497	514	3.1
3.2												1		1	1	4	3	3	2	2	17	17	3.3
N	1	3	13	20	30	57	87	119	120	174	215	247	294	269	239	188	99	29	14	2	2,220		
Cumulative *N*	2,220	2,219	2,216	2,203	2,183	2,153	2,096	2,009	1,890	1,770	1,596	1,381	1,134	840	571	332	144	45	16	2			
Mean	1.9	2.0	2.0	2.1	2.2	2.3	2,4	2.5	2.6	2.7	2.8	2.9	2.9	3.0	3.0	3.0	3.1	3.1	3.1	3.2			

Grades Predicted by HSR Alone	Grades Predicted by HSR plus SAT
Mean = 2.82	Mean = 2.82
SD = .278	*SD* = .322

	Blacks																				
	1.6	1.7	1.8	1.9	2.0	2.1	2.2	2.3	2.4	2.5	2.6	2.7	2.8	2.9	3.0	3.1	3.2	3.3	N	Cumula-tive N	Mean
1.9		1			1	1	1												4	232	2.0
2.0	1		2	1	1		1												6	228	1.9
2.1			1			1													2	222	2.0
2.2					2	2	6												10	220	2.1
2.3	N = 48				1	6	2	2	2								N = 16		13	210	2.2
2.4	(20.7%)					1	4	3	2	1	1						(6.9%)		12	197	2.3
2.5							3	4	3	5	1	1							17	185	2.4
2.6						1	2	6	2	6	3	1							21	168	2.4
2.7	N = 13						1	2	4	5	4	3	1	1			N = 155		21	147	2.5
2.8	(5.6%)							1	4	4	2	7	2	2		1	(66.8%)		23	126	2.6
2.9									1	4	12	10	7	2					36	103	2.7
3.0									1		3	3	3	9	3	1			23	67	2.8
3.1											1	6	8	9	7	8	2	1	42	44	2.9
3.2																1		1	2	2	3.2
N	1	1	3	1	5	12	20	18	19	25	27	31	21	23	10	11	2	2	232		
Cumula-tive N	232	231	230	227	226	221	209	189	171	152	127	100	69	48	25	15	4	2			
Mean	2.0	1.9	2.0	2.0	2.1	2.3	2.3	2.5	2.6	2.7	2.8	2.9	3.0	3.0	3.1	3.1	3.1	3.2			

Grades Predicted by HSR Alone

Mean = 2.73
SD = .319

Grades Predicted by HSR plus SAT

Mean = 2.57
SD = .322

Notes: Same sample as table 5.5. Sample includes 2,220 whites and 232 blacks in NLS who applied to a four-year college, had complete data on high school rank, SAT, the selectivity of the college applied to, and told NLS whether they were accepted by the college.

identical decisions for 76.4 + 15.4 = 91.8 percent of the white applicants and 66.8 + 20.7 = 87.5 percent of the black applicants.

Thus, for both whites and blacks, the two admissions policies make the same decision on most, but not all, of the applicants when the admissions cutoffs are set so that both policies admit the same number of applicants. This finding does not depend on the number of whites or blacks that are admitted so long as both policies admit the same number.[32]

The finding that the two admissions policies make the same admissions decision on the great majority of blacks and whites is virtually guaranteed by the fact that freshman grades predicted from rank alone and from rank plus SAT correlate 0.880 for blacks and 0.885 for whites. These high correlations mean that the same applicants are ranked in a sufficiently close order by rank only and rank plus SAT that the two policies admit and reject most of the same applicants. The fact that rank plus SAT predicts lower grades for most blacks than rank alone has little effect on the correlation between predicted grades since the means of the forecasted distributions are independent of their correlation. Overprediction therefore turns out to be irrelevant to a college's choice of students so long as a fixed and constant number of acceptances is to be made regardless of method.

Table 5.10 allows us to assess how many applicants are admitted by both a rank only and a rank plus SAT policy, and how many are rejected by both policies when a college admits the same number of applicants with each. We have not yet said anything about how the admitted students fare in college or how the rejected students might be expected to fare.

Nonetheless, the fact that the two policies make the same decision on so many of the same applicants suggests that they can make a difference in colleges' outcomes only for a small minority of applicants. It is possible that the two policies could make a substantial difference in college outcomes for the small minority of applicants on whom the two policies' admissions decisions differ. But it is likely that the two policies would have to lead to different admissions decisions on far more applicants than they do to make a large difference in college outcomes overall.

Effects on Admissions Outcomes

Table 5.11 presents our results. It shows that colleges' admissions outcomes for blacks are not affected in any important way if colleges

Table 5.11 Freshman Grade Point Average and B.A. Outcomes for High School Rank and High School Rank plus SAT Admissions Policies for Blacks (N = 201)

	FGPA: N (and %) of Cases ≤ 2.5 and N (and %) > 2.5					
	74.6% of Blacks Admitted (N = 150)			57.7% of Blacks Admitted (N = 116)		
	FGPA			FGPA		
	≤ 2.5	> 2.5	Total	≤ 2.5	> 2.5	Total
High school rank:						
Reject	38	13	51	61	24	85
	(18.9)	(6.5)	(25.4)	(30.3)	(11.9)	(42.3)
Admit	99	51	150	76	40	116
	(49.3)	(25.3)	(74.6)	(37.8)	(19.9)	(57.7)
Total	137	64	201	137	64	201
	(68.2)	(31.8)	(100.0)	(68.2)	(31.8)	(100.0)
High school rank plus SAT:						
Reject	42	9	51	66	19	85
	(20.9)	(4.5)	(25.4)	(32.8)	(9.5)	(42.3)
Admit	95	55	150	71	45	116
	(47.3)	(27.4)	(74.6)	(35.3)	(22.3)	(57.7)
Total	137	64	201	137	64	201
	(68.2)	(31.8)	(100.0)	(68.2)	(31.8)	(100.0)
	Bachelor's Degree: N (and %) of Cases					
	No B.A.	B.A.	Total	No B.A.	B.A.	Total
High school rank:						
Reject	25	26	51	37	48	85
	(12.4)	(12.9)	(25.4)	(18.4)	(23.9)	(42.3)
Admit	44	106	150	32	84	116
	(21.9)	(52.7)	(74.6)	(15.9)	(41.8)	(57.7)
Total	69	132	201	69	132	201
	(34.3)	(65.7)	(100.0)	(34.3)	(65.7)	(100.0)
High school rank plus SAT:						
Reject	26	25	51	40	45	85
	(12.9)	(12.4)	(25.4)	(19.9)	(22.4)	(42.3)
Admit	43	107	150	29	87	116
	(21.4)	(53.2)	(74.6)	(14.4)	(43.3)	(57.7)
Total	69	132	201	69	132	201
	(34.3)	(65.7)	(100.0)	(34.3)	(65.7)	(100.0)

Note: Same sample as table 5.4. Cell percentages may not add to marginals because of rounding.

use high school rank plus SAT to admit the number of blacks they want compared to rank alone. The table gives our results using two admissions standards, but we have studied both lower and higher admissions standards, and the results we present also hold for them. At the lower admissions standard both policies admit 150 (74.6 percent) of the blacks, and at the higher standard both policies admit 116 (57.7 percent) of them. One can compare the number (and percentage) of true positives, true negatives, false positives, and false negatives between the policies. The largest difference between corresponding cells is only five cases (2.5 percent).

Table 5.12 summarizes results computed from table 5.11. Line 1 shows the percentage of correct admissions forecasts. Correct admissions forecasts are accepted applicants who have successful freshman grades and eventually graduate (true positives) plus rejected applicants who would have unsuccessful freshman grades and not graduate (true negatives). With 74.6 percent of black applicants admitted, a high school rank admissions policy makes 44.2 percent correct admissions forecasts using actual freshman grades higher than 2.5 as a criterion of success. This is a 44.2 − 41.0 = 3.2 increment in correct forecasts per 100 above the number expected if high school rank had no relationship to actual freshman grades. Using the rank plus SAT policy results in an increment of 48.3 − 41.0 = 7.3 correct forecasts per 100 over the number expected if high school rank and the SAT had no relationship to actual freshman grades. The added value of the SAT and rank over rank alone is therefore 7.3 − 3.2 = 4.1 correct forecasts per 100.

The results are similar with the higher admissions standard that admits only 57.7 percent of the black applicants instead of 74.6 percent. The rank plus SAT policy improves the percentage of correct forecasts to 7.9 per 100 from 3.0 per 100 with rank alone.

Our results are even less supportive for the SAT when we look at correct admission forecasts using college graduation as the criterion instead of freshman grades. The number of correct forecasts for bachelor's degree attainment increases only 8.4 − 7.4 = 1.0 per 100 using the SAT to admit 74.6 percent of the applicants, and 10.8 − 7.8 = 3.0 per 100 using the SAT to admit 57.7 percent of the black applicants.

Lines 2 and 3 in table 5.12 show the estimated percentages of applicants who are rejected even though they would succeed (false negatives) and who are accepted even though they will fail (false positives). The largest gain from using the SAT is only 4.1 − 1.6 =

2.5 fewer errors per 100 when 57.7 percent of the black applicants are admitted.

Lines 4 and 5 show the percentage of successful students who are accepted (conditional percentage of acceptances) and the percentage of accepted students who are successful (conditional percentage of successes). The largest gain from using the SAT in addition to rank is 12.4 − 4.9 = 7.5 acceptances per 100 successful students using freshman grades as the criterion of success and admitting 57.7 percent of the blacks. This gain is not trivial, as it approaches the 10 percent range. But this gain falls to 8.2 − 5.9 = 2.3 when bachelor's degree is used as the criterion.

Our estimates from the University of Delaware's entering freshman class in 1983 are again very similar to the NLS, and are summarized in table 5.13. Admitting the top 69.8 percent of Delaware's blacks on the basis of freshman grades predicted from SAT plus high school grades does not increase correct admissions outcomes or decrease errors over admitting the same percentage of blacks with grades predicted from high school records alone. Adding the SAT does increase correct admissions outcomes and reduce errors with a higher admissions standard that admits only the top 42.5 percent of blacks. But the gain in correct admissions decisions is only 14.4 − 10.5 = 3.9 per 100. The improvement resulting from the SAT for the other outcomes is similarly small.

Taken together, our estimates suggest that the gains in correct admissions decisions and reductions in admissions errors for blacks from supplementing rank with the SAT rarely exceed 2–5 per 100 decisions. These gains are of the same order of magnitude we reported for whites in chapter 3. Our explanation for them is also the same. One can hardly expect large differences in actual admissions outcomes for the two policies when they make the same admissions decision, either to admit or reject, for as many of the same applicants as they do.

Conclusions about Use of the SAT with Blacks

Our results show that ETS's main justification for the SAT's use with black applicants—to help colleges admit black applicants who would succeed and reject black applicants who would fail—is not supported by the facts:

1. If selective colleges require blacks to have SAT scores at least equal to those of the whites they admit—no matter what else they

Table 5.12 Outcomes of High School Rank and High School Rank plus SAT Admissions Policies for Blacks

		74.6% of Blacks Admitted (N = 150)		57.7% of Blacks Admitted (N = 116)	
		High School Rank	High School Rank plus SAT	High School Rank	High School Rank plus SAT
		FGPA			
1. Percentage correct admission forecasts	*a.*	44.2 (41.0)	48.3 (41.0)	50.2 (47.2)	55.1 (47.2)
	b.	3.2	7.3	3.0	7.9
2. Percentage false negatives	*a.*	6.5 (8.1)	4.5 (8.1)	11.9 (13.5)	9.5 (13.5)
	b.	−1.6	−3.6	−1.6	−4.0
3. Percentage false positives	*a.*	49.3 (50.9)	47.3 (50.9)	37.8 (39.4)	35.3 (39.4)
	b.	−1.6	−3.6	−1.6	−4.1
4. Conditional percentage of acceptances	*a.*	79.6 (74.6)	86.2 (74.6)	62.6 (57.7)	70.1 (57.7)
	b.	5.0	11.6	4.9	12.4
5. Conditional percentage of successes	*a.*	34.0 (31.8)	36.7 (31.8)	34.5 (31.8)	38.6 (31.8)
	b.	2.2	4.9	2.7	6.8

		Bachelor's Degree			
1. Percentage correct admissions forecasts	*a.*	65.1 (57.7)	66.1 (57.7)	60.2 (52.4)	63.2 (52.4)
	b.	7.4	8.4	7.8	10.8
2. Percentage false negatives	*a.*	12.9 (16.7)	12.4 (16.7)	23.9 (27.8)	22.4 (27.8)
	b.	−3.8	−4.3	−3.9	−5.4
3. Percentage false positives	*a.*	21.9 (25.6)	21.4 (25.6)	15.9 (19.8)	14.4 (19.8)
	b.	−3.7	−4.2	−3.9	−5.4
4. Conditional percentage of acceptances	*a.*	80.3 (74.6)	81.1 (74.6)	63.6 (57.7)	65.9 (57.7)
	b.	5.7	6.5	5.9	8.2
5. Conditional percentage of successes	*a.*	70.7 (65.7)	71.3 (65.7)	72.4 (65.7)	75.0 (65.7)
	b.	5.0	5.6	6.7	9.3

Note: a = Observed percentages (and expected percentages given random admissions). b = Observed minus expected percentages from a. Same sample as table 5.4.

Line 1. Let decisions and outcomes be labeled as follows: A = applicants accepted and successful (true positives); B = applicants rejected and unsuccessful (true negatives); C = applicants rejected and successful (false negatives); D = applicants accepted and unsuccessful (false positives). Let all values be proportions of the total sample. The first value in Line 1a is then $A + B$ and the second value is $((B + D) * (B + C)) + ((C + A) * (D + A))$. Line 1$b$ is the first value minus the second value from line 1a.

Line 2. The first value in line 2a is C. The second is $(C + A) * (B + C)$. Line 2b is the first value minus the second value.

Line 3. The first value in line 3a is D. The second is $(B + D) * (D + A)$. Line 3b is the first value minus the second value.

Line 4. The first value in line 4a is $A/(C + A)$. The second is $D + A$. Line 4b is the first value minus the second value.

Line 5. The first value in line 5a is $A/(D + A)$. The second is $C + A$. Line 5b is the first value minus the second value.

Table 5.13 Freshman Grade Outcomes for University of Delaware Blacks

		69.8 % of Blacks Admitted (N = 74)		42.5 % of Blacks Admitted (N = 45)	
		High School GPA	High School GPA plus SAT	High School GPA	High School GPA plus SAT
1. Percentage correct admission forecasts	*a.*	60.3 (48.1)	60.3 (48.1)	61.3 (50.8)	65.2 (50.8)
	b.	12.2	12.2	10.5	14.4
2. Percentage false negatives	*a.*	7.6 (13.7)	7.6 (13.7)	20.8 (26.0)	18.8 (26.0)
	b.	−6.1	−6.1	−5.2	−7.2
3. Percentage false positives	*a.*	32.1 (38.2)	32.1 (38.2)	17.9 (23.2)	16.0 (23.2)
	b.	−6.1	−6.1	−5.3	−7.2
4. Conditional percentage of acceptances	*a.*	83.3 (69.8)	83.3 (69.8)	54.2 (42.5)	58.3 (42.5)
	b.	13.5	13.5	11.7	15.8
5. Conditional percentage of successes	*a.*	54.1 (45.3)	54.1 (45.3)	57.8 (45.3)	62.2 (45.3)
	b.	8.8	8.8	12.5	16.9

Notes: a = Observed percentages (and expected percentages given random admission). *b* = Observed minus expected percentages from *a*. Same sample as table 5.9. See notes to table 5.12 for method of calculating results.

look at—all but the least selective colleges in the country will have trouble enrolling even one qualified black for every ten qualified whites.

2. If selective colleges require blacks to have forecasted grades at least equal to those of whites, SAT scores do not appreciably improve their forecasts of successful and unsuccessful black applicants, and they greatly reduce black admissions.

3. If selective colleges give preference to blacks by admitting them with lower forecasted grades than whites, so that they do not reduce black admissions, SAT scores again do not improve their forecasts of successful and unsuccessful black applicants appreciably over using the high school record alone.

It does not follow from our conclusions, however, that colleges should drop the SAT for blacks, since eliminating all external standardized testing may have undesirable outcomes. But it also does not follow that the external examination system should include the SAT. (We discuss these issues and alternatives to the SAT in chapter 8.) Thus, in this chapter we do not argue that admissions tests should be dropped for blacks, only that the claim that the SAT helps colleges help blacks is false.

SIX

The SAT Has an Adverse Impact on Low-Income Applicants

The first part of this chapter looks at ETS's claim that the SAT benefits low-income students. Contrary to ETS, we find that using the SAT reduces selective colleges' acceptances of low-income applicants, just as it does with blacks. We then look at whether the SAT compensates for restricting admissions of low-income applicants by appreciably improving colleges' correct admissions decisions for them. We find no evidence that this happens. As with blacks, the SAT changes colleges' admissions outcomes for low-income students. But the changes are not an improvement, and the SAT does not help colleges significantly distinguish potentially successful low-income applicants from potentially unsuccessful ones. The changes arise almost entirely because fewer low-income applicants are admitted. Consequently, use of the SAT by selective colleges has added costs for low-income applicants that middle- and upper-income white applicants do not have, but it yields little compensatory improvement in admissions decisions.

ETS's Claim That the SAT Increases Admissions of Low-Income Students

"History indicates that selective admissions to higher education was (sic) far more a matter of class and economic status prior to the use of national admissions tests than it has been since," according to ETS. "The introduction of tests resulted in a substantial increase in opportunities for educational advancement of low-income students by providing a credible demonstration that many such students from schools without reputations for educational excellence could succeed in the demanding academic programs of the most selective institutions."[1]

ETS has done nothing, so far as we can discover, to try to show that this position is correct. Prior to the introduction of the SAT, most elite colleges used traditional achievement tests plus secondary school grades to make admissions decisions. These tests measured mastery of traditional academic subjects, including ancient languages. They therefore put students who had not studied these subjects at an overwhelming disadvantage. But ETS has never tried to determine whether students from secondary schools "without reputations for educational excellence" are at less of a disadvantage with the SAT than they are with traditional achievement tests.

Even if the SAT has reduced the handicap associated with coming from an obscure secondary school, it hardly follows that it has reduced the handicap associated with coming from a poor family. Just as predominately upper-middle-class high schools usually have a working-class minority, so, too, predominately working-class high schools usually have an upper-middle-class minority. Altering college admissions policies to admit more students from less well-known high schools may simply create additional opportunities for such upper-middle-class students—students from privileged families but not privileged communities. Such an admissions policy could easily increase the strength of the association between socioeconomic background and college admissions rather than reduce it. For example, some working-class students from well-known high schools might be replaced by upper-middle-class students from less-known high schools.

It is tempting to try to resolve these uncertainties with historical evidence. Robert Mare has examined the impact of socioeconomic background on whether American men who finished high school between 1925 and 1969 went on to college.[2] Using data from the 1973 replication of the "Occupational Changes in a Generation" survey, he shows that the impact of socioeconomic background on college entrance actually increased during these years. This is not to say that colleges grew more exclusive. On the contrary, college entrants became far more socially and economically heterogeneous. But the democratization of higher education was neither as rapid nor as complete as the democratization of secondary education. Among those who finished high school, therefore, socioeconomic background became a somewhat better predictor of college entrance.

One cannot, however, rely on evidence of this kind to assess the impact of tests like the SAT. Since virtually all high school graduates have always been able to get into some college regardless of their test scores, high school records, or anything else, the introduction of a test like the SAT is more likely to affect *where* low-income students are accepted than *whether* they are accepted. No good evidence exists for changes in the social and economic composition of highly selective colleges since they began relying on the SAT. Neither ETS nor the College Board has ever tried to collect such data. Even if this data did exist, we suspect that other factors, such as changes in the ratio of college costs to median family income, changes in the availability of scholarships and loans, and, perhaps most important, changes in the pattern of recruiting activity at elite colleges, have affected the composition of the student body at these colleges far more than the SAT has.

One does not, of course, have to assess the impact of the SAT on the socioeconomic composition of colleges historically. One can ask whether colleges that now select on the basis of both high school grades and SAT scores exclude more disadvantaged applicants than colleges that select applicants on the basis of high school grades alone. Unfortunately, however, ETS and the board have not investigated this question either.

Allan Nairn and Ralph Nader caused a minor public flurry over the issue of family income and college admissions in 1980 with their publication of *The Reign of ETS: The Corporation that Makes up Minds*. They charged that family income correlates so highly with SAT scores that the scores simply rank students by family income. Nairn and Nader claimed that SAT scores are "class in the guise of merit," adding: "If ETS scores really measure an important aspect of a person's 'merit' or, as ETS specifically calls it, 'scholastic aptitude,' then merit in the United States is distributed according to parental income."[3]

ETS vigorously denied that SAT scores and family income rank students in nearly the same way. They pointed out that the correlation of family income with SAT scores is "about 0.30."[4] "While *average* scores are higher for students from families with higher incomes, students from each income level obtain the full range of SAT scores."[5] ETS concluded that "the relationship is far from perfect and that a ranking of students by SAT scores is not a ranking by family income."[6] This is as far as ETS pursued the matter in response to Nairn and Nader in 1980, and it has not pursued it further since then.

The relationship between SAT scores and family income does not have to be perfect to be important. ETS and the board have claimed for years that the relationship between SAT scores and freshman grades is important even though it is not perfect. Yet the correlation between SAT scores and family income (0.30) is larger than the correlation between SAT scores and freshman grades at over 25 percent of the colleges participating in ETS's Validity Study Service.[7] It is nearly four times larger than the average improvement in prediction of freshman grades of 0.076 from the SAT over the high school record, which ETS and the board also claim is important.[8]

The next section looks in greater detail at whether colleges that select on the basis of both high school grades and SAT scores exclude more disadvantaged applicants than colleges that select applicants on the basis of high school grades alone. We find that they do. But the issues are more complex than the simplified debate between ETS and its critics.

Effects of the SAT on Admissions of Low-Income Students

Table 6.1 presents the cross-tabulation of SAT scores and family income for NLS applicants to four-year colleges. Average family

Table 6.1 Relationship of SAT Scores and Family Income among NLS Applicants to Four-Year Colleges

	Family Income (in Dollars)					
SAT Range	0–5,999	6,000–11,999	12,000–17,999	18,000+	*N*	Mean Family Income
1500–1600	0	2	4	2	8	14,375
1400–1499	1	5	15	17	38	16,349
1300–1399	4	30	39	47	120	15,290
1200–1299	10	55	73	93	231	15,234
1100–1199	13	92	84	113	302	14,700
1000–1099	29	116	132	135	412	14,248
900–999	31	129	133	117	410	13,683
800–899	29	100	71	82	282	13,172
700–799	29	75	65	55	224	12,742
600–699	35	44	23	12	114	9,454
500–599	15	24	10	4	53	9,307
400–499	4	2	0	0	6	5,000
N	200	674	649	677	2,220	
Mean (SAT)	862	965	1018	1045	996	
SD (SAT)	215	203	194	190	206	

Note: Sample consists of 2,200 NLS students who applied to a four-year college or university, had complete data on high school rank, SAT, college selectivity, family income, and told NLS whether they were accepted at the college.

income rises with each 100-point increase in SAT scores, except for the highest SAT category where the number of cases is small. The correlation between income and SAT is 0.286, very close to the correlation ETS reports.

The SAT obviously does not generate the same ranking of applicants as family income. Of the 166 NLS applicants who scored 1300 or above on the SAT, 25 percent reported family incomes below $12,000. Of the 173 who scored below 700, 28 percent reported family incomes of $12,000 or above. Nonetheless, colleges that select applicants above any SAT value and reject applicants below that value will exclude disproportionate numbers of low-income students. The higher the SAT value of the selected applicants, the higher will be their average family income.

Furthermore, table 6.2 shows that among college applicants who took the SAT in 1972, every measure of socioeconomic background is more strongly correlated with SAT scores than with high school class rank. The NLS data are not unique. A similar pattern is found for the high school class of 1980 in the national High School and Beyond study, the high school class of 1967 included in ETS's Academic Growth study, and the high school class of 1960 included in the Project Talent survey. Selecting on the basis of high school rank alone will therefore exclude fewer socioeconomically disadvantaged applicants than selecting on the basis of SAT scores.

While table 6.2 clearly shows that emphasizing high school rank rather than SAT in college admissions will equalize educational opportunities by socioeconomic background, it does not show what happens when colleges design admissions policies to maximize the academic success of their admitted students. Nevertheless, one should not play down the importance of the results presented in

Table 6.2 Correlations of SAT and High School Rank with Socioeconomic Background

	Family Income	Father's Occupation	Father's Education	Mother's Education
SAT	.286	.238	.296	.269
High school rank	.029	.043	.085	.067

Notes: Same sample as table 6.1. Correlations are pairwise within sample.

tables 6.1 and 6.2. Some colleges do set a minimum SAT cutoff, and others establish a preference ranking according to SAT score. Colleges may use the test scores by themselves, or combine them with high school grades or class rank. These policies are all alike in that they will exclude more economically disadvantaged applicants than advantaged applicants to the extent that they emphasize SAT scores over class rank.

To maximize the college success of admitted applicants, however, colleges must weigh applicants' high school records and SAT scores together to predict freshman grades, and then admit applicants by their predicted success according to the predicted performance model. With this model we can assess the effects of the SAT on admissions of economically disadvantaged applicants when colleges make the most efficient use of information in high school records and test scores to predict college success.

Few colleges make family income a major factor in admissions decisions or include it in their prediction equations. Most colleges find reasons for admitting applicants who are likely to inherit large family fortunes, but college application forms do not ask for parents' income or estimates of wealth. If colleges want to identify wealthy applicants, they must do so circuitously. Colleges can identify low-income applicants if they fill out financial aid forms, but no college we know of uses this information to help predict applicants' success. Over 80 percent of the four-year colleges in the College Board/American Association of Collegiate Registrars and Admissions Officers 1979 survey said that ability to pay was not a factor in their admissions decisions. Another 10 percent, mainly private colleges, said it was only a minor factor.[9]

Our analyses show that by excluding family income, colleges overpredict the freshman grades of lower-income students. Statistically, equations 3 and 4 in Table 6.3 add family income to the usual prediction equations, which include high school rank, SAT scores, and college selectivity (equations 1 and 2). The coefficient for family income is positive and statistically significant in both equations.[10]

To assess the consequences of overprediction, we used the unstandardized coefficients from equations 1 and 2 in table 6.3 to compute distributions of predicted freshman grades separately for lower-income NLS applicants and for all the others with higher family incomes. We defined lower-income applicants as ones who reported family incomes below $8,250 in 1972, which is about 1.1 standard deviations below the NLS sample mean of $13,943.[11]

Table 6.3 Prediction Equations Based on High School Rank, SAT Scores, College Selectivity, and Family Income for NLS Respondents

	Independent Variables						
Equation	High School Rank	SAT	College Selectivity	Family Income[a]	Constant	$\bar{R}^2$	SEE
1. B	.013174*		−.000065		1.9125	.170	.6065
beta	.417		−.013				
2. B	.009744*	.0010117*	−.0006511*		1.7616	.230	.5843
beta	.308	.303	−.126				
3. B	.013429*		−.0001778	.013278*	1.8257	.180	.6028
beta	.425		−.034	.105			
4. B	.010018*	.0009653*	−.0006762*	.006114*	1.7286	.231	.5836
beta	.317	.289	−.131	.048			

Notes: Sample consists of 1,950 NLS students attending four-year colleges or universities with complete data on high school rank, SAT, college selectivity, freshman grade point average, and family income.

[a]Coefficients multiplied by 1,000.

*Designates coefficients twice their standard error.

We then asked how using the SAT would affect high- and low-income students' admissions prospects in colleges of varying selectivity. Table 6.4 shows that adding the SAT to high school rank decreases the number of applicants admitted from lower-income families because more applicants fall below the selection cutoff value. At the most stringent admissions cutoff (3.1), or lowest selection ratio, the SAT reduces lower-income acceptances in the class from 20.7 percent to 16 percent. At every lower cutoff (3.0, 2.8, and 2.5), or higher selection ratio, a high school rank plus SAT policy also

Table 6.4 Expected Income Class Composition of Freshman Class When Selection Is Made from Top Down under High School Rank Only and High School Rank plus SAT Admissions Policies

	High School Rank			High School Rank plus SAT		
	High Income	Low Income	Total	High Income	Low Income	Total
GE 3.1	436 (79.3)	114 (20.7)	550	461 (84.0)	88 (16.0)	549
GE 3.0	740 (80.5)	179 (19.5)	919	670 (84.2)	126 (15.8)	796
GE 2.8	1,161 (80.0)	290 (20.0)	1,451	1,081 (82.6)	228 (17.4)	1,309
GE 2.5	1,509 (78.9)	403 (21.1)	1,912	1,476 (80.7)	352 (19.3)	1,828

Note: Numbers in parenthesis are percentage of total. Same sample as in table 6.1

reduces the proportional representation of students from lower-income families.

These effects of the SAT on lower-income applicants are smaller than the effects of the SAT on blacks (compare table 6.4 with tables 5.6 and 5.7). Nonetheless, they should not be ignored. They tell a very different story about the test's impact on low-income applicants from the one ETS and the board tell.

Effects of the SAT on Low-Income Students' College Outcomes

One way to justify the SAT's effect on lower-income applicants is to argue that the test improves colleges' admissions decisions for these students. This improvement might be sufficient to justify the test's lowering their acceptance rate. A necessary condition for this argument to hold, however, is that the SAT actually improve colleges' admissions outcomes appreciably for low-income applicants. All our evidence strongly suggests that the SAT does not do this.

Suppose a college has applicants whose predicted freshman grades are distributed like those of NLS students attending four-year colleges, and whose actual grades conditioned on these predicted grades would be distributed like those of attending students. If this college then admits all applicants whose predicted grades are above 2.5 and rejects all the rest, regardless of their family income, its admissions outcomes will be those in table 6.5. We also looked at admissions outcomes for other selection cutoffs between 2.3 and 3.0, but do not present the results because they lead to the same conclusions as table 6.5.

Supplementing high school rank with the SAT lowers the forecasted freshman grades of low-income students so that their acceptances fall from 82.2 to 71.9 percent. This, in turn, changes colleges' admissions outcomes for low-income students. The pattern of outcomes is the same as the one we found for blacks in chapter 5. The SAT reduces true positives from 41.8 to 39.4 percent, and reduces false positives from 40.4 to 32.5 percent. The test also increases the college's true negatives and false negatives.

A test that decreases both a college's true positive and false positive decisions and increases both its true negative and false negative decisions cannot be unequivocally said to improve its admissions outcomes. Nearly all these changes occur because adding the SAT to predictions based on high school rank lowers the admission of low-income students. Consequently, supplementing high school rank with the SAT has virtually no significant impact on colleges' true

Table 6.5 Freshman Grade Point Average Outcomes for High School Rank and High School Rank plus SAT Admissions Policies: Percentages (and Zero-Validity Base Rates)

	Income Groups					
	Higher Income (N = 1569)			Lower Income (N = 381)		
	≤ 2.5	> 2.5	Total	≤ 2.5	> 2.5	Total
High school rank:						
Reject	11.5	4.9	16.4	14.2	3.6	17.8
	(6.9)	(9.5)		(9.7)	(8.1)	
Admit	30.6	53.0	83.6	40.4	41.8	82.2
	(35.2)	(48.5)		(44.9)	(37.3)	
Total	42.1	57.9	100.0	54.6	45.4	100.0
High school rank plus SAT:						
Reject	12.9	5.0	17.9	22.1	6.0	28.1
	(7.5)	(10.4)		(15.3)	(12.8)	
Admit	29.2	52.9	82.1	32.5	39.4	71.9
	(34.6)	(47.5)		(39.3)	(32.6)	
Total	42.1	57.9	100.0	54.6	45.4	100.0

Notes: Same sample as in table 6.3. The predicted freshman grade point averages were computed from equations 1 and 2 in table 6.3. The selection cutoff is a predicted grade point average less than or equal to 2.5. The actual number of cases in each cell may be found by multiplying cell proportions by the appropriate N.

The base rates (in parentheses) are computed as follows.

Let decisions and outcomes be labeled as follows:

A = applicants accepted and successful (true positives);

B = applicants rejected and unsuccessful (true negatives);

C = applicants rejected and successful (false negatives); and

D = applicants accepted and unsuccessful (false positives). Let all values be proportions of the total sample. The true positive base rate is $100 * [(D + A) * (C + A)]$. The true negative base rate is $100 * [(B + C) * (B + D)]$. The false negative base rate is $100 * [(B + C) * (C + A)]$. The false positive base rate is $100 * [(D + A) * (B + D)]$.

positive, false positive, true negative, or false negative decisions once the base rate for these outcomes is controlled.

For example, the rank plus SAT policy increases a college's true negatives only (22.1 − 15.3) − (14.2 − 9.7) = 2.3 per 100 above the increase in base rate from the test's additional rejections of low-income applicants. The SAT increases true positives only (39.4 − 32.6) −

(41.8 − 37.3) = 2.3 beyond the decrease expected from the test's admission of fewer low-income applicants.

Nor are the results in table 6.5 unique to freshman grades. The same pattern of results occurs when we use bachelor's degree attainment as the criterion, except that the SAT looks a little less useful.[12]

All in all, our results show that addition of the SAT to high school rank rejects additional lower-income applicants, but not additional higher-income applicants. The test does this because it lowers the forecasted grades of low-income applicants so that fewer have forecasted grades that exceed the selection cutoff. Admission of fewer low-income applicants does change colleges' admissions outcomes for these students, but does not improve them overall. The outcomes change largely because the SAT affects the base rates for these outcomes, and not because the SAT appreciably improves colleges' ability to admit successful applicants or reject unsuccessful ones.

The SAT therefore acts with respect to admissions outcomes for low-income students much as it does for blacks. Colleges using a predicted grade cutoff for admissions could get admissions outcomes almost like those they get from the SAT by identifying low-income students admitted by high school rank alone and then randomly rejecting the same percentage of them the SAT rejects when it is added to high school rank.

For example, suppose a college whose applicants resemble our NLS sample in table 6.5 identifies low-income applicants admitted with a 2.5 cutoff by high school rank alone and then randomly rejects an additional (82.2 − 71.9)/82.2 = 12.5 percent of them. This college's admissions outcomes for low-income students would be very close to the ones it would get were it to add the SAT to high school rank. True positives would decrease from 41.8 percent to 41.8 × (1 − 0.125) = 36.6 percent, false positives would decrease from 40.4 percent to 40.4 × (1 − 0.125) = 35.3 percent, true negatives would increase from 14.2 percent to 14.2 × (1 + 0.579) = 22.4 percent, and false negatives would increase from 3.6 percent to 3.6 × (1 + 0.579) = 5.7 percent. These admissions outcome percentages are very close to the percentages in table 6.5 when the college uses the SAT and high school rank together.

The SAT therefore acts with respect to admissions outcomes much as a zero-validity supplement to high school rank that increases rejection of low-income students. There is thus not only adverse impact on economically disadvantaged applicants, but also little improvement in ability to predict their college success. A good admissions test ought to supplement the high school record to help colleges admit low-income students who will be successful and reject those who will be unsuccessful. A good test should be appreciably better than a zero-validity supplement to the high school record that randomly rejects low-income students.

SEVEN

The Effects of the SAT Have Not Changed since 1960

This chapter discusses the changes in secondary and postsecondary education and their clientele since 1960 that could affect the importance of the SAT. First, we compare estimates of the academic benefits of the SAT to colleges from the 1980 High School and Beyond survey to our findings from the National Longitudinal Study in 1972. Despite nearly a decade of fluctuations in SAT means and standard deviations, and possible grade inflation in both high school and college grades, we find that colleges' academic benefits from using the SAT to select applicants do not appear to differ in any significant way from 1972 to 1980.

Next, we look at students from the 1960 Project Talent survey. Even at this early date, we find a high correlation between admissions decisions made from a high school record only policy and a high school record plus SAT policy. We therefore conclude at three separate intervals over a twenty-year span that the SAT has added a substantively insignificant increment to the accuracy of colleges' admissions decisions from their applicant pools.

Changes in Secondary and Postsecondary Education since 1960

In 1960 slightly over 1,000,000 students entered college as first-time freshmen. By 1970 over 1,800,000 freshmen enrolled. And in 1980 the number of first-time freshmen had increased to over 2,600,000.[1] These enrollments increased partly because the number of 18-year-olds grew steadily from the early 1960s through the early 1970s, and partly because the percentage of 18-year-olds entering college increased from the 1960 level.

With this substantial expansion of college enrollment, some dilution of the overall academic ability of college-bound seniors was inevitable. As the advisory panel on the SAT score decline put it in 1977: "It would be pleasant to think that as increased percentages of vastly larger numbers of young people stay in school longer and go on to college, the college entrance examination averages achieved before by a favored fraction of students could be held constant. Yet any such expection would be ruefully unrealistic."[2]

As nearly everybody knows by now, SAT scores started to decline in 1963, and continued their decline every year through 1981. Every year since 1981–82, the national SAT math averages have shown slight increases, and the national verbal SAT averages have increased every year but one.[3] The College Board's advisory panel on the SAT decline estimated that 66–75 percent of the decline during the 1960s and 20–30 percent of the decline during the 1970s was due to compositional changes in the population of test takers.[4] This conclusion is a controversial one, since almost everything from open education and nuclear fallout to junk food and smoking by pregnant mothers has been advanced as a possible cause.[5]

Whatever the causes of the erosion in SAT scores, colleges over the past twenty years have had to reconcile the two conflicting trends of vastly increased numbers of applications and less-qualified college applicants. The glut of applications throughout the 1960s and early 1970s presented admissions offices with the problem of how to evaluate properly the large volume of applications from an increasingly heterogeneous group of students. But as at other times in its past, ETS offered colleges at least a partial solution to their problems.

ETS started its Validity Study Service in 1964 to assist colleges with the prediction of their applicants' college performance. But ETS has also used the Validity Study Service to promote the SAT: "In practice . . . the SAT-verbal score and the SAT-mathematical score are often made part of a formal regression equation that may include information from the high school record (and) from the results of the College Board Achievement Tests. . . . In such equations the test has clearly demonstrated that it makes a unique contribution to the prediction of college success."[6] In addition, ETS considered the SAT a "leveling agent":

> In addition to its supplemental and incremental value, the SAT has a value of its own in confirming the grades from different schools. Since the high school record is a reflection of locally controlled curricula and local grading practices . . . there are variations from school to school in the meaning of the grades. This fact inevitably works to the advantage of some college applicants and to the disadvan-

> tage of others. The SAT, on the other hand, represents a standardized measure of the same mental tasks. . . . Thus, it operates as a "leveling agent," cutting across differences in local customs and conditions and affording the admissions officer a single metric for considering the records of all applicants. Especially in the case of students coming from little-known schools, the SAT provides information about the student that would otherwise be unavailable, or at best, difficult to obtain.[7]

Many colleges responded to ETS on their own by requiring applicants to submit SAT scores for admission. But some colleges were also required to use the SAT if they wanted to be members of the College Board. In 1954 the College Board instituted a "test use" requirement that forced all members to use at least one of its exams.[8] As the board's membership grew, so did the SAT-taking population.

In 1960 there were 350 collegiate members of the College Board, and that year over 560,000 SATs were taken. Ten years later collegiate membership in the board had grown to 850. Since most of these schools required applicants to take the SAT to be considered for admission, it is not surprising that the numbers of SAT takers also grew tremendously. Between 1960 and 1970, the number of students taking the SAT increased to 1,605,900.[9] During the 1970s the number declined slightly, but held steady at around 1,400,000. By 1985, however, SAT volume had climbed again to 1,705,000.

Long-term growth in college enrollments led to increased heterogeneity of SAT scores in colleges' student bodies. The SAT standard deviation increased 20 points between 1964 and 1976 in the typical college in ETS's Validity Study Service.[10] This is not a huge gain, since the median standard deviation in 1964 was about 140. But since selective colleges are overrepresented in the Validity Study Service, it may understate the average increase in SAT standard deviations. It seems clear that with vastly greater numbers of students attending postsecondary institutions since 1960, some increase in the heterogeneity of the student body's test scores is inevitable.

Since 1960 most colleges have also experienced some grade inflation. Numerous studies have documented the rise in undergraduate grade point averages since the 1960s.[11] This trend is disturbing to many educators because it occurred at the same time that other evidence pointed to declines in high school seniors' preparedness for college work. Note that high schools may also have experienced grade inflation, which may lead to a restriction in range for the high school record.[12]

What are the consequences of expanding equality of opportunity, increasing enrollments, and grade inflation for higher education and the predictiveness of the SAT? One might expect that greater ranges in colleges' freshman classes' SAT scores would have increased the SAT's correlation with college grades since 1960.[13] And if high school grades decreased in variance from grade inflation, then the predictiveness of high school grades for college grades might have declined since 1960, while the contribution of the SAT increased.

In fact, when we looked at the existing data on historical trends in the contribution of the SAT and the high school record, evidence for a significant trend was very small. In our opinion, one could easily argue that the changes are simply random fluctuations from year to year. In one of the few published analyses of such trends, Isaac Bejar and Edwin Blew claim that the correlation of high school grades with college freshmen grades in the Validity Study Service declined from 1964 to 1973.[14] Inspection of their figure 9, however, shows that any decline was probably less than 0.10. Given the changing composition of colleges that contribute data to the Validity Study Service, we have little confidence that such a decline is indicative of a change in all colleges. And even Bejar and Blew believe that the correlation has remained stable since 1973.[15] The most recent analysis of the Validity Study Service data by ETS researchers also shows no substantively important change in the year-by-year correlation between high school grades (or class rank) and freshman grades between 1964 and 1982.[16]

Bejar and Blew also argue that the correlation of SAT scores with freshman grades has shown a slight increasing trend since 1970. But inspection of the fluctuations in their time series from 1964 suggests that random year-to-year variation is at least as plausible an explanation.[17] The same is true for the more recent analysis of the Validity Study Service data by ETS researchers.[18]

Finally, Bejar and Blew state that it is "evident" that after controlling for the high school record, the SAT's contribution to the prediction of freshman grades has fluctuated yearly since 1964. But in their search for a trend, they go on to say that the "clearest trend seems to be that the contribution of the SAT has been greatest in most recent years."[19] Our assessment of their figure 11 is that their first observation of year-to-year fluctuation is probably the most accurate description of the time series. Nor has there been an upward trend in the contribution of the SAT to prediction of freshman grades after the high school record is controlled. We again reach a similar conclusion from the more recent analysis of ETS's Validity Study Service data for the years between 1964 and 1982.[20]

Having stated that these changes are probably best described as random fluctuations, we wish to stress that determining a trend for most of these statistics is not very important. As we argued in chapter 3, the contribution of the SAT to R^2 with the high school record controlled gives a very misleading view of the benefits to colleges of using the SAT to make selection decisions. This is because the predictions that a college makes from the high school rank plus SAT policy correlate very highly with those made from high school rank alone. As a result, the two selection policies lead to the same admissions decisions for the vast majority of applicants.

Consequently, to assess the benefits to colleges of using the SAT in 1980, 1972, and 1960, we use the methods we have developed in the previous chapters to compare the outcomes of different admissions policies.

Empirical Results: 1980 versus 1972

We constructed freshman grade equations with the 1980 High School and Beyond survey (HSB) using high school rank and high school rank plus the SAT, which we then compared to our findings in chapter 3 from the 1972 NLS survey.[21] Table 7.1 shows the results. The effects of the SAT in 1972 and 1980 appear to be very similar as indicated by the beta coefficients of 0.294 and 0.325 in equation 4. Comparing betas across different samples can be problematic because the beta weights change when the variance of a predictor

Table 7.1 Regressions of College Grade Point Average

		Independent Variables					
Equation		High School Record	SAT	College Selectivity	Constant	$\bar{R}^2$	SEE
1. *a*. HSB	B	.529*			1.104	.214	.520
	beta	.463					
b. NLS	B	.0127*			1.875	.168	.602
	beta	.411					
2. *a*. HSB	B	.376*	.000828*		.811	.276	.499
	beta	.329	.286				
b. NLS	B	.0092*	.000786*		1.347	.211	.587
	beta	.298	.235				

(*continued*)

Table 7.1 (*continued*)

Equation		High School Record	SAT	College Selectivity	Constant	R^2	SEE
		Independent Variables					
3. *a*. HSB	B	.512*		.000252	.892	.216	.519
	beta	.448		.058			
b. NLS	B	.0129*		−.000136	1.999	.168	.602
	beta	.418		−.026			
4. *a*. HSB	B	.379*	.000943*	−.000343*	1.059	.280	.497
	beta	.331	.325	−.079			
b. NLS	B	.0096*	.000982*	−.000697*	1.851	.224	.582
	beta	.310	.294	−.134			

Notes: The NLS sample is the same as in table 3.1. The HSB sample consists of 1,010 men and women who attended a four-year college from September 1980 through January 1982 for at least three semesters, and had data on self-reported high school grades, college grades, college selectivity, and SAT scores. We coded the variables as follows:

SAT is the sum of scores on the verbal and math sections of the SAT. Students' SAT scores were reported by ETS and merged with the HSB file by student ID.

High School Record is the students' self-reporting of cumulative grades earned in high school. Students could select from eight categories. We coded grades on a four-point scale as follows: mostly A (90–100) = 3.87; about half A and half B (85–89) = 3.5; mostly B (80–84) = 3.0; about half B and half C (75–79) = 2.5; mostly C (70–74) = 2.0; about half C and half D (65–69) = 1.5; mostly D (60–64) = 1.0; mostly below D (below 60) = 0.5.

College Grades is the students' reporting of how well they had done in coursework since leaving high school. Since this question was asked in the spring of 1982, students would be reporting the equivalent of three semester's grades (fall 1980; spring 1981; fall 1981). Students could select from seven grade categories, which we coded as follows: mostly A (3.75–4.0) = 3.87; about half A and half B (3.25 – 3.74) = 3.5; mostly B (2.75–3.24) = 3.0; about half B and half C (2.25–2.74) = 2.5; mostly C (1.75–2.24) = 2.0; about half C and half D (1.25–1.74) = 1.5; mostly D or below (less than 1.25) = 1.0.

College Selectivity. As an estimate of selectivity, we used the average SAT scores (verbal plus math) of enrolling freshmen at a given college. For the NLS sample, this information was available from the 1971 American Council on Education's Institutional Characteristics File. Unfortunately, ACE tapes compiled after 1976 do not include freshman SAT score averages, so 1980 selectivity information was not available for the HSB data. After exploring several options, we decided to merge the 1971 ACE data with the 1980 HSB file. While the average SAT scores of entering freshmen would be likely to decline over the eight-year period from the NLS to the HSB, the relative rankings between colleges are not likely to change much. To check this, we extracted fifty colleges at random from the ACE file and compared their 1971 freshmen SAT scores with more recent, published SAT averages. The correlation between scores was 0.88, which supports our decision to use the 1971 ACE selectivity measure for the HSB.

*Designates coefficients twice their standard error.

variable changes.[22] It is perhaps more informative to note that the unstandardized coefficients for the SAT remain similar in the two surveys: 0.000943 in HSB, 0.000982 in NLS. Thus, despite the obvious differences in samples of college freshmen in 1972 and 1980, the SAT has had a remarkably consistent effect over the high school record in predicting college grades in these two surveys.

The results in the two national surveys compare favorably with evidence from ETS's Validity Study Service and are consistent with our interpretation of no trend over time in the contribution of the SAT beyond high school record to the prediction of freshman grades. The increment in validity added by the SAT is 0.063 in the 1972 NLS and 0.07 in the 1972 Validity Study Service data. The comparable values for the 1980 HSB and 1980 Validity Study Service data are 0.064 and 0.08.

Our argument, however, is that the important issue for college admissions is not how much the SAT increases a multiple correlation coefficient, but how much the test affects selection. To make this determination, we compared admissions selections with a high school record only policy against a high school record plus SAT policy.

The admissions policies agree on approximately 91 percent of the decisions in both surveys using a 2.5 forecasted freshman grade cutoff for admissions (table 7.2). In the NLS, when each student's freshman grade point average is predicted using rank alone, these predictions correlate 0.881 with those made from rank plus SAT. In the HSB, the correlation between admissions selection policies is 0.880.[23]

Table 7.3 compares a high school rank only policy against a high school rank plus SAT policy for the prediction of five freshman grade admissions outcomes at two standards of admission. Line 1 shows that at an admissions selection cutoff above 2.5, the high school rank policy results in 62.2 percent correct decisions, compared to 64.6 for rank plus SAT in the NLS. The increment over a zero-validity base rate for rank alone in the NLS is 62.2 − 53.0, or 9.2; for rank plus SAT it is 64.6 − 52.7, or 11.9. Therefore, the added value of the SAT over high school rank alone is only 2.7 (11.9 − 9.2) correct forecasts per 100. The comparable figure for the HSB sample is an additional 3.4 correct forecasts. At the higher admissions cutoff of above 3.0, the increment due to the SAT in the NLS is only an additional 2.2 correct decisions per 100. In the HSB, the SAT adds less than one additional correct decision per hundred.

The SAT is also not very helpful in either survey for colleges concerned with minimizing acceptances of students likely to fail

Table 7.2 Agreement between Admissions Selection Strategies

Data Survey	Total Agreement (Percentage Accepted plus Percentage Rejected)	Percentage Accepted by High School Record plus SAT and Not by High School Record Alone	Percentage Accepted by High School Record and Not by High School Record plus SAT	Correlation between High School Record and HSR plus SAT
HSB	90.7	2.8	6.5	.880
NLS	90.8	2.9	6.3	.881

Notes: NLS sample same as table 3.4. HSB sample consists of 1,684 seniors who applied to a four-year college or university in the fall of 1980, and who had complete data on self-reported high school grades, SAT, and college selectivity. Admissions selection cutoff is above 2.5 in both samples.

Table 7.3 Outcomes and Zero-Validity Base Rates (in Parentheses) of High School Record and High School Record plus SAT Admissions Policies

	Standard for Admissions and Admissions Policy					
	Above 2.5			Above 3.0		
Freshman Grade Outcomes[a]	HSR	HSR plus SAT	Δ[b]	HSR	HSR plus SAT	Δ[b]
1. Percentage Correct Decisions						
HSB	65.5 (57.0)	68.5 (56.6)	3.4	62.7 (47.1)	63.8 (47.6)	0.6
NLS	62.2 (53.0)	64.6 (52.7)	2.7	61.7 (47.7)	64.0 (47.8)	2.2
2. Percentage False Negatives						
HSB	4.4 (8.6)	4.2 (10.1)	1.7	30.9 (38.7)	29.0 (37.1)	0.3
NLS	4.6 (9.2)	4.7 (10.6)	1.3	34.0 (41.0)	32.3 (40.4)	1.1
3. Percentage False Positives						
HSB	30.1 (34.3)	27.3 (33.3)	1.8	6.4 (14.2)	7.2 (15.3)	0.3
NLS	33.2 (37.8)	30.7 (36.6)	1.3	4.2 (11.2)	3.7 (11.8)	1.1
4. Percentage of Conditional Acceptances						
HSB	92.7 (85.6)	93.2 (83.1)	3.0	48.4 (35.4)	51.6 (38.1)	0.5
NLS	91.6 (83.1)	91.4 (80.5)	2.4	37.4 (24.7)	40.7 (25.9)	2.1
5. Percentage Conditional Successes						
HSB	64.8 (59.9)	67.1 (59.9)	2.3	81.9 (59.9)	81.1 (59.9)	−0.8
NLS	60.1 (54.5)	61.9 (54.5)	1.8	82.6 (54.5)	85.7 (54.5)	3.1

Notes: Same samples as table 7.1 Percentages in parentheses are expected percentages for a zero-validity base rate. See table 3.5 for method for computing base rates.

[a]See table 3.5 and notes for definitions and computation of correct and incorrect admission decisions in lines 1–5.

[b]This column summarizes gains in correct decisions from the SAT controlling for base rates in both admissions policies.

(false positives) or reducing denials of students who would succeed (false negatives). The largest reduction observed in the NLS sample is 1.3 fewer errors per 100 (at the 2.5 cutoff). The use of the SAT in the HSB results in an only slightly higher percentage reduction in errors of 1.8 at the 2.5 cutoff. In either survey, the gains in correct admissions decisions and reductions in errors with the SAT plus rank policy over rank alone are not very impressive.

Nor does the SAT help colleges in either sample to admit an overall higher quality freshman class. Table 7.4 shows that using an admission cutoff of 2.5, the rank plus SAT policy would only boost the observed grade point average from 2.91 to 2.93 on a four-point scale in the NLS, and from 2.96 to 2.99 in the HSB survey. The results are similar for a more rigorous cutoff of 3.0.

Table 7.4 Comparison between HSB and NLS of Average Freshman Grade Point Average

Decision Made by High School Record	Decision Made by High School Record plus SAT		
	Reject	Accept	Overall
	Admission Standard: Predicted Grades above 2.5		
Reject			
HSB	2.40	2.90	2.49
NLS	2.40	2.60	2.43
Accept			
HSB	2.46	2.99	2.96
NLS	2.46	2.94	2.91
Overall			
HSB	2.42	2.99	2.89
NLS	2.42	2.93	2.83
	Admission Standard: Predicted Grades above 3.0		
Reject			
HSB	2.67	3.05	2.71
NLS	2.64	3.10	2.69
Accept			
HSB	2.97	3.25	3.21
NLS	2.97	3.37	3.26
Overall			
HSB	2.69	3.21	2.89
NLS	2.67	3.29	2.83

Note: Same samples as table 7.1.

Empirical Results: 1960 versus 1972 and 1980

To investigate a year earlier than 1972, we turned to the 1960 Project Talent base-year and one-year follow-up surveys of high school seniors.[24] We analyzed 2,212 Project Talent seniors with complete data on SAT, high school grades, and college grades. Unfortunately, no college selectivity information is available for the Project Talent data, and it is, therefore, impossible to control for college selectivity. Not controlling for selectivity violates common sense because every student's grade point average is treated as having been earned at a single college. For this reason, we do not present detailed cross-tabulations of predicted grade distributions or actual outcomes of admission decisions as we did for the NLS and HSB.

However, controlling for college selectivity does not appear to make large alterations in the prediction equations for college grade point averages. This can be seen by comparing equations 1 and 3 with equations 2 and 4 in table 7.1. For example the NLS equation for high school rank only (eq. 1*b*) and high school rank plus college selectivity (eq. 3*b*) have identical R^2s and standard errors of estimate. In fact, the coefficient for college selectivity is not statistically significant at the .05 level in equation 3*b*. The unstandardized coefficient for high school rank differs by only 0.0002 between equations 1*b* and 3*b*.

Somewhat larger differences are apparent in the coefficient for SAT when equations 2 and 4 are compared. In the HSB, controlling selectivity (eq. 4*a*) boosts the standardized coefficient of the SAT about 14 percent over the coefficient in equation 2*a*. In the NLS, the corresponding SAT coefficient is about 25 percent larger. However, the interested reader can insert values into equations 2 and 4 and see that controlling selectivity has only a trivial impact on individuals' predicted grade point average. Thus, the predicted grades for any individual will vary little whether equation 2 or 4 is used.

For example, a hypothetical NLS individual whose high school rank is at the eightieth percentile, whose SAT scores total 1000, and who attends a college of 1000 selectivity will have a predicted freshman grade average of 2.869 when equation 2*b* is used. Predicted grades will be 2.904 when equation 4*b* is used. The difference between the predicted scores is only 0.035 of a grade point. While it would be preferable, other things being equal, to control for college selectivity, the lack of this variable in the Project Talent data should not affect our results in any important way.

Table 7.5 presents results of regressions of college grade point average on high school grades and SAT for the Project Talent sample.

Table 7.5 Regressions of College Grade Point Average on High School Grades and SAT Scores for 2,212 Project Talent Students

Equation	High School Grades	SAT	Constant	*R*	SEE
1. B	.0444*		0.0985	.485	.578
beta	.485				
2. B		.00121*	1.3036	.355	.618
beta		.355			
3. B	.0374*	.00061*	−0.1241	.511	.568
beta	.408	.178			

Notes: Sample includes 2,212 Project Talent seniors with complete data on high school grades, SAT, and college grades. We coded variables as follows:

SAT. ETS located the student's last SAT result prior to high school graduation in May or June 1960.

High school record. The high school grade measure is the grade obtained from averaging high school grades in English, social studies, foreign language, mathematics, and science. These are student-reported grades. We calculated the percentage of respondents in each grade category and assigned everyone in that category the *Z* score for the percentile midpoint of the category. *Z* scores were then standardized to a mean of 50 and a standard deviation of 10.

College GPA is the average grade students received in any combination of the following courses: mathematics, physical science, biological science, social studies, English composition and grammar, English literature, foreign language, fine arts, music, psychology, philosophy, religion, education, engineering, business administration, home economics, and/or agriculture and forestry. These are also student-reported grades on a four-point scale.

*Designates coefficients more than twice their standard error.

The equations are again similar to those observed in the HSB and NLS. The high school record is the best single predictor of college grade point average, but the SAT increases the validity coefficient 0.03 (.511 - .485).

The earliest year for which any national data is available for comparison with Project Talent is 1964, the first year of the Validity Study Service. The Project Talent sample has a larger SAT standard deviation than the 1964 ETS Validity Study Service data, but less variability on college grades. The lower variability of the Project Talent measure of freshman grade point average probably offsets the increased variance on SAT, thereby producing results that are not out of line with the Validity Study Service. Thus the average increment in *R* in 1964 for the colleges participating in ETS's Validity Study Service was 0.08. The increment in the Project Talent data is 0.03.

The important question is, how highly correlated are freshman grades predicted from high school record alone (table 7.5, eq. 1) and freshman grades predicted from the high school record plus the SAT (table 7.5, eq. 3)? The correlation is 0.922. This correlation should be treated cautiously, since it is obtained from students whose college grade point averages could not be adjusted for college selectivity. Nonetheless, the correlation is in line with others we observed in national and local samples, which indicate that the SAT does not greatly increase colleges' ability to make more accurate admissions decisions over the high school record alone.

We therefore conclude that the SAT has added little to colleges' ability to make admissions decisions about applicants at three divergent periods in the recent history of American postsecondary education. Although there are obvious differences in the samples of students attending college in 1960, 1972, and 1980, the SAT appears to have equally modest benefits in all three years.

EIGHT

What Is to Be Done?

This chapter discusses steps to reform college admissions testing. Unlike many previous critics of the SAT and ETS, we do not argue that standardized college admissions testing should be eliminated. We argue for more experimentation, for improved information about the costs and benefits of admissions testing to colleges, for improved achievement tests, and for rethinking what admissions testing can and cannot accomplish. We develop the outlines of our suggestions in this chapter. The groups most able to pursue them further are ETS, the College Board, and the more than 2,500 colleges and educational organizations that comprise their constituencies. But given the past responses of the College Board and ETS to criticism, none of this is likely to happen without external pressure on both organizations to take the lead in these tasks. We conclude with a few suggestions on steps to do this.

Experiments That Drop the SAT

College admissions officers sometimes shudder at the thought of colleges dropping the SAT and relying on applicants' high school grades, class ranks, academic courses, high schools attended, and other information to make admissions decisions. ETS has often repeated their concerns to help reinforce the importance of the SAT. More than twenty years ago, for example, Henry Chauncey, ETS's first president, and John Dobbins, an ETS program director, wrote:

> To the college admissions officer, the transcript of grades from one high school looks very much like the transcript from any other. An A average earned in a highly academic high school where most graduates go on to college may mean something quite different from an A average earned in a high

> school where academic learning is secondary to vocational training. With candidates' transcripts coming from as many as a thousand different high schools each year, however, the college admissions officer has no infallible way of knowing what the reported grades mean. Lacking a method for interpreting the information sent to him about the candidates for admission, he needs some means for deciding which ones are the ones most likely to succeed in the studies offered by his college.[1]

ETS's current president, Gregory Anrig, describes dire consequences if colleges were to drop the SAT:

> Do we really want to go back to "the good old days" in American higher education? Those were the days when admission to many colleges and universities depended on the prestige of your private or public high school, who your parents were, whether a relative was an alumnus/a (and a donating one at that), and whether you would "fit in" with a student body much like its predecessors over the years.[2]

These reactions seem exaggerated and oversimplified, however. Many selective colleges in the country are very small, with a total undergraduate enrollment of fewer than 2,000. They may receive 1,500 or fewer freshmen applications every year. Even small admissions staffs at these colleges could easily read everyone's application and make admissions decisions without the SAT. The important question is how well they could evaluate a candidate's credentials without the SAT.

We think they could evaluate them quite well. Admissions professionals have, in the vast majority of cases, detailed knowledge of applicants' high schools and how other students from those schools have fared, and in some cases may even be on a first-name basis with the guidance counselor, principal, or headmaster. When an applicant is from a completely unknown high school, the admissions officer can simply pick up a telephone and request information such as rank in class, course syllabi, or college attendance rates for other graduating classes. Or the admissions officer could contact a colleague whose college has experience with the school in question.

During the fall of 1986, SAT scores were delayed at Amherst College for about 10 percent of their early decision candidates. Henry Bedford, dean of admissions, read the applications without ETS reports. After the scores arrived, other members of Bedford's staff evaluated the candidates. Bedford wrote us: "In no case did the academic rating vary from mine; the only serious difference was a question of the magnitude by which one candidate was not qualified for admission."[3] Although Amherst's experience is obviously unsystematic, anecdotal, and based on only about forty cases, it certainly does not portend disaster if Amherst were to drop the SAT.

A little more problematic, in our opinion, are the larger colleges and universities that receive thousands of applications annually. Of course, the number of applications that must be studied in fine detail at these colleges may be much smaller than the thousands received, since many decisions to admit or reject are clear at the outset. Moreover, the highly selective colleges that receive large numbers of applications from well-qualified persons have sufficient admissions staffs to make selection decisions with the same care as small selective colleges. Still, in many larger, but relatively unselective, colleges and universities, it is not practical for admissions officers to give every applicant's folder the same careful study that small selective colleges can.

These are the colleges and universities that out of practical necessity rely on selection formulas to aid their decision making. The best of these formulas use information about applicants' high school work and test scores to forecast their academic success. Our findings in chapter 3 show, however, that adding applicants' SAT scores to formulas based on their high school record changes very few admissions decisions and improves colleges' admissions outcomes by only a very small amount.

Consequently, we think that both small and large selective colleges and universities that now use the SAT could drop the test with no serious negative consequences. Their admission rates for blacks and lower-income applicants would probably increase if they do not now use a quota. In general, we are inclined to side with David Owen's conclusion: "If the SAT simply disappeared tomorrow, admissions officers would squawk for a year or so, the foundations of the Henry Chauncey Conference Center [at ETS] would tremble, and life would go on as before. The SAT plays virtually no useful role in college admissions right now. Getting rid of it would not, by itself, make admissions very different."[4]

However, one must be very careful in reaching conclusions like these about the future. College admissions testing with the SAT is now widespread, and predictions about the effects of dropping the SAT from data collected at a time when many colleges rely on admissions testing are an uncertain guide about the long-run effects of selection without the SAT.

Consequently, our estimates in chapters 3 and 4 that the SAT does not improve colleges' correct admissions decisions and does not help applicants select academically appropriate colleges and our estimates in chapters 5 and 6 that admissions of black and economically disadvantaged applicants would increase are guides to the consequences of colleges dropping the SAT in the future. The fact that our findings were as true in 1960, when admissions testing was less widespread than it is now, suggests that these estimates may be an accurate depiction of a future with less admissions testing. But they are still only estimates. Three examples illustrate conditions that could change them.

First, suppose that selective colleges that now use the SAT began to drop the test. Peter Mueser, an economist at the University of Missouri, has suggested to us that colleges that drop the SAT might experience a change in the composition of their applicant pools.[5] Their applicant pools might increasingly consist of applicants with good high school records but low SAT scores. Among applicants with the same high school grades, these colleges would presumably attract more than their share of persons with low SAT scores. Applicants with higher test scores would apply to colleges that still required test scores, because their test scores would increase their competitive advantage in admissions.

Suppose—to take an extreme case—that a college dropped the SAT and attracted only applicants whose forecasted grades from high school rank were as high or higher than when forecasted from rank and the SAT. This college would have an applicant pool consisting solely of applicants below a northwest to southeast diagonal line in table 3.4. Were this college to admit all these applicants (or a random sample of them), their freshman class would have grades that averaged 2.71. This constitutes a decline of 0.12 of a grade point in freshman grades from the 2.83 that we estimated in the absence of any compositional change in the college's applicant pool (table 3.8).

If our hypothetical college then admitted only those applicants from its truncated applicant pool whose predicted grades with high school rank were above 2.5, its freshman class would have grades that averaged 2.77. This is considerably lower than the average grades of 2.91 (table 3.8) we estimated this college to have if it used only high school rank in the absence of a compositional change in its applicant pool. Thus, when this college drops the SAT and admits by high school rank alone, the average grades of its freshmen fall by $2.93 - 2.77 = 0.16$, which is a larger drop than the 0.02 decline in freshman grade point average we estimated in chapter 3.[6]

If colleges that drop the SAT were to experience changes in their applicant pools such as these, our estimates of the effects of dropping the SAT would be understated. But it is uncertain which kinds of colleges, and how many of them, might be affected this way. On the one hand, most high school students probably do not develop detailed, rational application strategies based on guesses about how differing colleges weight the SAT in their admissions policies. Also, many colleges—even highly selective ones—probably have somewhat determinate applicant pools based on geographical residence, family ties, and ability to pay tuition and other costs. Consequently, applicant response to a change in SAT requirements may be slight. On the other hand, if colleges that drop the SAT are about equally preferred to other colleges that do not drop the test by relatively large numbers of applicants having similar admissions potential, the shifts in applicants' perception of their competitive advantage will influence which college they apply to. Our estimates of the effects of these colleges dropping the SAT could therefore be understated.

A second condition that could modify the accuracy of our estimates is that high school grades may become less accurate predictors of academic success if more and more colleges drop admissions tests. The board's president, George Hanford, makes this argument:

> It might be asked, What would occur if admissions tests were no longer used and the importance given to high school grades in deciding admissions were increased? Certainly students would feel greater pressure to take easier courses to boost their high school grades, and teachers and schools would experience considerable pressure to ease grading standards as well. . . . [The] suggestion that the school record could be used alone . . . assumes that these data would retain their current predictive power even if the checks and balances provided by test scores were no longer available to colleges.[7]

This is one of the more specious of the board's claims for the SAT. The argument is completely speculative and denigrates teachers. Hanford cannot know that high school grades would lose their predictive power in the absence of college admissions tests, and he has never offered any evidence that they might. There is no evidence that high school grades had less predictive power in the 1960s or earlier when admissions testing was not as common as it is now. Nor is there any convincing evidence that the predictive power of high school grades has declined in the period of grade inflation since the early 1970s.[8] Nonetheless, one cannot prove that Hanford's claim has no merit.

Another argument against drawing conclusions about a future without the SAT is the assertion that the SAT or some test like it is inevitable, and that if it did not exist, it would have to be invented. In its most sophisticated form, this view contends that there were good reasons historically for the growth of the SAT that would reassert themselves if colleges tried to abandon the test.

We have never found this argument very compelling, despite having heard it many times from people at ETS and from some of our colleagues. However, when we encountered it recently in a note by Howard Wainer, one of ETS's leading experts in measurement and statistics, we decided that it merited at least a brief mention. Wainer writes:

> The scenario I imagine has Greg Anrig wandering dejectedly around central New Jersey with worries about *None of the Above*, James Crouse, the Justice Department, the Golden Rule Insurance Company, and who knows what else. Just as he begins to worry that perhaps he ought to reconsider the previously rejected plan of turning ETS into a combination hay farm and parking lot his guardian angel (perhaps in the form of L. L. Thurstone) came by to take him on a tour of what an SATless world would be like.
>
> While there are many of these subjunctive worlds that crowd one's imagination, the most prominent one looks just like the one he left. The hustle and bustle of the controlled mayhem involved in turning out of the SAT has been relocated from Princeton to Iowa City (or maybe Monterrey [*sic*]), but except for minor changes the rest continues. The reason for this is that if the SAT didn't exist it would have to be invented. In the vacuum created by the absence of an SAT the ACT expanded. Why this should happen is quite clear and parallels the reasons for the development of an SAT and its subsequent growth.[9]

This is not as clear to us as it is to Wainer. In our view, the only way to be certain about what the future would be like without the SAT is for colleges to stop using the test and evaluate the results. Some undergraduate colleges have made the SAT optional recently, most notably Bowdoin and Bates. Harvard Business School has also dropped its admissions test, and Johns Hopkins Medical School has made the Medical College Admissions Test optional. Both Bowdoin and Bates collected data and published what happened.

Bowdoin allowed applicants to submit or withhold SAT scores starting in 1970. However, since most of the applicants had taken the SAT, Bowdoin could later obtain scores from the students who matriculated. Paul Schaffner, a psychology professor at Bowdoin, analyzed the Bowdoin experiment and published the results in 1985.[10]

Schaffner found a steady increase in applications from 1970 to 1974, due almost entirely to an increase in applicants who withheld their SAT scores. In 1974 Bowdoin's admissions committee modified the policy slightly to recommend submission of SAT scores. The change was introduced because the committee was concerned that the rising number of SAT-withholding applicants were less qualified than other applicants. The size of the applicant pool and the percentage of withholders declined for one year after the policy modification and remained relatively steady after that.

The initial rise in the number of SAT-withholding applicants from 1970 to 1974 was most likely the result of the policy's effect on expanding Bowdoin's applicant pool to more applicants with both lower SAT scores and lower high school class ranks. Schaffner does not report applicants' SAT scores or class ranks for 1970–74, so one cannot be certain of this. He does report matriculated students' test scores and class ranks from 1976 to 1982, both of which were slightly lower for withholders than submitters. This suggests that during these later years, at least, withholding applicants also had lower SAT scores and class ranks than submitters, unless Bowdoin selected and enrolled the more promising of its submitters and the less promising of its withholders, which seems unlikely.

The most important finding from Bowdoin's experiment is that the optional SAT policy had no negative effect on the quality of admissions decisions. Schaffner did find that the college grades of admitted students who withheld their SAT scores averaged a fifth to a quarter of a grade point below those of their classmates who submitted SAT scores. But this was not because the admissions committee needed withholders' SAT scores to admit the best students. Rather, the admissions committee admitted withholders who had both lower SAT scores and lower high school class ranks than submitters, and these differences in credentials explain the difference between the college grades of the withholders and submitters. Consequently, the effects of Bowdoin's SAT-optional admissions policy are somewhat confounded with a lowering of admissions standards for withholders.

Despite the lack of definitiveness in Bowdoin's experiment, it has so far found no reason to change its policy. Schaffner reports:

> The feasibility of the policy has been demonstrated. Administrative aspects have worked smoothly; virtually all ma-

> triculants were aware of the option to submit or withhold their SAT scores and knew their scores in advance so as to have been able to make informed choices. . . . The policy was overwhelmingly endorsed by students. More important than administrative considerations, though, is that virtually all students in both groups have proven capable of meeting the college's educational requirements. Of the dozen students permanently dismissed for academic and/or disciplinary reasons in the four academic years since fall 1979, only two had withheld SAT scores upon application.[11]

Bates's SAT-optional policy results are more preliminary than Bowdoin's, but William Hiss reports results from the first two years of Bates's SAT-optional policy that confirm Bowdoin's in important respects.[12] Hiss reports that Bates's applicant pool increased 17.6 percent in the two years following the decision to make SATs optional, with a significant increase in geographical diversity, minority applications, and foreign applications.

Hiss also reports that there was no evidence that growth in Bates's applicant pool was only from persons with lower SAT scores. Still, he did find that applicants who chose not to submit their SAT scores did average 80 points lower on both the SAT verbal and math sections than submitters. However, Bates did not make poorer admissions decisions in admitting these applicants, since the admitted nonsubmitters, despite their lower scores, did not differ significantly in first semester grade point average or academic standing from the submitting students.

Hiss concludes that "enrolling non-submitters have done markedly better than one would have predicted from their SATs." He adds: "We acknowledge a very small sample and a short time line, but are solidly pleased with the results of the optional SAT policy to date."[13]

Bowdoin's and Bates's SAT-optional policies and Schaffner's and Hiss's reporting of them stand as models for colleges to assess the effects of dropping the SAT. Along with the analyses in this book, they provide a clear direction for colleges and universities to follow in analyzing the usefulness of the SAT.

To begin, colleges could replicate the analyses we present in chapters 3–6. All these analyses can be conducted with widely available statistical packages. If an institution has conducted a validity study of its own, or if a study has been undertaken by the Validity Study Service, a college can easily use these data for its analyses. Alternatively, colleges could request the Validity Study Service to do the analyses for them.

Colleges could also take a variety of SAT policy steps similar to Bowdoin's and Bates's—such as making the test optional for a year or two; dropping use of the test for everyone, or a random sample of applicants; or admitting students who normally would be rejected by addition of the SAT to their high school record—and evaluate the results of the experiment.[14]

If our analyses prove correct and generalizable, the results of these research strategies should confirm the conclusions we reach in this book. The next step would be an institutional decision about whether to drop the SAT. Bates and Bowdoin made affirmative decisions once they marshaled the evidence against the SAT. But a major obstacle stands in the way of many colleges dropping the test. Bates and Bowdoin could initiate an SAT-optional policy partly because they are prestigious institutions with strong competitive positions in the admissions marketplace. They did not have to worry as much as some other colleges that the public might misread their policies.[15]

Other colleges, particularly less selective and less esteemed ones, run the risk of the public interpreting their dropping the SAT as an admissions gimmick. Admissions officers with whom we have spoken often acknowledge privately that the SAT provides only marginal academic benefits, and that they could get along quite well without it. But given the uncertain consequences of how high schools and the general public would view such a move, the officers are content to maintain the status quo, especially since the cost of the SAT is paid by applicants and not by them.

We realize that admissions personnel need to be concerned about the impact of policy changes. For this reason, we hope that other highly selective colleges will begin to explore the SAT's impact on admissions outcomes more carefully than they have in the past. If a few influential and prestigious universities did this, the results could provide the best impetus for less selective institutions to explore admissions without the SAT.

Suppose that American colleges that now use the SAT were to begin dropping the test over the next few years, and suppose further that nothing suffered as a result. It would then follow that colleges could drop the SAT and make their admissions decisions from applicants' high school records. But it would not follow that colleges *ought* to drop the SAT and rely only on applicants' high school records. One reason not to drop all admission tests is that other kinds of admissions tests may have virtues the SAT does not have.

Experiments That Replace the SAT

The College Board's main tests for more than forty years were achievement tests. Over its first two decades, the board offered examinations in subjects like history, chemistry, mathematics, physics, Greek, Latin, and English. Then, for the reasons discussed in chapter 2, the board began to embrace aptitude testing and its own SAT for college admissions. The board now offers fourteen achievement tests in five broad subject areas.[16] But only about a fifth of the SAT population takes one or more achievement tests, and the board does not encourage colleges to give them the same emphasis as the SAT. Since the advent of the SAT, the board and ETS have stressed the advantages of the SAT and ignored the advantages of achievement tests.

One advantage frequently cited by the board and ETS for the SAT over achievement tests is that the SAT "is not tied to a particular course of study." As a result, says Rex Jackson, a former vice president at ETS, the SAT "is more broadly appropriate than subject-matter achievement tests for students with different patterns of educational preparation."[17]

There is no doubt that the SAT is less dependent on specific instruction than the early achievement tests used by the College Board. The board's original achievement examinations were based on highly detailed course syllabi. Often the instruction for a syllabus was given in only a handful of preparatory schools. But as time passed, the board developed achievement tests based on much broader curricular areas.

Since the 1960s the board has made greater efforts within broad curricular areas to construct achievement tests that are fair to students having, say, one biology curriculum but not another. The board has tried to include test items at various levels of difficulty from a common core of knowledge, and thus test abilities basic to all curricula in a given area, as well as content from each identifiable curriculum in the subject area. And according to the board, it has succeeded: "The scores [on achievement tests] are particularly appropriate for use in admissions because they are independent of specific textbooks, grading procedures, and methods of instruction. This independence allows comparison of students whose course preparation and backgrounds vary widely."[18]

Despite these claims, neither the board nor ETS has ever tried to assess directly whether the SAT is less tied to high school curricula than its current achievement tests. Admittedly, it is difficult to identify all the curricula used to teach a subject in American high schools. Nonetheless, if the SAT were less sensitive than the board's current achievement tests to all the curricular and instructional variations among schools, we should find that schools' average SAT scores varied less relative to individual scores than schools' average achievement scores do. Indeed, if the SAT were truly insensitive to the curricular and instructional characteristics of the school an individual had attended, schools' average SAT scores should not vary at all once we control for the characteristics of entering students.

ETS has undertaken research that bears on this question. The ETS Academic Growth study surveyed ninth graders in 1965 and followed them up in eleventh grade.[19] Seventeen communities in the United States participated in the study. They were selected to vary in geographical location, school system size, and the proportion of their high school seniors continuing to college. ETS administered its School and College Ability Test (SCAT), which uses many items similar to the SAT, to both ninth and eleventh graders. ETS also administered its Sequential Tests of Educational Progress (STEP), which uses many items similar to the subject-matter achievement tests in its admission testing program to both ninth and eleventh graders.

The Academic Growth study has been analyzed by a number of investigators, but most thoroughly by Karl Alexander and his colleagues at Johns Hopkins University.[20] Alexander found that after controlling for socioeconomic background and test scores of ninth graders, school-to-school differences in average SCAT scores relative to individual scores were no less than school-to-school differences in average STEP scores. These results do not suggest that so-called "aptitude" tests are less tied to a particular course of study than achievement tests.

Additional evidence for a larger sample of high schools comes from the longitudinal testing program carried out by Project Talent. In 1963 Project Talent retested twelfth graders who had been initially tested as ninth graders in 1960 in more than one hundred comprehensive public schools. After controlling ninth grade test scores, family background, college plans, and high school curriculum, Christopher Jencks and Marsha Brown found that school-to-school variation in schools' average score on Project Talent's twelfth grade social studies and history information test was no greater relative to individual scores than schools' average vocabulary, reading comprehension, and arithmetic reasoning scores, all of which contain questions similar to the SAT.[21] This does not suggest that conventional achievement tests are any more sensitive to curriculum and instructional variations among high schools than so-called "aptitude" tests are.

Both of these studies raise serious doubts about the College Board's traditional assumption that the SAT places applicants from high schools of varying curricula and instruction on a more equal footing than achievement tests do. This assumption may have been true half a century ago, when the SAT was instituted, and it may still be correct today if one compares the SAT to achievement tests in subjects that are only taught in a limited number of secondary schools. But so far as we can tell from the limited available evidence, it is probably not true for achievement tests in subjects like mathematics and social studies that are taught, albeit in very diverse ways, in all secondary schools.

A second advantage widely touted by the board and ETS of the SAT over achievement tests is that the SAT places individuals from low-income, poorly educated families and nonwhite backgrounds on a more equal footing than achievement tests that measure the secondary school curriculum. "I am unable to see how the ideals of . . . increased access to higher education for those who have been traditionally underrepresented in our society can be advanced by moving to a system based on achievement tests," Stephen Ivens, a College Board representative, told an American Educational Research Association symposium in Los Angeles in 1981.[22]

So far as we can discover, the College Board and ETS have not investigated whether race and socioeconomic background affect conventional achievement scores more strongly than they affect SAT scores. The work of Barbara Heyns on summer learning, however, suggests that both race and socioeconomic status have more impact on what students learn outside the classroom than inside it.[23] Thus, if the SAT were less tied to classroom learning than conventional achievement tests, we would expect race and socioeconomic status to have more impact on SAT scores than on conventional achievement scores. But, as we have just seen, the SAT may be just as tied to classroom learning as conventional achievement tests are.

The Academic Growth study provides further evidence on this point. Data made available to us by Karl Alexander indicate that father's education, father's occupation, mother's education, and race have roughly the same correlations with the two aptitude scores and two achievement scores described above and with the SAT that was taken by twelfth graders. For those concerned with equality of opportunity, then, aptitude tests seem to offer no clear advantage over achievement tests.

A third traditional virtue of the SAT over conventional achievement tests, according to ETS, is that the SAT "is designed to assist in predicting future academic performance."[24] The SAT is designed to differ from achievement tests in biology or American history that are retrospective measures of school achievement. Regardless of the SAT's design, however, our evidence strongly suggests that achievement tests in traditional secondary school subjects predict freshman grades, college completion, and adult economic success as well as the SAT. We therefore see no grounds for preferring the SAT to achievement tests in high school subjects on grounds of its greater predictive power.

The College Board did not investigate whether the SAT predicted college grades more or less accurately than traditional achievement tests when it first introduced the SAT. Since then there have been a few studies in specific colleges, but these results are not generalizable. Harvard, for example, received some publicity a few years ago when it was considering a modification of its undergraduate admissions policies that would permit the student the option of substituting two achievement tests for the SAT. In a recent issue of *Change*, Harvard's Dean Whitla notes: "College Board achievement tests have long been better predictors of grades at Harvard than have the SATs."[25] Bates College also finds similar results. Bates's analysis indicates that achievement tests explain more variance in college grades beyond high school rank than the SAT does.[26]

Results from ETS's own Validity Study Service also show that achievement tests predict freshman grades at least as well as the SAT does. Based on validity studies conducted for colleges with College Board achievement test takers between 1964 and 1981, the average of all achievement tests taken correlates 0.37 with freshman grades. The English composition test correlates 0.36 and the mathematics level 1 test correlates 0.35. Correlations of the SAT with freshman grades are about the same magnitude: 0.32 for the SAT verbal test, 0.30 for the SAT math test, and 0.38 for the best weighted sum of them both.[27]

The best data we have found on the predictive validity of achievement tests for freshman grades are, however, from a study ETS conducted in 1979 of twenty-two highly selective colleges and universities. Seventy-eight percent of the freshmen in these colleges had taken at least one achievement test. Table 8.1 summarizes our analyses of these data. It shows that, on average, SAT and achievement scores predict freshman grades equally well, though the pattern varies significantly from college to college. In most colleges, scores on ETS's achievement tests are almost interchangeable with SAT scores.[28]

We also computed the correlations between distributions of predicted freshman grades based on high school record, high school record plus the SAT, and high school record plus achievement test average. The SAT-added distribution correlates 0.831 with that based on high school record alone and the achievement-added distribution correlates 0.839 with that based on high school record alone. The distributions of predicted grades by high school record plus SAT and high school record plus achievement correlate 0.934. This suggests that colleges should choose between the two sorts of tests on grounds other than their ability to predict freshman grades.

ETS has never investigated whether its traditional achievement tests predict college completion better or worse than the SAT does, but one can get some relevant evidence from Project Talent, which surveyed a representative national sample of students who were in grades 9 through 12 of a public or private secondary school in 1960 and followed them up eleven years after their expected high school graduation, when they were around twenty-nine years old. We analyzed data on a representative subsample of those who had attended college.[29] To estimate college applicants' "aptitude" scores, we summed their scores on the Project Talent tests of vocabulary, reading comprehension, and arithmetic reasoning.[30] To estimate their

Table 8.1 Mean R^2 in Regressions of Freshman Grade Point Average on Selected Student Characteristics in Twenty-two Colleges

Independent Variables	R^2
1. SAT_v + SAT_m	.134
2. Achievement Scores	.134
3. High School Grades	.150
4. SAT_v + SAT_m + High School Grades	.215
5. Achievement Scores + High School Grades	.213
6. SAT_v + SAT_m + High School Grades + Achievement	.227
7. SAT_v + SAT_m + Achievement	.151

Note: Achievement tests differ from college to college, and high school grades are based on grade-point average in some colleges and rank in class in others. We are indebted to Len Ramist of ETS for supplying us with the original data.

overall "achievement" scores, we summed their standardized scores on the Project Talent tests covering English, history and social studies, mathematics, and natural sciences.[31]

Table 8.2 shows correlations of the Project Talent "aptitude" and "achievement" composites, the number of years of higher education completed, and whether respondents earned a bachelor's degree. Among those initially tested in twelfth grade who entered college, the standardized regression of the bachelor's degree (B.A.) variable on the "aptitude" and "achievement" composites is:

$$\text{B.A.} = 0.376 \text{ achievement} + 0.026 \text{ aptitude } (R^2 = 0.158) \quad (8.1)$$

Since both coefficients have standard errors of 0.044, the "achievement" coefficient is highly significant, whereas the "aptitude" coefficient is not at all significant.[32] This pattern recurs for respondents tested in ninth, tenth, and eleventh grades. It also recurs when one predicts years of higher education rather than the earning of a bachelor's degree, and when one adds high school grades to the equation.[33] These results suggest that, at least in the 1960s, selective colleges probably would not have seen increased attrition rates if they had substituted a battery of achievement tests for the SAT.[34]

All in all, our results give little reason to defend the SAT over achievement tests on grounds of predictive validity, freedom from curricular influence, or the effects of race and socioeconomic background. The choice between the SAT and subject-matter achievement tests in all these areas seems to be a toss-up; the two types of standardized tests are quite similar. If we are correct, this means that replacing the SAT with achievement tests would not let colleges select a more able freshman class than if colleges used only their applicants' high school records. Nor would we expect an increase in the influence of curricular differences between high schools on test scores. Also, achievement tests would not be likely to lower the rejection of applicants from low-income and nonwhite backgrounds compared to the SAT. The best way to increase the acceptance rates of blacks and low-income applicants in the long run is to make sure they learn as much as middle-class white applicants and that their high school records and test scores accurately assess this learning.

That some things would not change if colleges replaced the SAT with achievement tests does not mean that nothing would change, however. Since achievement tests are not widely used, the effect of using them is hard to predict. However, achievement tests would

Table 8.2 Statistics on College Entrants in Project Talent

			Correlations				
	Mean	*SD*	Aptitude	Achievement	High School Grades	Years of Higher Ed.	B.A. Degree
Aptitude							
9th–12th	106.48	13.20	1.000				
12th only	111.53	11.56	1.000				
Achievement							
9th–12th	105.98	11.16	.859	1.000			
12th only	110.58	10.91	.824	1.000			
High school grades							
9th–12th	51.62	7.64	.318	.340	1.000		
12th only	51.21	7.40	.362	.379	1.000		
Years of higher ed.							
9th–12th	3.39	1.78	.355	.414	.327	1.000	
12th only	3.46	1.78	.361	.426	.325	1.000	
B.A. degree							
9th–12th	.52	.50	.356	.396	.331	.816	1.000
12th only	.55	.50	.336	.398	.324	.818	1.000

Note: Top rows cover 5,333 respondents who were initially surveyed in grades nine through twelve, attended college, and had complete data. Bottom rows cover 1,365 respondents initially surveyed in grade twelve who attended college and had complete data.

seem likely to accomplish a number of desirable things in college admissions that the SAT has no chance to accomplish. The advantages of achievement tests over the SAT depend both on the kinds of achievement tests colleges use, and how they use them.

Advantages of Achievement Testing

CERTIFYING COMPETENCE

One of the things a test does is certify competence. What kind of competence does the SAT certify? Is it what colleges want? Initially, Henry Chauncey and others thought of the SAT as an intelligence test. "For all practical purposes, and in all of their uses," Chauncey wrote, "they are the same kind of test."[35] By the late 1950s ETS stopped equating the SAT with intelligence, though it did little to discourage others from thinking of the SAT that way. In 1959, for example, ETS published a booklet titled *You: Today and Tomorrow*, which was benevolently supposed to help ten-year-olds interpret their aptitude test scores. "In making their decisions," the text suggested, "the first questions that John, Andy, Betsy and Bill have to ask themselves are these: How much general scholastic aptitude have I? What special abilities have I?" The booklet then went on to say: "Your scholastic ability is like an engine. It is the source of your power and speed in school: It tells you how fast and how far you can go."[36] Since ETS gave tests that purported to measure scholastic ability, it seems reasonable to suppose that ETS—or its brochure writer—thought scores on these tests were, in fact, like horsepower ratings on an engine.

ETS does not make such claims today. Samuel Messick, an ETS vice president for research, is the company's leading spokesman for what traits the SAT measures. Messick formulates ETS's description of the SAT as follows: The SAT "measures developed abilities of verbal and mathematical reasoning and comprehension that are acquired gradually over many years of experience and use in both school and nonschool settings."[37]

This description makes it clear that in ETS's current view the SAT measures neither innate intelligence nor fixed endowments. And the definition is clear as far as it goes. But when Messick describes in more detail what he means by "developed abilities," the definition gets cloudy:

> Overall, then, a person's developed ability structure is conceptualized here as a multidimensional organization of stable

> assemblies of information-processing components that are combined functionally in task performance, learning, problem solving, and creative production. . . . Thus, developed abilities influence the structuring and restructuring of knowledge while developed knowledge structures influence the organization and application of abilities, leading to increasingly more complex structures of each. . . . Furthermore, the distinction between developed abilities and developed knowledge structures cuts across this aptitude-achievement contrast, as does Anastasi's continuum of experiential specificity and Snow's pyramid of referent generality.[38]

We will stick with Messick's unelaborated view that the SAT measures "developed abilities of verbal and mathematical reasoning and comprehension." We think most colleges would do the same thing, since few would be moved to defend the need to measure their applicants' "multidimensional organization of stable assemblies of information-processing components that are combined functionally in task performance, learning, problem solving, and creative performance."

But even if colleges take the view that the SAT measures developed abilities of verbal and mathematical reasoning and comprehension, we doubt whether colleges are interested in having *only* these abilities certified. If colleges were interested in certifying only the verbal and mathematical reasoning and comprehension of their applicants, they would have stopped looking at high school grades in academic courses a long time ago.

It is precisely because achievement tests certify knowledge of particular high school subjects that they have an advantage over the SAT. Both college teachers and the general public have become increasingly concerned in recent years with the fact that college freshmen know less than they used to. Most educators agree that changes in college preparation in our nation's high schools are at least partly responsible for this problem. Since the early 1970s, observers of American high schools have noted the proliferation of college preparatory elective courses that do not appear to demand thoughtful and critical reading, let alone careful writing. An A or B now seems to mean a great deal less than it used to. Promotion to the next grade has become almost automatic. Homework is less frequently assigned, and when it is assigned it is often not completed or graded. Absenteeism is up, and students' motivation seems down. Teachers are charged with incompetence or, worse, illiteracy. Nor are administrators immune from criticism.

Although we have no quantitative data on the number of hours secondary school students in different countries spend studying, most observers agree that American high school students do less academic work than their counterparts in Europe or Japan.[39] Most observers also agree that one reason European and Japanese teenagers work hard is that they must take achievement tests at the end of secondary school that largely determine whether and where they will be allowed to obtain higher education. We would not want to see American teenagers become as preoccupied with academic success and standardized exams as, say, Japanese teenagers, but we do not believe that this is a real danger. We *would* like to see American teenagers do more academic work than they now do. If selective colleges were to base admission on high school grades and tests that certify mastery of the secondary school curriculum instead of basing it on grades and tests that measure vocabulary, reading comprehension, and basic mathematics, high school students who want to attend college might be encouraged to take their academic work more seriously.

Incentives for Educational Improvement

Changing admissions testing from the SAT to achievement tests can hardly be a remedy for what many regard as a crisis in the quality of secondary education. But substituting achievement tests for the SAT could have beneficial effects on both the college preparatory curriculum and the students in it.

One point that is clear about any college admissions testing program is that students who want to be selected are going to try to improve their chances of being selected. To see this, one has only to look at the power of admissions tests to shape schools and lives in Japan. Much of Japan's educational system prepares students for these examinations. Students prepare for the examinations very seriously over a long period of time since the prestige of one's university strongly influences an individual's future.[40]

College entrance examinations in Japan have a large impact on schools and students largely because admission to Japanese universities is based solely on test scores. This is not true in the United States even for our most selective universities. Colleges and universities in the United States have never experimented collectively with a broad admissions testing program that tried to create desirable incentives for high schools to upgrade their courses and for high school students to take these classes more seriously than they now do. Colleges have instead focused almost pathologically on using the SAT to select the best and the brightest—incorrectly as far as we can see, since the marginal gains of the SAT over applicants' high school records are small to nonexistent.

As a result, admissions tests have had only a modest impact on high school instructional programs in the United States. The impact they have had has been largely in training or prep classes for the SAT. In a survey reported in the NEA *Research Bulletin,* schools were asked whether nationwide testing programs such as merit scholarship exams and college entrance exams exerted an influence on their instructional programs. Forty-one percent of the schools answered "yes" and said the influence is desirable. About 5 percent said "yes," but termed the influence undesirable. Thirty-two percent detected no influence, and 21.3 percent were undecided.[41]

The incentives created by tests to bring quality instruction in line with what the tests measure have great potential. In the case of minimum competency testing, for example, parents do not want their children to fail, and students do not want to do poorly. Many educators also realize that if too many of their students do not get promoted, or do not graduate, they themselves will come under fire. Courts even help the tests influence schools when they declare that the tests violate the equal protection and due process clauses of the U.S. Constitution if appropriate preparation has not been provided to students.

The present emphasis on the SAT now creates incentives for instruction and learning both within and outside of schools, but for only a small portion of the secondary school curriculum covering verbal and mathematical reasoning and comprehension. Thus, one finds that high school SAT cram courses and commercial preparation courses often give a great deal of attention to memorizing long lists of "SAT words" and reviewing high school algebra and geometry word problems. Were admissions testing to stress more of the secondary school curriculum, we might expect that preparation would take place more than it now does within the entire college preparatory curriculum and probably over a longer period of time.

A college admissions testing program that emphasizes achievement tests would also create incentives for high schools to offer more demanding academic courses, and for college-bound students to take them. A high school senior trying to decide between a European history course and a nonacademic elective, for example, is more likely to choose the history course if he knows he must compete favorably against others on a history achievement test to get into a selective college.

Furthermore, emphasizing tests that measure mastery of the secondary school academic curriculum would encourage high school students to believe that taking advanced academic courses counts for something in the future. One might argue that college-bound students are now encouraged to take advanced courses because selective colleges look at their transcripts and grades to see what courses they have taken and how well they did. We believe this is true. But we also believe that having to compete favorably against others on nationally normed achievement tests would strengthen students' beliefs that taking advanced courses and working hard in them is important.

Encouraging Diversity

The effect of replacing the SAT with conventional achievement tests would depend, of course, on how the system worked. If colleges were to ignore the tests completely, in the long run the tests would have little effect on anything, and would not be taken by many people. But if colleges in large or even moderate numbers were to require conventional achievement tests, and were able to convince students and the rest of the educational community that their scores were important, more secondary schools would feel obliged to offer courses explicitly tailored to the tests. This is, of course, one of the things a good college preparatory program in high school ought to do. It should at a minimum prepare high school students for the competencies that colleges think are important and that the tests measure.

Some who would be likely to oppose the use of conventional achievement tests for college admissions argue that preoccupation with tests will create a tendency for teachers to teach only to the tests, will encourage cramming, and will concentrate attention on skills amenable to measurement by the multiple choice format.[42] We also would not like to see teachers preoccupied with teaching only to tests, with these results. We do not, however, see these outcomes as very likely if the tests cover sufficiently broad areas, test items are kept secure as they now are prior to their use, and a variety of item types with essays are used as they now are.

Offsetting these potential problems, we see the advantages of an admissions testing program that creates a tighter articulation than now exists between what colleges want entering freshmen to know and the high schools that must teach this material. Since most colleges want their applicants to know something beyond verbal and mathematical reasoning and comprehension, we think that an admissions testing program that rewards students for learning these additional things has much in its favor. If selective colleges were to base admission on high school grades and tests that measured mastery of the secondary school curriculum, instead of basing it on grades and the SAT, which measures verbal and mathematical reasoning and comprehension, high school students who wanted to attend selective colleges might take their academic work somewhat more seriously.

Likely opponents of replacing the SAT with achievement tests also argue that even if the tests did not create an excessive amount of teaching toward them, they would create a long-run tendency toward curricular uniformity.[43] They point with horror to the consequences of achievement testing in England and France and especially Japan. But we believe this fear is overstated. The use of achievement tests could create more curricular diversity. The College Board and its member colleges could easily establish a set of achievement tests more flexible than those in England, France, or Japan.

The College Board now offers achievement tests in fourteen subjects. If more colleges were concerned with measuring achievement, ETS could easily double this number, even giving several types of exams in the more popular subjects. If the College Board allowed students to take as many exams as they wanted, while only reporting their highest scores, students could take a lot of unorthodox courses without jeopardizing their admissions prospects. Many colleges would embrace a system that encouraged diversity in academic interests. Such a system would still reward verbal and mathematical reasoning and comprehension, as the SAT now does, but it would also require and reward sustained application in at least a few additional areas, which the present admissions testing system does not.

New Kinds of Achievement Tests

Simply expanding the fourteen achievement tests produced by ETS for the College Board to twenty or even thirty, however, will not be adequate. David Owen, for example, criticizes ETS's achievement tests on grounds of their superficiality and the ease with which they can be coached.[44] Nor does the College Board, as far as we know, do any serious searching to find out whether the material tested on its current achievement tests is covered by the courses students actually take.

A better model for subject-matter achievement testing that tries to ensure a match between what is tested and what is taught is the College Board's Advanced Placement Program (AP). This program could provide a better foundation on which to build new achievement tests than the board's existing achievement tests. The Advanced Placement Program could also lead to new ways of thinking about college admissions testing.[45]

High schools that participate in the Advanced Placement Program offer courses based on course descriptions and detailed specifications worked out by representatives of both colleges and high schools. "The program's major components are curriculum materials in 24 college-level courses in 13 subjects, AP workshops and institutes for teachers, and annual college-level examinations for students."[46]

A recent survey of Advanced Placement teachers provides encouraging results for the AP program as "a model for improving educational quality." The survey, done for the College Board by Research and Forecasts, Inc., surveyed 1,513 Advanced Placement teachers from 600 high schools. Teachers gave positive ratings on a number of important criteria that benefit schools, students, school systems, and teachers:

> Nine in ten (89 percent) of the AP teachers indicate that AP courses can help improve the quality of instruction within an entire school or school system. . . . Eight in ten (81 percent) believe AP courses provide incentives, goals, and models to younger students in the school; . . . [and] almost half (49 percent) believe AP courses can help improve the quality of teaching in earlier grades. . . .
>
> Ninety-two percent of teachers in schools with more than 25 percent minority enrollment believe AP courses can help raise the standard of education within a school or system. . . .
>
> Teachers notice many improvements in their students as their AP courses progress. Most important, in their opinion, is an increase in students' abilities to analyze and synthesize information (71 percent), and to express themselves orally and in writing (47 percent). . . . Students also improve their study, research, and planning skills (45 percent). . . .
>
> The survey found that Advanced Placement teachers are highly satisfied, dedicated, and motivated professionals who are challenged by their AP courses. Nine in ten (92 percent)

> say their AP courses can increase teachers' interest, motivation, and enthusiasm for teaching. AP courses can also increase teachers' morale (89 percent) and a sense of teacher dedication and professionalism (83 percent). . . .
>
> More than half (65 percent) agree strongly and somewhat that AP courses help a school or system retain good teachers.[47]

Why not extend the idea of Advanced Placement courses to college preparatory courses generally? A new admissions achievement testing program built on the Advanced Placement idea of standardized tests covering specified curricula in a large number of areas, but with tests and curricula pitched at differing difficulties, could encourage greater diversity, foster the idea that taking challenging high school courses is a good thing, and give admissions officers as much common ground as they now have for judging applicants from different high schools.

Using the Advanced Placement model, the College Board might host various constituencies to work out principal objectives of the high school curriculum. In fact, the College Board has already started this process with its Project Equality program. Project Equality could easily be expanded to coordinate with the AP model to develop the testing program we propose.

The College Board's Project Equality, begun in 1980, goes further than the board has gone since the 1920s toward emphasizing the importance for college-bound high school students of a wider range of skills and subjects than are measured by the SAT. The College Board has brought together hundreds of school and college educators, lay people concerned with education, and subject-matter specialists to draft and build a consensus for a new statement of "Preferred Patterns of Preparation" for college in the 1980s and beyond. Project Equality has identified six areas in the secondary school curriculum that "can be defined in measurable terms" and that "provide a way to tell students what is expected of them": reading, writing, speaking and listening, mathematics, reasoning, and studying skills. The Project Equality statement also emphasizes that college-bound students should have a record of achievement in English, foreign or second language, history and social studies, mathematics, science, and the visual and performing arts.

Project Equality essentially rediscovers the board's long-standing goal of establishing tighter links between high school and college preparation, a goal that dates from the founding of the College Board. The board's strategy is to build a consensus within the educational community about the nature of desirable college preparation in the 1980s and to use that agreement as leverage to influence and strengthen the quality of secondary education. This strategy was reborn in the wake of a 17-year decline in SAT scores, the proliferation of elective courses in the high school curriculum, grade inflation, the tendency of many students to reduce the number of academic courses taken in the senior year, and the growing number of remedial English and mathematics courses offered by colleges.

Given the seemingly inevitable difficulties that accompany efforts to achieve consensus, and its debatable status as a desirable goal, there is no important reason to restrict achievement tests to just a few subjects. Nor is there any disadvantage to constructing two or three levels of AP-like exams and curricula within a given subject. ETS could, for example, develop three levels of an American history test and associated curriculum. Level 1 would measure what is generally regarded as minimum knowledge or skills in American history. Level 2 might be an intermediate level test. Level 3 could remain similar to the current AP program. Exams could also be added in subjects covered occasionally in high school, such as psychology, sociology, and philosophy.

Such a diverse system of standardized achievement tests covering specified curricula might prove a boon for college admissions officers. In many ways, of course, the admissions process would not change. Most colleges would still ask applicants to submit an application form, high school transcript, personal recommendations, and perhaps a writing sample. The main purpose of the achievement exams would still be to confirm the high school record and to assist admissions officers in interpreting transcripts from less familiar high schools.

But a system of diverse achievement tests based on well-defined curricula would lend itself to many interesting wrinkles in the college admissions process. For example, a college could require students to submit a total of say, six achievement test scores. Two or three subjects could be required by the college, with the rest being selected by the candidate. Colleges could also specify that certain exams must be level 2, while the remaining ones might be any level. Perhaps one of the exams might be level 3—evidence of advanced preparation and a serious academic commitment.

If students have some choice of tests to take, and if colleges encouraged students to take as many exams as they wanted while reporting only their highest scores, students could take unconventional courses without harming their admissions chances. Admissions officers could judge the academic interests and capabilities of their applicants by the number, diversity, and levels of achievement examinations presented by the candidate.

Such a system would still reward verbal and mathematical reasoning and comprehension, as the SAT now does, but it would also reward sustained effort in additional areas, which the SAT does not. In other words, were the College Board to expand Project Equality to include the development of achievement tests and curricula along the lines of the Advanced Placement Program, it would encourage changes in our college admissions testing system that would reward those who learn the most in secondary school. As long as the tests are nationally normed, the system would provide admissions officers with a common yardstick, but have all the other advantages we have presented in this chapter—certify competence, encourage educational improvement, provide curricular diversity, and emphasize academic content learned in schools. Given the failure of the SAT to do what ETS says it is intended to do, such a system could represent a vast improvement over the present one.

A Final Note on the Board and ETS

The mounting evidence over the years that the SAT may not accomplish its intended purposes has not, unfortunately, sparked creative energy from the College Board and ETS to review the purposes of admissions testing or to modify their tests. Quite the contrary, their reaction to criticism has often been defensiveness and a quick repetition of the party line about the SAT's virtues without any new supporting evidence. We know firsthand the high level of talent that exists at ETS and the board, and believe it is a shame they have not taken the lead over the years in examining the issues we raise in this book. But we are not naive enough to think that this will change easily.

Recent history shows that the board and ETS do respond when faced with legal challenges, legislation, and public pressure. Test disclosure, originally legislated in New York, and the out-of-court settlement between the Golden Rule Insurance Company and ETS are two examples.[48] This book may provide ammunition to individuals who wish to pursue these avenues with the SAT against the board, ETS, and colleges that require the test. But we think these approaches are unlikely to bring about the kind of examination we would like to see. After all, it is the self-proclaimed responsibility of the board and ETS to serve the "public interest," and as holders of most of the necessary data, they can, theoretically at least, examine the SAT better than anyone else. A better way to accomplish this examination is for colleges and professional associations concerned with admissions testing to encourage the board and ETS to undertake it.

Our prescription rests on the belief that good information can change people's understandings about the outcomes of admissions testing, and that when this happens on a large scale, consumer desires to bring about needed changes will eventually prevail. ETS and the College Board are not immune to market demands in the long run, and these can be changed by dependable information. In the long run, information may be a more powerful source of institutional change than anything else.

A time-honored method for examining complicated issues and educating the public on important matters is the blue-ribbon panel. The United States has a long and relatively successful tradition of panels and committees that have helped to shape education. For example, the Committee of Ten's recommendations in 1893 about the high school curriculum helped focus debate for nearly twenty-five years. The *Cardinal Principles of Secondary Education* of the National Education Association provided guidance for vocational education in the high school curriculum during the 1920s and 1930s. Just a few years ago, in 1983, the National Commission on Excellence in Education charged that our educational system was being eroded by a rising tide of mediocrity.

About ten years ago, the College Board itself appointed a "blue-ribbon panel" to investigate what was then a most controversial educational concern: the unexplained decline in SAT scores of college-bound seniors. Several points about the panel's origins from its final report bear repeating, and are relevant to our proposal for a panel to study further the issues we raise in this book.

> The trustees and the officers of the College Board believe that we must do all that we can to investigate and interpret this phenomenon [SAT score decline] to the public at large. . . .
>
> We are appointing a blue-ribbon panel to assist in making sense out of the complex and interrelated issues involved. The panel will be asked to audit the steps already taken to insure the psychometric integrity of the tests, to suggest additional ones if appropriate, to examine other kinds of research already done, and to identify research that still

> needs to be done in order to deal effectively with the score decline issue as it relates to candidate population, secondary education, and society. . . .
>
> Although the panel was technically appointed to advise the College Board and Educational Testing Service, its mission from the start emphasized its independence, including the freedom to deliberate such issues as it chose to consider and to report its findings in the public interest, whether or not they might be critical of the College Board or ETS.[49]

The College Board and ETS could themselves achieve an impressive public relations move by calling for a panel to study the SAT and admissions testing. A major university president or foundation chairman could also initiate the project. So could respected organizations like the National Council on Measurement in Education, the American Educational Research Association, the American Psychological Association, or the National Academy of Sciences.

Whatever its actual genesis, a careful report from a first-rate panel may hold the most promise for a further examination of the use and misuse of the SAT and other admissions tests at American colleges and universities.

Notes

Chapter 1

1. *The Times* (London), 30 August 1981.

2. Educational Testing Service, *ETS International Activities* (Princeton, N.J.: ETS, n.d.), p. 1.

3. Ibid., p. 4.

4. *Forbes,* 15 November 1976, p. 89.

5. Educational Testing Service, *Charter and Bylaws* (Princeton, N.J.: ETS, 1984), p. 17.

6. Educational Testing Service, *1985 Annual Report* (Princeton, N.J.: ETS, 1985), p. 6.

7. Educational Testing Service, *Trustees' 1984 Public Accountability Report,* (Princeton, N.J.: ETS, 1984), p. 1.

8. Educational Testing Service, *1983 Annual Report,* (Princeton, N.J.: ETS, 1983), p. 7.

9. Response Analysis Corporation, *SAT Monitor Program: High School Students View the SAT and College Admissions Process* (Princeton, N.J.: Response Analysis Corporation, 1978), p. 19.

10. Educational Testing Service, *What the Polls Say* (Princeton, N.J.: ETS, n.d.), p. 2.

11. George H. Hanford, *Testing the Tests* (New York: The College Board, n.d.). Adapted from a speech to the Middle States Regional Assembly of the College Board in Philadelphia, 6 February 1980.

12. College Entrance Examination Board, *National College-Bound Seniors, 1982* (New York: CEEB, 1983), p. 4.

13. Educational Testing Service, *Trustees' 1984 Public Accountability Report,* p. 1.

14. Even a 1985 visiting committee, which was otherwise very friendly to ETS, urged ETS to "expand its role in research related to racial, ethnic, and gender differences" (Educational Testing Service, *Report of the 1985 ETS Visiting Committee* [Princeton, N.J.: ETS, June 1985], p. 9).

15. Letter from Warren W. Willingham to James Crouse, 25 June 1985.

16. Educational Testing Service, *Educational Testing Service Annual Report, 1960–61* (Princeton, N.J.: ETS, 1961), pp. 25–26.

17. Educational Testing Service, *Test Scores and Family Income: A Response to Charges in the Nader/Nairn Report on ETS* (Princeton, N.J.: ETS, 1980), p. 2.

18. Educational Testing Service, *Trustees' 1984 Public Accountability Report,* p. 3.

19. Walter Haney, "Trials of Admissions Testing" (paper presented at the annual meeting of the American Psychological Association, Montreal, 1 September 1980), p. 2.

20. Ibid., p. 2.

21. Gerald W. Bracey, "ETS as Big Brother: An Essay Review of *None of the Above,*" *Phi Delta Kappan* 67 (September 1985): 76.

22. Winton H. Manning and Rex Jackson, "College Entrance Examinations: Objective Selection or Gatekeeping for the Economically Privileged," in *Perspectives on Bias in Mental Testing,* ed. Cecil R. Reynolds and Robert T. Brown (New York: Plenum Press, 1984), p. 190. Emphasis added.

23. Ibid., p. 215. Emphasis added.

24. Gretchen W. Ricol, executive director, Access Services, College Entrance Examination Board, to Kerry D. Marsh, 28 February 1986.

25. Educational Testing Service, *Developing a Test* (Princeton, N.J.: ETS, 1983), p. 2.

26. College Entrance Examination Board, *1983–84 Student Bulletin* (New York: CEEB, 1983), p. 15.

27. Educational Testing Service, *1983 Annual Report,* p. 7.

28. David Owen, *None of the Above: Behind the Myth of Scholastic Aptitude* (Boston: Houghton Mifflin, 1985), pp. 48–60.

29. David Owen to Gregory Anrig, 10 May 1983.

30. Gregory Anrig to David Owen, 25 May 1983.

31. Memorandum from Gregory Anrig to ETS executive advisory board, 25 May 1983.

32. David Owen, "Response to ETS's Response to *None of the Above*" (photocopy, n.d.), p. 7.

33. Educational Testing Service, "Statement of Educational Testing Service on Certain Key Issues in *None of the Above: Behind the Myth of Scholastic Aptitude* by David Owen" (Princeton, N.J.: ETS, 18 April 1985, photocopy.)

34. George H. Hanford, memo to College Board members, May 1985.

35. Steven Brill, "The Secrecy behind the College Boards," *New York,* 7 October 1973, p. 74.

36. Warner Slack and Douglas Porter, "The Scholastic Aptitude Test: A Critical Appraisal," *Harvard Educational Review* 50 (1980): 169.

37. Allan Nairn and associates, *The Reign of ETS: The Corporation That Makes Up Minds* (Washington, D.C.: Ralph Nader, 1980).

38. Educational Testing Service, *ETS Standards for Quality and Fairness* (Princeton, N.J.: ETS, 1983), p. 23.

39. James Crouse to ETS executive, 5 June 1984.

40. Ibid. The request that Crouse write this letter is puzzling to us even now, since it came from a person in whom we have a great deal of respect and personal admiration, and who has otherwise been of considerable assistance to us. Furthermore, ETS had no reason to believe that we had already decided what these data would show. Nor had we previously made a multitude of requests for data from ETS. Nor was there any great cost in supplying us information that had already been assembled.

41. Hanford, *Testing the Tests,* p. 6.

42. Educational Testing Service, *Accountability, Fairness, and Quality in Testing* (Princeton, N.J.: ETS, 1980), p. 1.

43. George H. Hanford, memo to College Board members, April 1985, p. 2.

Chapter 2

1. Few American colleges admitted students by examination in the nineteenth century. Most admitted nearly anyone or relied on preparatory departments or admitted by certificate. Admission by certificate spread rapidly after its initiation by the University of Michigan in 1870. By 1900 certificate colleges outnumbered examination colleges. Even most Ivy League colleges, including Brown, Cornell, and Pennsylvania, admitted some students on certificate by the turn of the century or shortly after, though they all retained examinations as well. Only Harvard, Yale, and Princeton never admitted students on certificate. See Harold S. Wechsler, *The Qualified Student* (New York: John Wiley and Sons, 1977), chaps. 1–3, for further discussion.

2. For further discussion, see Wechsler, *Qualified Student,* chap. 3.

3. See Wechsler, *Qualified Student,* chaps. 4 and 5; and John A. Valentine, *The College Board and the School Curriculum* (New York: College Entrance Examination Board, 1987), chaps. 1 and 2.

4. For a good general discussion of the origins of the College Board, see Wechsler, *Qualified Student,* chaps. 4 and 5. For "house histories" of the board's origins, see Claude M. Fuess, *The College Board: Its First Fifty Years* (New York: Columbia University Press, 1950), and Valentine, *College Board and the School Curriculum.* For a more critical history, see Michael S. Schudson, "Organizing the 'Meritocracy': A History of the College Entrance Examination Board," *Harvard Educational Review* 42 (1972).

5. For good discussions of the board's early examinations and who took them, see College Entrance Examination Board, *The Work of the College Entrance Examination Board: 1901–1925* (Boston: Ginn and Co., 1926); Fuess, *College Board;* and Schudson, "Organizing the 'Meritocracy.' "

6. See Fuess, *College Board,* chap. 4, for discussion of the board's comprehensive examinations, their content, and schools' and colleges' reaction to them.

7. Henry Pritchett, "Has the College Entrance Examination Board Justified Its Quarter-Century of Life?" in CEEB, *Work of the College Entrance Examination Board,* p. 13.

8. For more detailed discussion of Columbia's changing undergraduate environment after the turn of the century, see Wechsler, *Qualified Student,* chap. 7.

9. Quoted from Frederick P. Keppel, dean of Columbia College from 1910 to 1918, in Wechsler, *Qualified Student,* p. 135.

10. See ibid., chap. 7, for more detailed description of Columbia's reaction to these changes in its student body.

11. See David O. Levine, *The American College and the Culture of Aspiration, 1915–1940* (Ithaca, N.Y.: Cornell University Press, 1986), chap. 7, and Marcia Graham Synnott, *The Half Opened Door: Discrimination and Admissions at Harvard, Yale, and Princeton, 1900–1970* (Westport, Conn.: Greenwood Press, 1979) for excellent further discussion.

12. Wechsler, *Qualified Student,* p. 155.

13. Ibid., p. 158.

14. Ibid., p. 158.

15. Ibid., p. 159.

16. Harry McKown, "The Trend in College Entrance Requirements, 1913–1922," Department of Interior Bureau of Education Bulletin no. 35 (Washington, D.C.: Government Printing Office, 1925), p. 26.

17. See, for example, the reprinted papers of Carl Brigham, Frank N. Freeman, H. H. Goddard, Lewis M. Terman, and Edward L. Thorndike in Clarence Karier, ed., *Shaping the American Educational State: 1900 to the Present* (New York: Free Press, 1975).

18. For two studies that strongly associate many founders of modern testing and measurement with eugenics and Social Darwinism, and that argue for the influence of those movements on public policy, see Stephen J. Gould, *The Mismeasure of Man* (New York: Norton, 1981) and Leon J. Kamin, *The Science and Politics of IQ* (Potomac, Md.: Lawrence Erlbaum, 1974). For important criticism of these studies, see Bernard D. Davis, "Neo-Lysenkoism, IQ, and the Press," *Public Interest* 73 (1983); Arthur Jensen, "The Debunking of Scientific Fossils and Straw Persons," *Contemporary Education Review* 1 (1982); Franz Samelson, "H. H. Goddard and the Immigrants," *American Psychologist* 37 (1982); and Mark Snyderman and Richard Herrnstein, "Intelligence Tests and the Immigration Act of 1924," *American Psychologist* 38 (September 1983).

19. McKown, "College Entrance Requirements," pp. 26–27.

20. Fuess, *College Board,* p. 102.

21. Carl Campbell Brigham, *A Study of American Intelligence* (Princeton, N.J.: Princeton University Press, 1923), p. 210.

22. College Entrance Examination Board, *Work of the College Entrance Examination Board,* p. 44.

23. Ibid., p. 44.

24. Ibid., p. 55.

25. Gary Saretzky, "Carl Campbell Brigham, the Native Intelligence Hypothesis, and the Scholastic Aptitude Test" (Princeton, N.J.: Educational Testing Service, research memorandum, December 1982), p. 10.

26. College Entrance Examination Board, *Work of the College Entrance Examination Board,* p. 44.

27. Ibid., p. 44.

28. Ibid., p. 55.

29. Lewis M. Terman, *Intelligence Tests and School Reorganization* (New York: World Book Co., 1923), pp. 27–28.

30. For references to these papers and discussion of their influence, see Karier, ed., *Shaping the American Educational State*.

31. For more on the Eight Year Study, see Wilford M. Aikin, *The Story of the Eight Year Study* (New York: Harper and Brothers, 1942).

32. For additional context, see Valentine, *College Board and the School Curriculum,* chaps. 3, 4, and 5.

33. Ibid., p. 53.

34. For discussion of the origins of ETS and the relationship of ETS to its founding organizations, see Fuess, *College Board,* chaps. 8 and 9; Ellen Lagemann, *Private Power for the Public Good: A History of the Carnegie Foundation for the Advancement of Teaching* (Middletown, Conn.: Wesleyan University Press, 1983), chap. 5; Nairn and associates, *Reign of ETS;* and Schudson, "Organizing the 'Meritocracy.' "

35. For example, George F. Zook, president of the American Council on Education; Edward S. Noyes, chairman of the College Board; Oliver C. Carmichael, president of the Carnegie Foundation for the Advancement of Teaching; Raymond Allen, president of the University of Washington; Joseph W. Barker, president of the Research Corporation of New York City; James B. Conant, president of Harvard University; Senator James W. Fulbright of Arkansas; Superintendent Herold C. Hunt of the Chicago Public Schools; Katharine McBride, president of Bryn Mawr College; Dean Thomas R. McConnell of the University of Minnesota; Lester E. Nelson, principal of Scarsdale High School; and Commissioner Frank T. Spaulding of New York.

36. For example, E. F. Lindquist, Ralph W. Tyler, Lee J. Cronbach, John C. Flanagan, Paul Horst, Irving Lorge, Henry A. Murray, L. L. Thurstone, Dael Wolfle, W. J. Brogden, Henry S. Dyer, Frederic M. Lord, Harold Guilliksen, and William Angoff.

37. ETS says: "From the start, these bodies have been made up of the representatives of major organizations concerned with schools and colleges across the nation and, indeed, around the world. Therefore, they have brought to their deliberation both knowledge of the issues and experience in shaping problem-solving policies" (Educational Testing Service, *Annual Report, 1973–74* [Princeton, N.J.: ETS, n.d.], p. 17). For a more detailed description and more critical assessment of ETS's ties with major figures

in the higher education, political, and measurement and research communities, see Nairn and associates, *Reign of ETS,* especially chaps. 2, 4, 7, 8, and 9.

38. See, for example, R. Hartnett and D. Feldmesser, "College Admissions Testing and the Myth of Selectivity: Unresolved Questions and Needed Research," *AAHE Bulletin* 32 (March 1980). In this case, ETS's encouragement was apparently not very strong. David Owen, who has looked into the aftermath of this publication, reports the following: "Hartnett and Feldmesser's paper was really a call for further research, a call that ETS was understandably reluctant to heed. ETS and the College Board, Hartnett says, pressured them to reconsider their findings. They refused. Later, both were given the choice of either leaving the company or accepting jobs outside of research. Hartnett, who had been at ETS fifteen years, quit. Feldmesser decided to stay and was put to work writing test questions, something ETS also hires college students to do. Both actions were officially described as cost-cutting moves, but because ETS has a university-style tenure system, Hartnett had to be given a generous severance settlement and Feldmesser continued to be paid his old salary. More recently, he also quit" (Owen, "The Last Days of ETS," *Harper's,* May 1983, p. 36).

39. See David Tyack and Elisabeth Hansot, *Managers of Virtue* (New York: Basic Books, 1982) for examples of other networks in education.

40. Educational Testing Service, *Annual Report, 1949–50* (Princeton, N.J.: ETS, n.d.), p. 11.

41. Educational Testing Service, *Annual Report, 1950–51* (Princeton, N.J.: ETS, n.d.), p. 10.

42. Ibid., p. 10.

43. Educational Testing Service, *Annual Report, 1949–50,* p. 11.

44. Ibid., pp. 11–12.

45. Educational Policies Commission, *Education for All American Youth* (Washington, D.C.: National Education Association, 1944), p. 142.

46. "Flapdoodle," *Time,* 19 September 1949, p. 64.

47. Educational Testing Service, *Annual Report, 1950–51,* p. 10.

48. Ibid., p. 11.

49. Ibid., pp. 14–15.

50. Ibid., p. 12.

51. Educational Testing Service, *Annual Report, 1949–50,* p. 9.

52. Ibid., pp. 9–10.

53. Educational Testing Service, *Annual Report, 1957–58* (Princeton, N.J.: ETS, n.d.), p. 20.

54. Ibid., pp. 27–28.

55. Ibid., p. 28.

56. James B. Conant, "J. B. Conant's First Thoughts on Criteria for a Satisfactory Public High School," November 1957, (folder 25, box 1, Conant Papers, Harvard University Archives, Cambridge, Mass.).

57. Henry Chauncey to James B. Conant, 11 April 1958.

58. Ibid.

59. Memorandum from Martin R. Katz to Henry Chauncey, 10 April 1958.

60. College Entrance Examination Board, *On Further Examination: Report of the Advisory Panel on the Scholastic Aptitude Test Score Decline* (New York: CEEB, 1977), p. 4.

61. Educational Testing Service, *Annual Report, 1973–74,* p. 21.

62. Educational Testing Service, *Annual Report, 1960–61,* pp. 25–26.

63. Educational Testing Service, *Annual Report, 1973–74,* p. 21; and letter from Dennis Kelley, corporate publicity associate, Educational Testing Service, to James Crouse, 14 August 1986.

64. After the SAT, the American College Testing Program's (ACT) assessment tests are the most used tests for admissions into American colleges and universities. Candidate volume for this program has increased from 133,065 at its first administration in 1959 to 738,836 in 1985, and the number of testing sites has increased from about 300 to more than 3,400. See American College Testing Program, *Executive Summary: National ACT Assessment Results, 1984–1985* (Iowa City: ACTP, n.d.) and *25 Years of Service to Education: 1984 Annual Report* (Iowa City: ACTP, n.d.).

65. For example, in the Cooperative Institutional Research Program Freshman Survey conducted annually by the Higher Education Research Institute at UCLA, colleges are categorized by their "selectivity," so that individual institutions can compare their freshmen to those of similar colleges. Average freshman SAT scores at each college are the measure of selectivity. See Alexander W. Astin et al., *The American Freshman: National Norms for Fall 1985* (Los Angeles: UCLA Higher Education Research Institute, December 1985), pp. 101–3.

66. For an excellent discussion of these issues, see the Committee on Ability Testing's report to the National Research Council: Alexandria Wigdor and Wendell Garner, eds., *Ability Testing: Uses, Consequences, and Controversies* (Washington, D.C.: National Academy Press, 1982).

67. Nairn and associates, *Reign of ETS.*

68. Hanford, *Testing the Tests.*

69. John Weiss, executive director of FairTest, quoted in *Education Week,* 30 October 1985.

70. In 1979 New York became the first state to adopt "truth-in-testing" legislation for college and graduate school admissions exams. The legislation required test makers to provide test takers with copies of their tests and corrected answer sheets, upon request, and to publish complete editions of tests. In November 1984, ETS, the state of Illinois, and the Golden Rule Insurance Company agreed in an out-of-court settlement to follow the "Golden Rule" procedures to select items for the Illinois Insurance Agent Licensing Test (Circuit Court of the Seventh Judicial Circuit, Sangamon County, Illinois, no. 419-76, 20 November 1984). The main provision of the procedures is designed to eliminate items that are potentially racially biased from the test. In April 1986, building upon "truth-in-testing" and the "Golden Rule," legislative leaders in New York State, supported by test reformers,

civil rights groups, and consumer advocates, introduced a sweeping six-bill package. The proposed New York legislation extends "truth-in-testing" to professional and occupational tests (Senate Bill no. 9015); applies the Golden Rule test construction procedure to New York's professional and occupational standardized tests (Senate Bill no. 8985); requires test makers to make public statistical information on college and graduate school admissions tests (Senate Bill no. 9020); enables students to request their "truth-in-testing" rights when they register for the exam (Senate Bill no. 9021); requires test makers to make challenges public (Senate Bill no. 9022); and applies New York's "truth-in-testing" law to the Test of Standard Written English (Senate Bill no. 9023). Similar, though less sweeping, legislation has been introduced in California (Assembly Bill no. 4045) and Massachusetts (Senate Bill no. 2530).

Chapter 3

1. College Entrance Examination Board, *Taking the SAT: A Guide to the Scholastic Aptitude Test and the Test of Standard Written English* (New York: CEEB, 1978), p. 48.

2. Educational Testing Service, *Test Use and Validity: A Response to Charges in the Nader/Nairn Report on ETS* (Princeton, N.J.: ETS, 1980), p. 5.

3. Hunter Breland, "An Examination of State University and College Admissions Policies" (Princeton, N.J.: Educational Testing Service, Research Report RR-85-3, January 1985), pp. 4, 9.

4. Ibid., p. 5.

5. College Entrance Examination Board, *Guide to the College Board Validity Study Service* (New York: CEEB, 1982), chaps. 2–4.

6. College Entrance Examination Board, *Undergraduate Admissions: The Realities of Institutional Policies, Practices, and Procedures* (New York: CEEB, 1980), table 13.

7. For quantitative data on colleges' use of these sources of information, see College Entrance Examination Board, *Undergraduate Admissions,* tables 14 and 15, and Warren W. Willingham and Hunter M. Breland, *Personal Qualities and College Admissions* (New York: College Entrance Examination Board, 1982).

8. Any other weights that colleges assign to the SAT and high school record will result in lower overall academic benefits from selection than the predicted performance model weights (see Breland, "University and College Admissions Policies," p. 18, and Arthur Jensen, *Bias in Mental Testing* [New York: Basic Books, 1980], chap. 9, for further discussion). Furthermore, if the college uses other information on the applicant in addition to SAT scores and high school record (HSR), such as interview ratings, for example, the best method for predicting freshman grades will weight high school record and SAT scores lower than their weights when this other information is missing. In particular, if

$$\text{Best prediction of freshman grades} = B_1\text{SAT} + B_2\text{HSR} \quad (1)$$

and

$$\text{Best prediction of freshman grades} = C_1\text{SAT} + C_2\text{HSR} + C_3 \text{ other information} \quad (2)$$

then in general B_1 will be larger than C_1 and B_2 will be larger than C_2. Both equations maximize freshman grade predictions given the information they use assuming that nonlinearities are not present. Equation 2 will usually explain freshman grades better than equation 1, since it uses more information. But the independent contribution of the SAT to prediction in equation 1 will exceed its contribution in equation 2 if all variables have positive correlations, as they nearly always do, since adding the other information in equation 2 will lower the SAT coefficient in equation 2 compared to equation 1 and raise the R^2.

9. Hunter M. Breland, Gita Wilder, and Nancy J. Robertson, *Demographics, Standards, and Equity: Challenges in College Admissions* (N.p.: AACRAO, American College Testing Program, CEEB, ETS, and National Association of College Admission Counselors, 1986), table 3.8.

10. See, for example, S. F. Ford and S. Campos, ''Summary of Validity Data from the Admissions Testing Program Validity Study Service'' (Princeton, N.J.: College Entrance Examination Board, 1977); ETS, *Test Use and Validity,* pp. 15–16; and Leonard Ramist et al., ''The Predictive Validity of the ATP Tests,'' in *The College Board Technical Handbook for the Scholastic Aptitude Test and Achievement Tests,* ed. Thomas F. Donlon (New York: College Entrance Examination Board, 1984).

11. See John C. Flanagan et al., *The American High School Student* (Palo Alto, Calif.: American Institutes for Research, 1964) for information about the Project Talent Survey, conducted initially in 1960. See J. R. Levinsohn, L. B. Henderson, J. A. Riccobono, and P. Moore, *National Longitudinal Study Base Year, First, Second, and Third Followup Data File Users Manual* (Research Triangle, N.C.: Research Triangle Institute, 1978), for information about the National Longitudinal Study, conducted initially in 1970. See *High School and Beyond, 1980, Senior Cohort First Followup (1982): Data File User's Manual* (Washington, D.C.: National Center for Education Statistics, 1983) for information about the 1980–82 High School and Beyond Survey.

12. ETS reports a median increment of 0.06 from 827 studies in its Validity Study Service (*Test Use and Validity*). Len Ramist (personal communication) of ETS reports a median increment of 0.074 for colleges reporting in the Validity Study Service between 1976 and 1980. When the increments are ranked for these colleges from lowest to highest, the increments at the 16th, 25th, 50th, 75th, and 90th percentiles are 0.017, 0.043, 0.074, 0.107, and 0.147.

13. See, for example, Slack and Porter, ''Scholastic Aptitude Test,'' and Nairn and associates, *Reign of ETS*.

14. Since the equations in table 3.3 predict the dichotomous variable of bachelor's degree attainment, we additionally estimated them with maximum-likelihood probit analysis. The results did not change in any substantively important way, so we used the ordinary least-squares estimates in table 3.3.

15. For readers unfamiliar with regression equations, b_1 represents the average change in FGPA associated with a one-point increase in SAT scores among persons with the same HSR value; b_2 represents the average change in FGPA associated with a one-point increase in HSR among persons with the same SAT score; b_3 represents the estimated FGPA of persons whose SAT and HSR are zero; and e is an error term.

16. This potential bias has been known for a long time. See for example, John P. Campbell, "Psychometric Theory," in *Handbook of Industrial and Organizational Psychology,* ed. Marvin Dunnette (Chicago: Rand McNally, 1976); Karl Pearson, "Mathematical Contributions to the Theory of Evolution, XI: On the Influence of Natural Selection on the Variability and Correlation of Organs," *Philosophical Transactions of the Royal Society* (A), 200 (1903); and Robert L. Thorndike, *Personnel Selection: Test and Measurement Techniques* (New York: John Wiley and Sons, 1949).

17. See, for example, Robert L. Linn, "Range Restriction Problems in the Use of Self-selected Groups for Test Validation," *Psychological Bulletin* 69 (1968): 69–73.

18. In effect, admissions officers usually truncate applicant pools on an unmeasured variable (Z) that is a composite of some measured variables (X), such as SAT scores and high school class rank, and a host of unmeasured variables (U), such as unscored letters of reference and interview impressions. The selection process is approximated by the following equation:

$$Z = b_4 X + U \qquad (1)$$

where X is the vector of measured variables affecting selection of an applicant, such as SAT score and class rank, and U is a composite of unmeasured characteristics affecting selection. If the composite score Z is greater than some value, the applicant is accepted. Otherwise he or she is not accepted. The college admissions process therefore truncates applicant pools on Z. But Z is not directly observed. All one knows is that when Z is greater than some threshold value for an individual, that individual is in the sample of attending college students with freshman grades. Otherwise he or she is not.

Estimation of the coefficients for the SAT and for class rank in the applicant pool with equation 3.1 in the text therefore implicitly includes another equation like equation 1. Equation 3.1 describes the predictive effectiveness of the SAT and high school rank for freshman grades in the applicant pool, and equation 1 in this note describes the nonrandom selection of applicants into the sample of attending college students who actually have freshman grades. In addition, the two equations describe a selection process that allows the unmeasured determinants of an applicant getting selected and continuing throughout the freshman year in equation 1 of this note to correlate with the unmeasured determinants of his or her freshman grades in equation 3.1 in the text. That is, *U* and *e* may be correlated.

19. The most promising techniques we know for estimating and correcting the potential bias in coefficients from incompletely truncated samples have come from the work of James Heckman—for example, "The Common Structure of Statistical Models of Truncation, Sample Selection, and Limited Dependent Variables and a Sample Estimator of Such Models," *Annals of Economics and Social Measurement* 5 (1976), and "Sample Selection Bias as a Specification Error," *Econometrica* 47 (1979). For a general introduction to these techniques, see Richard Berk, "An Introduction to Sample Selection Bias in Sociological Data," *American Sociological Review* 48 (1983). For an introduction to these techniques for psychologists working on selection test validation, see Craig A. Olson and Brian E. Becker, "A Proposed Technique for the Treatment of Restriction of Range in Selection Validation," *Psychological Bulletin* 93 (1983). For their use in models of college application and admissions, see Charles Manski and David Wise, *College Choice in America* (Cambridge, Mass.: Harvard University Press, 1983).

20. We have tested nearly a dozen models of sample selection bias using Heckman's techniques (see preceding note); the results, however, are less than satisfying. The probit models for selection of applicants into the sample of attending students in tables 3.2 and 3.3 have included applicants' SAT scores, their high school class ranks, and the selectivity of the college to which they apply. When values of lambda from the probit equations are inserted in equation 7 in tables 3.2 or 3.3, the coefficient for lambda is sometimes positive and sometimes negative, but never significant. Coefficients for other variables change dramatically, but inconsistently, from their values in equation 7 and often become negative and insignificant.

Using the NLS data—but with different endogenous variables and a population of all high school seniors instead of college applicants—Manski and Wise found more consistent evidence of sample selection bias. They also estimated SAT scores for at least a third of NLS's high school seniors who did not take the test, most of whom did not go on to college from high school. In addition, they used different methods of estimation from the ones we used. Any of these factors could be responsible for the differences in our results. Finally, it is worth noting that Manski and Wise found, as we did, a high degree of predictiveness for the SAT (*College Choice in America,* pp. 129–58). Consequently, their corrections do not alter the substantive conclusions we reach from table 3.1.

21. See, for example, College Entrance Examination Board, *Validity Study Service Data Analyses and Interpretation* (New York: CEEB, n.d.), p. 3.

22. Table 3.4 is actually a composite of predicted grades for applicants at many different colleges, but the composite never differs in any substantive way from the distributions at individual colleges. We have checked this in two ways.

First, we constructed versions of table 3.4 separately for NLS applicants to the most selective American four-year colleges, to the middle range of selective four-year colleges, and to the least selective four-year colleges. We divided the 2,781 NLS applicants into 968 who applied to the nation's most selective colleges, where freshman SAT scores averaged 1,100 or over; the 1,061 who applied to moderately selective colleges, where freshman SAT scores averaged between 1,000 and 1,099; and the 752 who applied to the country's least selective colleges, where freshman SAT scores averaged less than 1,000. The mean predicted freshman grade point averages from SAT scores and high school rank were 2.886, 2.733, and 2.768 at the most selective, moderately selective, and least selective colleges respectively. The standard deviations were 0.298, 0.352, and 0.329. Predicted from high school rank, the means were 2.887, 2.744, and 2.781, and the standard deviations were 0.224, 0.319, and 0.287. Thus, the mean predicted freshman grade point average is slightly higher and the standard deviation is slightly smaller for the most selective colleges compared to the others, but the difference is small for any practical purpose. The correlations of the two distributions of predicted freshman grade point averages are 0.808, 0.915, and 0.879 respectively.

Second, we constructed versions of table 3.4 for several individual colleges. These separate tables do not differ in any important way from the composite of the distributions in table 3.4. We therefore believe that the distributions in table 3.4 are typical of the distributions of applicants' predicted freshman grades at many American colleges.

23. Our emphasis on freshman grades and graduation does not mean we think colleges should be concerned only with those outcomes. The objectives colleges seek to attain vary greatly from college to college. See Robert Klitgaard, *Choosing Elites* (New York: Basic Books, 1985), and Warren W. Willingham, *Success in College: The Role of Personal Qualities and Academic Ability* (New York: College Entrance Examination Board, 1985), for good discussions of colleges' many objectives in relation to admissions. We focus on freshman grades and graduation because ETS, the College Board, and colleges themselves use these outcomes to build a case for the SAT. Colleges do not use the SAT to forecast the academic or social value-added they produce, or their applicants' accomplishments in nonacademic endeavors.

24. This is a well-established principle in selection theory. See Breland, "University and College Admissions Policies," and Jensen, *Bias in Mental Testing*, chap. 9, for further discussion.

25. One might expect that the mean predicted grade would be higher for students attending a given college than that college's applicants, because the college would reject the applicants with the lowest predicted grades. But applicants with high predicted freshman grades at any given college may go elsewhere. This pattern of selection might result in very small differences in predicted grade means between individual colleges' pools of

applicants and attending students, although the standard deviation may be slightly smaller for attending students.

In fact, we find a pattern of roughly equal means for applicants and attending students and smaller standard deviations for attending students that is consistent with this interpretation. But as far as we can tell the difference in standard deviations is so small as to be of no substantive importance, as the interested reader can see by comparing the results for attending students below with those presented in note 22 above for applicants. We divided the 2,470 NLS students attending college into 706 who attended the most selective colleges in the country, where freshman SAT scores averaged between 1,100 and 1,600; the 1,008 who attended the moderately selective colleges, where freshman SAT scores averaged between 1,000 and 1,099; and the 756 who attended the least selective colleges, where freshman SAT scores averaged between 400 and 999. The mean freshman grade point average predicted from both admissions policies must be identical, unlike the applicant predictions, since the data on which the equations and the predicted freshman grade point averages are computed are the same. The means are 2.928, 2.788, and 2.792 respectively. The standard deviations are 0.268, 0.327, and 0.321 predicted from rank plus SAT, and 0.205, 0.294, and 0.278 predicted from rank. The correlations between the two distributions are 0.768, 0.901, and 0.865. These values are all quite close to the values reported for applicants in note 22.

26. Table 3.5 compares a high school rank admissions policy with a rank plus SAT policy for five admissions outcomes. Two admissions standards are used here with cutoffs above 2.5 and 3.0 respectively. *a.* shows two percentages for each policy at both admissions standards. The first percentage is the observed percentage of cases conforming to each admissions outcome. The second percentage, in parentheses, is the proportion of cases conforming to each admissions outcome that one would expect if the applicants were admitted with high school rank and SAT scores having no relationship to freshman grades or earning a bachelor's degree. *b.* shows the differences between these two percentages, or the gains in each outcome resulting from use of a rank only or rank plus SAT admissions policy at each of the two admissions standards. The interested reader can follow the notes to table 3.5 to see how we calculated each of the summary results.

27. The problem with proportional improvements typically used by ETS, in our judgment, is that they can seem large because the base (in this case 9.2) from which the proportional improvement is calculated is small. Thus, while the proportional improvement of 29.3 percent can give the impression that the SAT is more important than 2.7 additional forecasts per hundred, the proportional improvement still amounts only to an improvement of 2.7 correct forecasts per hundred, which we believe most colleges would not be likely to notice. One would think, on the other hand, that ETS would want to avoid the charge that it uses proportional improvements in a self-serving way to magnify the importance of the SAT.

ETS often cites proportional improvements in response to critics who point out that absolute improvements resulting from the SAT are small (see, for example, ETS, *Test Use and Validity,* and Rex Jackson, "The Scholastic Aptitude Test: A Response to Slack and Porter's 'Critical Appraisal,' " *Harvard Educational Review* 50 [1980]). In fact, ETS has accused us of denigrating the usefulness of the SAT while failing to stress proportional improvements (see Warren Willingham and Leonard Ramist, "The SAT Debate: Do Trusheim and Crouse Add Useful Information?" *Phi Delta Kappan* 64 [November 1982]). Yet we have never seen a discussion from ETS of whether proportional improvements give a misleading magnification of the importance of absolute gains from the SAT.

28. Given the decision to use a base rate, one must then choose which base rate to use. We finally settled on a base rate that is the correct forecasts one would make with predictors having zero validity. The main advantage of this approach is that it is perhaps the standard approach to contingency tables and is therefore well known. Given fixed marginals, the probability of falling into a particular cell is computed, and then the percentage of correct forecasts is the sum of the percentages of successful acceptees and unsuccessful rejects. The only drawback is that when the margins differ for rank only and rank plus SAT admission policies, using a fixed predicted grade cutoff, the base success rates of 53.0 and 52.7 differ slightly because the marginals from which they were computed differ slightly. But this is not a problem once one sees how the calculations are made.

Another approach is to think of the base as the percentage of all applicants who would succeed were they all to be admitted or were a random sample to be admitted. This approach has the advantage of not requiring fixed and equal marginals for the two admissions policies in order to have identical base rates. Since 54.5 percent of the cases are successful with the 2.5 admissions standard, one infers that if all applicants or a random sample of them were admitted, the success rate would be 54.5 percent. Using this base rate, the added value of the SAT would be $(64.6 - 54.5) - (63.2 - 54.5) = 2.4$ additional correct forecasts per 100. With this approach, one can essentially ignore the base rate since it is the same for both admissions policies.

One could also argue that the base rate of 54.5 follows self-selection of applicants to colleges, and that if all SAT takers applied randomly to colleges, the base rate would be far smaller than 54.5. But even if we choose a small base rate, the value added by the SAT would still be only 2.4 additional correct admissions decisions per 100 that a college would make from its applicant pool. So, as far as we can tell, the choice of base rate has little effect on substantive results. We chose the one we thought most people would be familiar with.

29. It is possible to tell a much longer story about the numbers from tables 3.6 and 3.7 than is given in the text. First, one can focus on the admitted applicants who are successful for each admissions policy. Using the top panel of table 3.6 as an example, note that 2.9 percent of the sample were rejected by the rank policy but admitted by the rank plus SAT policy.

Of these seventy-one cases, thirty-one, or 43.7 percent, were successful, so that an additional (.0291)(.437) = 1.3 percent of the cases in the entire sample were admitted by the rank plus SAT policy who were successful, though they were rejected by the rank only policy. Similarly, 5.4 percent of the sample was admitted by the rank only policy but rejected by the rank plus SAT policy. Thirty-four, or 25.4 percent, of these individuals were successful in college, so that an additional (.054)(.254) = 1.4 percent were admitted by the rank only policy who were successful, though they were rejected by the rank plus SAT policy. The difference between 1.3 and 1.4 reported in the text is therefore a composite of differences in percentages of eligible applicants admitted by the two policies and success rates in college for those admitted. If the interested reader takes the trouble to make these computations for both admissions policies in tables 3.6 and 3.7, he or she will see that both of the numbers in the composite are sometimes higher for the rank plus SAT policy compared to the rank only policy, and sometimes lower. That is why the composite results in the text are so similar for the two policies.

Another way to look at the same results is to focus on the successful students who would be admitted. Again using the top panel of table 3.6, 4.6 percent of the sample are successful students rejected by the rank only policy who could be admitted by the rank plus SAT policy; 27.4 percent of these 113 successful students are admitted, so that an additional 1.3 percent of successful students are admitted by a rank plus SAT policy who are not admitted by a rank only policy. Similarly, 4.7 percent of the sample are successful students rejected by the rank plus SAT policy who could be admitted by the rank only policy; 29.3 percent are actually admitted, so that an additional 1.4 percent of successful students are admitted by a rank only policy who are not admitted by a rank plus SAT policy. This is, therefore, a second way to see why the composite results in the text for each admissions policy comparison are so nearly the same. Since both of these exercises lead to the same numbers that the text gives, except to develop the explanation a bit, no doubt all but the most obsessive/compulsive readers will conclude that the text tells them as much as they need to know.

30. The values in table 3.8 for random admissions, 2.83 and 15.82, could be lower if observed college outcomes for individuals with differing predicted freshman grade point averages who actually attend college were higher than the college outcomes applicants with these same predicted freshman grade point averages who do not attend college would have. But this would not change the estimated gains from using the SAT. In order for the estimated gains from using the SAT to be accurate, one must assume, along with ETS and most American colleges, that actual college outcomes observed for individuals with differing predicted freshman grades who actually attend college are identical to the outcomes one would observe for applicants with these same predicted freshman grade point averages who do not attend college. One must assume, in other words, that sample selection bias is minimal.

31. The difference between the two admissions policies depends on the outcomes for the cases in which they make different admissions decisions. The difference is always small. Table 3.8 shows that with the lower admissions standard 71/2470 = 2.9 percent of all applicants are admitted with the SAT plus rank policy and are not admitted by the high school rank only policy, whereas 134/2470 = 5.4 percent of all applicants are admitted with a rank only policy and are not admitted with the rank plus SAT policy. The average freshman grades of these two groups differ by only 2.60 − 2.46 = 0.14 points on a four-point scale. Their average educational attainment differs by only 15.55 − 15.48 = 0.07 years.

The differences are also very small when the higher admissions standard is used: 201/2470 = 8.1 percent of all applicants are admitted by the high school rank plus SAT policy and rejected by the rank only policy, and 6.9 percent of all applicants are admitted only by the high school rank policy. Average freshman grades for these two groups differ by 0.13 points on a four-point scale. Their average educational attainment differs by only 0.21 years.

ETS has pointed out a different interpretation of these findings. Taking the case of average grades, one can argue that if the average freshman grade point average increases by 0.14, this could mean that one out of seven students' grades increase by a whole letter grade (1.0), while the other six have no increase. This is possible, of course, but we do not think admissions tests would ever work this way. Carried further, this argument implies that the 0.14 average gain in freshman grade point averages is large because one out of twenty-one student's grades is three letter grades (3.0) higher, while the other twenty show no difference.

32. We computed these values from correlations, means, and standard deviations supplied to us by ETS for 412 colleges participating in the VSS from 1976 to 1980. Readers who have access to these same statistics for their own colleges can easily make the same calculations and compare their results to what we find in the VSS data. The equations for the two admissions policies in standardized form are:

$$\hat{Y} = B_1 R \qquad (1)$$

$$\hat{Z} = C_1 R + C_2 V + C_3 M \qquad (2)$$

where R = high school grades or rank, V = SATV, and M = SATM. The covariance between $\hat{Y}$ and $\hat{Z}$ is:

$$\text{Cov}(\hat{Y}, \hat{Z}) = B_1 C_1 + B_1 C_2 r_{R,V} + B_1 C_3 r_{R,M}$$

and the correlation between $\hat{Y}$ and $\hat{Z}$ is:

$$r_{\hat{Y},\hat{Z}} = \text{Cov}(\hat{Y},\hat{Z})/((R_{\text{Eq.1}})(R_{\text{Eq,2}}))$$

which equals 0.868 for all colleges, 0.801 for the most selective colleges and 0.840 for the least selective colleges.

33. The correlations in the VSS and NLS are also quite close to the correlation of 0.843 we calculate between freshman grades predicted from high school grades alone and from high school grades plus ACT scores for 258 colleges reporting data to the American College Testing Program. Thus, the nation's other large college admissions testing program illustrates the same redundancy from addition of the ACT to high school grades as the SAT illustrates in the College Board's admissions testing program. Michael Valiga kindly supplied us the correlations for this computation: self-reported high school grades in English, mathematics, social studies, and science have a median multiple correlation of 0.487 with freshman grade point average for these 258 colleges; ACT scores in these same subject tests have a median multiple correlation of 0.480 with freshman grade point average; the average median correlation of ACT scores in English, mathematics, social studies, and science with high school grades in the corresponding subject is 0.402.

34. See Educational Testing Service, *Test Use and Validity,* and Willingham and Ramist, "SAT Debate."

35. Ramist et al., "Predictive Validity of the ATP Tests," p. 146n. Actually, the regression coefficient value presented therein is incorrect. The correct value is the cited value divided by a hundred.

36. Ibid., pp. 144–46.

37. A good example of a correction in range restriction that makes the SAT look impressive is in the 6 November 1985 issue of *The Chronicle of Higher Education,* where Harvard's director of instructional research and evaluation, Dean K. Whitla, says that if Harvard were to admit students at random, the correlation between SAT scores and first-year grades would be 0.93 (*Chronicle of Higher Education,* no. 10, p. 3). Whitla also says that "the multiple correlations, when corrected for restriction of range, would jump from .57 to the high eighties; my last estimate went to .90." (*Measures in the College Admissions Process: A College Board Colloquium* [New York: College Entrance Examination Board, 1986], p. 18). We wrote Whitla twice asking how he corrected for restriction of range to get these values, but he did not reply to our letters.

38. See Ramist et al., "Predictive Validity of the ATP Tests," table 8.13.

39. See Peter Spiro. "Test Prep Panic," *New Republic,* 20 December 1982, p. 13.

40. Quoted in *Education Week,* 4 December 1985, p. 4.

41. Response Analysis Corporation, *SAT Monitor Program,* p. 22.

42. Educational Testing Service, *Test Scores and Family Income,* p. 10.

Chapter 4

1. See, for example, College Entrance Examination Board, *National College Bound Seniors, 1982,* p. 4; *About Your 1983 PSAT/NMSQT Scores* (New York: CEEB, 1983); and *Profiles, College-Bound Seniors, 1981* (New York: CEEB, 1982).

2. Breland, Wilder, and Robertson, *Demographics, Standards, and Equity,* table 2.1.

3. For an excellent summary of admissions requirements at public colleges and universities in all fifty states, see Margaret E. Goertz and Linda M. Johnson, "State Policies for Admission to Higher Education," College Board Report No. 85-1 (New York: CEEB, 1985).

4. See tables 4.10, 4.11, and 4.12 in *Demographics, Standards, and Equity*. Also see table 17 in the 1979 AACRAO/CEEB study *Undergraduate Admissions*. For example, when the 1979 AACRAO/CEEB study asked colleges to identify the single most important or very important applicant characteristic they consider in admissions decisions, 82 percent of the four-year colleges identified academic performance in high school, measured by grades or rank in class, whereas 58 percent identified aptitude test scores like the SAT. When asked what applicant characteristics they routinely looked at, 73 percent of the four-year colleges said they routinely considered admissions test scores in judging the admissibility of practically all freshman applicants. Only 9 percent said they did not require or regularly use admission test scores.

5. See Breland, Wilder, and Robertson, *Demographic, Standards, and Equity,* table 4.12, and *Undergraduate Admissions,* p. 36. For example, some 50 percent of the most competitive colleges in the 1979 AACRAO/College Board survey required three or four years of high school mathematics, whereas only 16 percent of the less competitive colleges required that much. At least two years of a foreign language were required by 49 percent of the most competitive colleges, but by only 27 percent of the less competitive ones. And when they had minimum SAT requirements, the most competitive colleges' minimums averaged 838, while the less competitive colleges minimums averaged 733.

6. See, for example, Richard Moll, *Playing the Private College Admissions Game* (New York: Times Books, 1979), and Willingham and Breland, *Personal Qualities and College Admissions*.

7. At least twenty other states have admissions requirements at some public colleges and universities that are very explicit. See Goertz and Johnson, "State Policies for Admission to Higher Education." No summary comparable to theirs exists for private institutions. The best sources of summary information for private institutions are the commercially produced guides to colleges.

8. College Entrance Examination Board, *Undergraduate Admissions,* table 9.

9. Response Analysis Corporation, *SAT Monitor Program,* p. 17.

10. Willingham and Breland, *Personal Qualities and College Admissions,* pp. 4–5.

11. Breland, Wilder, and Robertson, *Demographics, Standards, and Equity,* table 4.13; see also College Entrance Examination Board, *Undergraduate Admissions,* table 14.

12. Since the end of World War II, the College Board has encouraged colleges to make more formal quantitative predictions of academic success, and in 1964 the board established the Validity Study Service to help member

colleges assess the validity of their predictions. By 1979 the AACRAO/College Board found that almost half of the four-year colleges it surveyed used quantitatively calculated predicted grades in admissions and placement. In 1985 AACRAO found that 20 percent of the four-year public colleges and 12 percent of the four-year private colleges it surveyed provided prospective students either upon request or routinely with equations to estimate probable first-year achievement. But because most colleges do not publish how they calculate predicted grades, or how predicted grades are used along with other information, or the distribution of predicted grades for successful applicants, prospective applicants can only estimate how their predicted grades compare with a college's average.

13. Even though prospective applicants do not know exactly how colleges will forecast their academic success and count their nonacademic assets, they are likely to have a good idea about their probable academic performance at colleges of differing selectivity. Prospective applicants to a college usually know something about its academic requirements for admissions and the difficulty they pose. Colleges and numerous guides and directories also publish the average SAT scores of colleges' freshman classes, and the average high school grade point average and rank in class of their freshman classes so that prospective applicants can estimate their likely success. Many applicants will make informal assessments based on the academic experiences of older friends who attend the college. And at least one guide even gives computational aids for students to use their high school record and test scores to calculate their estimated freshman grades, chances of earning a B, and chances of dropping out at colleges of differing selectivity. See Alexander Astin, *Predicting Academic Performances in College* (New York: Free Press, 1971).

14. College Entrance Examination Board, *About Your 1983 PSAT/NMSQT Scores,* p. 14.

15. Leonard L. Baird, "Relationships between Ability, College Attendance, and Family Income," *Research in Higher Education* 21 (1984).

16. Manski and Wise, *College Choice in America,* p. 82.

17. Baird, "Ability, College Attendance, and Family Income," pp. 380–81.

18. Hartnett and Feldmesser, "College Admission Testing and the Myth of Selectivity." Table 2.3 in Breland, Wilder, and Robertson, *Demographics, Standards, and Equity,* indicates that 17 percent of the four-year public colleges surveyed by AACRAO in 1985 admitted more than 95 percent of their applicants, 49 percent admitted more than 80 percent, and 92 percent admitted more than 50 percent. The comparable values for four-year private colleges were 17 percent, 51 percent, and 91 percent respectively.

19. Moll, *Playing the Private College Admissions Game,* p. 5.

20. R. A. Weitzman ("The Prediction of College Achievement of the Scholastic Aptitude Test and the High School Record," *Journal of Educational Measurement* 19 [1982]) reports values for the standard deviation between colleges, SD(B), the standard deviation within colleges, SD(W),

and the total standard deviation, SD(T), of 0.20, 0.57, and 0.60 for high school grade point average, and 50, 88, and 101 for SAT verbal scores. These values are from 1980 and 1981 ATP Validity Study Service data for between 650 and 1851 colleges summarized by ETS. The values of SD(B) imply that the top and bottom fifths of colleges differ by (2.8)(0.20) = 0.56 points on the four-point high school grade point average scale and (2.8)(50) = 140 points on the 200–800 SAT verbal scale.

21. Using the values reported by Weitzman ("Prediction of College Achievement") implies that colleges explain VAR(*B*)/(VAR(*B*) + VAR(*W*)) = 0.04/(0.04 + 0.325) = 11 percent of the total variance in high school grade point averages and 2500/(2500 + 7744) = 24 percent of the total variance in SAT scores. The standard deviation within colleges of high school grade point averages is therefore SQRT (1 − 0.11) = 94 percent of the overall standard deviation. The standard deviation within colleges of SAT verbal scores is SQRT (1 − 0.24) = 87 percent of the overall standard deviation.

22. Since the equations in table 4.1 predict a dichotomous variable of acceptance vs. nonacceptance with ordinary least squares, we also estimated the equations with maximum likelihood probit analysis. The results did not change in any substantively important way. Furthermore, since respondents who apply to four-year colleges are a nonrandom sample of those who apply to any college, and those who apply to any college are a nonrandom sample of all those who take the SAT, and all those who take the SAT are a nonrandom sample of all high school graduates, one ought in principle to correct coefficients in acceptance equations like those in table 4.1 for sample selection bias. We have not done this. Steven Venti and David Wise ("Test Scores, Educational Opportunities, and Individual Choice," *Journal of Public Economics* 18 [1982]) found results very similar to ours with a sample of NLS respondents, and did make sample selection bias corrections in coefficients of acceptance equations. The simulated admissions probabilities after correction for sample selection bias were very close to those based on uncorrected coefficients (ibid., pp. 55–56). This is probably as it should be, since, as Venti and Wise expect a priori, the unobserved determinants of respondent's application decisions (which are made by applicants) should correlate poorly with the unobserved determinants of admissions decisions (which are made by institutions). Venti and Wise estimate this correlation at 0.08 (ibid., p. 49). Since Venti and Wise's results were not affected by their corrections for sample selection bias, and since the methods of making the corrections employ assumptions that are difficult to test, we chose to use uncorrected coefficients.

23. We limit our discussion to academic benefits of self-selection because colleges look at their applicants' high school grades and test scores for academic reasons. Colleges do not, for example, look at high school grades and SAT scores to encourage individuals to apply who will excel on the lacrosse field or baseball diamond.

24. Because for these analyses we wanted to predict freshman grades at colleges of differing selectivity as accurately as possible from high school

rank and SAT scores, we checked to see whether these variables had important nonlinear relationships with freshman grades, and whether the relationships of SAT and class rank to freshman grades depended on the selectivity of the college. We did not look at nonlinearities and interactions in chapter 3 because colleges do not look at them for admissions predictions. We first estimated equations 5 and 7 in table 3.2 for subsamples stratified by college selectivity, but the minor differences between the equations were too small to affect any substantive result. We then added squared terms for college selectivity, SAT, and high school rank to equation 7, plus product terms between all pairs of variables, and R^2 increased only 0.03. We therefore retained the linear versions of equations 5 and 7 for our computations.

25. See for example, Daniel Kahneman, Paul Slovic, and Amos Tversky, eds., *Judgment under Uncertainty: Heuristics and Biases* (Cambridge: Cambridge University Press, 1982).

26. The average difference is only 0.09 of a grade; 5.7 percent of the applicants have a 0.4 grade point difference, 2 percent have a 0.5 grade difference, and 0.3 percent have a 0.6 difference.

27. This is because controlling for college selectivity at different values changes only the intercepts of equations 4.1 and 4.2, which does not affect the correlation between the predicted freshman grades.

28. The standard deviation in observed freshman grade point averages conditional upon the predictions from equation 4.1 is SQRT (1 − 0.168) = 91 percent as large as the standard deviation of actual freshman grade point averages in the entire NLS sample. It is SQRT (1 − 0.224) = 88 percent as large conditional upon the predictions in equation 4.2 that add SAT scores. These are similar to values of SQRT (1 − (0.52) (0.52)) = 85 percent and SQRT (1 − (0.58) (0.58)) = 81 percent, respectively, computed from 827 Validity Study Service studies summarized in Educational Testing Service, *Test Use and Validity,* p. 16.

29. Response Analysis Corporation, *SAT Monitor Program,* p. 37.

Chapter 5

1. Hunter Breland, "Population Validity and College Entrance Measures" (College Entrance Examination Board Research Bulletin, November 1978), p. 44.

2. Arthur Jensen, *Straight Talk about Mental Tests* (New York: Free Press, 1981), pp. 43, 45 51.

3. Nairn and associates, *Reign of ETS,* p. 110.

4. College Entrance Examination Board, *Profiles, College-Bound Seniors, 1981,* p. iii.

5. Between 1976 and 1984 white college-bound seniors' SATV scores averaged 451, 448, 446, 444, 442, 442, 444, 443, and 445. Black college-bound seniors' SATV scores averaged 332, 330, 332, 330, 330, 332, 341, 339, and 342. White college-bound seniors' SATM scores averaged 493, 489, 485, 483, 482, 483, 483, 484, and 487. Black college-bound seniors' SATM scores averaged 354, 357, 354, 358, 360, 362, 366, 369, and 373. The mean SATV

score of blacks thus increased 10 points over these years, and the mean SATM score increased 19 points. Because the average SAT verbal and math scores of whites declined by 6 points over these years, the black-white difference fell 16 points on the SATV and 25 points on the SATM between 1976 and 1984.

Educators often assume that SAT score increases result from improved schools. George Hanford, president of the College Board, said about SAT score increases in 1985 that recent education-reform initiatives "have begun to pay off," that "instruction in the schools has been improving," and that "high school students are giving greater attention to academic study" (*Education Week,* 2 October 1985). Secretary of Education William J. Bennett said: "Bravo, . . . We begin to see here the impact of the reform movement of the past several years" (*Morning News,* [Wilmington, Del.], 24 September 1985).

We are less optimistic that SAT score increases result from improved schools. All the black SATV score increase and half the SATM score increase has occurred since 1981, during which time the black standard deviations have remained very stable, while the number of college-bound blacks who took the SAT declined steadily from 75,434 in 1981 to 71,177 in 1984. Some part of the black SAT increase may result from changes in the composition of the black SAT-taking population. The median size of the families in which college-bound blacks who took the SAT lived declined each year from 4.2 in 1981 to 3.9 in 1984. The median educational level of their parents also increased by a tenth of a year. How much these changes arise from changing marginals and from changing test-taking propensities is unknown, as is how much of the black-white gap these changes might explain. For discussion of these issues, see Howard Wainer, "An Exploratory Analysis of Performance on the SAT," *Journal of Educational Measurement* 21 (1984), and Lawrence Stedman and Carl Kaestle, "The Test Score Decline Is Over: Now What?" *Phi Delta Kappan* 67 (November 1985).

6. Among white SAT takers, 8.4 percent got verbal scores of 600 and above, and 18.7 percent got math scores that high. The comparable values for blacks are 1.3 percent and 2.6 percent. Lest we be accused of being unaware of the problems faced by other minorities, Mexican-Americans and Puerto Ricans fare worse than blacks numerically at and above 600, although slightly better as a percentage of their population of SAT takers. Only 415 (2.6 percent) and 1,045 (6.5) of the Mexican-American SAT takers got verbal and math scores, respectively, of 600 and above. The comparable values for Puerto Ricans were 206 (2.7 percent) and 433 (5.8 percent).

7. Len Ramist, head of ETS's Validity Study Service, reports an average SAT standard deviation of 80 for twenty-two selective colleges that participated in the Validity Study Service and whose freshman verbal plus math scores averaged over 1200 (personal communication). Assuming a mean SATV or SATM score at these colleges of 650, and a normal distribution of SAT scores for students attending them, only about 3 percent of the students' SAT scores would be lower than the *Z*-score corresponding to 500

of (500 − 650)/(80) = −1.88. This is, of course, only an approximation since the distributions cannot be normal. The SAT ceiling is 800, which is only 150/80 = 1.875 standard deviations above a 650 mean.

8. The values of 30 and 3 reported in the text are after adjustment of the actual number of correct answers for guessing.

9. See Goertz and Johnson, "State Policies for Admission to Higher Education," for a good discussion of differing admissions policies based on high school grades (or class rank) and test scores.

10. Breland, "An Examination of State University and College Admissions Policies." Breland studied the impact on whites and blacks of four admissions policies that combined or separately used unweighted SAT scores, high school grades, and class ranks: single-index minimum, in which a test score, or class rank, or grade point average is used alone to determine eligibility; multiple-index minimums, in which eligibility depends on satisfying minimums on at least two of these indexes; either-or minimums, in which eligibility depends on satisfying minimums on either of one or more indexes; and sliding scales, which set minimums on one index that depend on an applicant's score on another of the indexes. At all except the lowest admissions standards, each of these policies resulted in a lower percentage of blacks being eligible for admissions than whites.

11. Goertz and Johnson, "State Policies for Admission to Higher Education," pp. 9–10.

12. Ibid., p. 9. Note that most states have special admissions policies for applicants not meeting admissions standards. Nevertheless, these published standards illustrate the high potential for the SAT to have a negative impact on blacks' admissions opportunities.

13. See Breland, "University and College Admissions Policies."

14. Breland, "Population Validity and College Entrance Measures," p. 36.

15. Since the equations include college selectivity, they allow for the fact that grading standards vary among colleges differing in selectivity. Consequently, a student with a given rank and SAT score who earns lower average freshman grades than another student with the same rank and SAT score because he or she attends a more selective college will also have lower predicted freshman grades.

16. Statistically, equations 3 and 4 in table 5.4 show that a race dummy variable (coded 1 if black, 0 if white) is negative and significant when added as a final step to equations 1 and 2. We checked whether overprediction changed at differing high school rank, SAT, and selectivity levels by comparing equations 3 and 4 with equations that added interaction terms between each variable and race. Adding the interactions increased the adjusted R^2 only 0.01 in equation 3 and 0.005 in equation 4. Furthermore, predictions made from these equations differed very little from equations 3 and 4 for selected values of the independent variables that spanned combinations of their observed values. Thus, overprediction does not seem to vary systematically by SAT, high school rank, and selectivity levels.

17. In favoring this explanation we de-emphasize the importance of several other explanations that we believe are of less general importance. If racial differences in high school records and test scores are large enough to explain racial differences in freshman grades, blacks' freshman grades will be overpredicted if high schools report students' records with random measurement error, or if the SAT is unreliable (see Robert L. Linn, "Selection Bias: Multiple Meanings," *Journal of Educational Measurement* 21 [1984]). Since the SAT has a reliability in the 0.89–0.92 range (see Donald A. Rock and Charles E. Werts, "Construct Validity of the SAT across Populations—An Empirical Confirmatory Study," Research Report RR-79-2, [Princeton, N.J.: Educational Testing Service, 1979], p. 27), Linn's explanation could account for part of the black overprediction if high school reports are unreliable. But we think the care that high schools take in reporting student records and the pervasiveness of overprediction makes this an unlikely general explanation.

Statistical regression of black and white predictors to different means could also account for some of the overprediction at selective colleges (see Klitgaard, *Choosing Elites,* p. 247, for further discussion). But since overprediction occurs at open-admissions colleges as well as at selective ones, this explanation may not be generally useful (see Bernie Silverman, Florence Barton, and Mark Lyon, "Minority Group Status and Bias in College Admissions Criteria," *Educational and Psychological Measurement* 36 [1976]).

Ceiling effects in which colleges create a wide "A" range for grades could create nonlinearities in freshman grade predictions. These could lead to overprediction of blacks' grades because of their lower means on the predictors. But we have not seen evidence of these nonlinearities in the data for colleges we have examined. We also doubt that ceiling effects are a widespread phenomenon in most American colleges.

Affirmative action favoring blacks in admissions could also explain part of the overprediction. Suppose that among blacks and whites with the same test scores and high school records, admissions officers admit a higher percentage of blacks than whites. If one assumes that whites are more advantaged than blacks on unmeasured traits that affect college performance (because a lower percentage are selected), then omitting these traits from the prediction equations could overpredict blacks' grades.

However, there are also problems with this explanation. Whites may not be more advantaged on unmeasured traits than blacks even though fewer whites relative to the total number are selected. Also, Willingham and Breland's *Personal Qualities and College Admissions* shows that twenty-three background and achievement measures raise R^2 by only 0.04 when added to the typical prediction equation including high school record and SAT (see table 9.6).

Finally, blacks' grades may be biased downward compared to equally performing whites, but we suspect that "affirmative" college grading is at least as widespread as "discriminatory" grading. Blacks may also enroll more than whites in "hard" courses where they earn lower grades than whites with the same high school records and test scores do in the "easier" courses in which they enroll. But we have no evidence that this is true and suspect that the opposite argument is equally plausible.

18. ETS researchers and others sometimes assume that overprediction based on the high school record alone arises mainly because high school education is of lower quality for blacks than it is for whites even though blacks and whites have the same high school grades. One way this can happen is if blacks attend racially isolated metropolitan schools in which college-bound students with any given high school GPA or rank have a lower quality education than whites with the same GPAs or ranks who attend other schools. It can also happen when blacks attend racially mixed schools if blacks are isolated in inferior classes but are given grades comparable to whites. Or blacks could be given grades equal to whites in the same classes when they have learned less. Overprediction is reduced when SAT scores are added to the high school record, by this account, because the SAT provides an indirect measure of the quality of education that is lower for blacks even when their high school records are the same as whites'. Unfortunately, however, strong empirical support for these explanations does not exist.

19. Note that blacks with grades predicted from high school rank of any average almost always have a lower average when they are predicted from rank plus the SAT (compare row and column means, table 5.5).

20. College Entrance Examination Board, *Undergraduate Admissions,* table 37, presents frequency data on colleges' use of these selection procedures.

21. The cross-tabulations are very similar. We checked the cross-tabulations of predicted freshman grade distributions for black and white attending students, and they do not differ greatly from the ones in table 5.5 for applicants. We therefore assume that if table 5.5 is a good approximation to the predicted grade point averages of students who apply to typical American colleges, so are the ones for attending students.

We computed predicted mean grade point averages, standard deviations, and correlations between predicted grade distributions for blacks and whites who attended college at three selectivity levels: highly selective (average freshman SAT scores between 1100 and 1600), selective (average freshman scores between 1000 and 1099), and least selective (average freshman SAT scores between 400 and 999). The statistics are quite similar to those reported for applicants. There are larger discrepancies for the black sample, but sampling variability may cause some of the fluctuation.

22. We discuss this aspect of sample selection bias in more detail in chapters 3 and 4. Colleges assume that applicants with any given predicted freshman grade would have the same distribution of actual freshman grades as do their attending students with the same predicted grade. We tried to estimate the extent of nonrandom sample selection bias in the NLS prediction equations, but our results were inconclusive. We constructed several sample selection bias models for whites and blacks separately using the

techniques described in chapters 3 and 4. The probit models for selection of applicants into the sample of attending students included applicants' high school rank, SATs, selectivity of college applied to, and family income. When the correction factor (lambda) was added to the OLS prediction equations, the coefficients for rank, SAT, and college selectivity fluctuated, and sometimes became negative. Consequently, we will assume that applicants with given predicted freshman grades at colleges of known selectivity would have the same observed grades as students actually attending these colleges whose predicted grades are the same.

23. See notes to table 5.8 for method of computing these base rates. Also see chapter 3 for the rationale for zero-validity base rates.

24. Using bachelor's degree as the criterion in table 5.8, random rejection of 22.7 percent of the blacks admitted by high school rank decreases true positives from 52.7 percent to 52.7 × (1 − 0.227) = 40.7 percent, decreases false positives from 21.9 percent to 21.9 × (1 − 0.227) = 16.9 percent, increases true negatives from 12.4 percent to 12.4 × (1 + 0.665) = 20.6 percent, and increases false negatives from 12.9 percent to 12.9 × (1 + 0.665) = 21.5 percent. These values are very close to the percentages of 43.3, 14.4, 19.9, and 22.4 respectively in table 5.8 for the SAT and high school rank together.

25. For example, we estimate using the 2.0 cutoff in table 5.9 that randomly rejecting (69.8 − 62.3)/69.8 = 10.7 percent of the blacks admitted using high school grades would decrease Delaware's true positives from 37.7 percent to 37.7 × (1 − 0.107) = 33.7 percent, which is very close to the 33.0 percent true positives expected using the SAT along with high school grades. The interested reader who makes the calculations for each of the other outcomes, and at both selection cutoffs, will see that adding the SAT to high school grades produces outcomes very close to those expected from rejecting a similar percentage of blacks randomly from those admitted using high school grades.

26. These conclusions depend, of course, on the assumptions we have discussed that allow us and ETS to treat attending students as though they are applicants. The assumption that a college's attending students' forecasted freshman grades are distributed similarly to its applicants' forecasted grades seems to be met at the University of Delaware. Delaware admits about 90 percent of its state applicants, so the predicted grade distributions of attending students resemble those of applicants. The average forecasted grade of attending students exceeds the applicant average by no more than 0.166, and the standard deviation is lower by no more than 0.077.

The other main assumption is that the freshman grade distributions conditioned on forecasted grades are the same for applicants as they are for attending students. If these assumptions are not met, the cell counts, marginals, and base rates in tables like table 5.9 for attending students will differ from the ones the college would have if the table was based on applicants. The results will, however, still be applicable to other colleges that do have applicant distributions like the ones we look at for attending students. This is why it is important to replicate these findings in many colleges in order to have added confidence in them. It is also why we try to state our findings in the conditional form for colleges with applicant pools resembling the ones we examine for attending students.

27. Manski and Wise, *College Choice in America,* p. 85.

28. College Entrance Examination Board, *Undergraduate Admissions,* tables 41 and 42.

29. Willingham and Breland, *Personal Qualities and College Admissions.* The nine colleges were Bucknell, Colgate, Hartwick, Kalamazoo, Kenyon, Occidental, Ohio Wesleyan, Richmond, and Williams.

30. Ibid., tables 6.3 and 6.8.

31. Breland, Wilder, and Robertson, *Demographics, Standards, and Equity,* tables 4.8 and 4.9.

32. Changing the selection ratio to admit fewer than 170 blacks or more than 170 blacks by either policy changes the percentages in the four segments of the table. The same is true if more or fewer than 1,800 whites are admitted by either policy. But changing the number of blacks or whites admitted does not change the finding that the two admissions policies make the same admissions decisions for the vast majority of blacks as well as whites.

Chapter 6

1. Educational Testing Service, *Test Scores and Family Income,* p. 10.

2. Robert Mare, "Change and Stability in Educational Stratification," *American Sociological Review* 46 (1981).

3. Nairn and associates, *Reign of ETS,* p. 204.

4. Educational Testing Service, *Test Scores and Family Income,* p. 9.

5. Ibid., p. 6.

6. Ibid., p. 7.

7. Ramist et al., "Predictive Validity of the ATP Tests," table 8.1.

8. Ibid., table 8.6. The 0.076 is the increase in multiple correlation.

9. College Entrance Examination Board, *Undergraduate Admissions,* p. 22.

10. Nonlinearities and interactions are of only minor importance in equations 3 and 4. We added squared terms for each predictor variable and product terms for each pair of variables. Only one nonlinearity and one interaction were twice their standard error. Adjusted R^2 was increased only 0.03 by nonlinear and interaction terms.

11. These distributions of predicted grades from the SAT and rank together and from rank alone for higher and lower income applicants are typical of those found in individual colleges. So are the cross-tabulations of predicted grades by the two policies. We trisected applicants into students who applied to highly selective colleges (average freshman SAT scores of 1100 and above), selective colleges (average freshman SAT scores between 1000 and 1099), and less selective colleges (average freshman SAT scores below 1000). The means, standard deviations, and correlations differed by selectivity level and income category, but the differences were always small.

12. As expected, adding the SAT to high school rank decreases the percentage of true positives and false positives and increases the percentage of true negatives and false negatives. At some selection cutoffs, more than 100 percent of the changes in these outcomes brought about by the SAT is because the SAT decreases admissions of low-income students. Supplementing high school rank with the SAT at some cutoffs thus has a slightly negative effect on each outcome once the base rate is controlled. The SAT never has a positive effect on B.A. degree attainment as large as it does for freshman grades.

Chapter 7

1. U.S. Department of Health, Education and Welfare, *Digest of Education Statistics, 1975* (Washington, D.C.: Government Printing Office, 1976), and U.S. Department of Education, *Fall Enrollment in Higher Education, 1982* (Washington, D.C.: U.S. Department of Education, 1982).

2. College Entrance Examination Board, *On Further Examination,* p. 14.

3. Ibid., table 2; and College Entrance Examination Board, *National College-Bound Seniors, 1985* (New York: CEEB, 1985), p. 4.

4. College Entrance Examination Board, *On Further Examination,* pp. 18–20.

5. See Stedman and Kaestle, "Test Score Decline is Over," for a good discussion of the extent of the decline and some of the methodological problems in assessing its causes. See Owen, *None of the Above,* pp. xvii–xix, for an entertaining and useful discussion of causes that have been advanced. For a more scholarly discussion of these same issues, see Christopher Jencks, "Declining Test Scores: An Assessment of Six Alternative Explanations," *Sociological Spectrum* 1 (December 1980): 1–16.

6. Thomas F. Donlon and William H. Angoff, "The Scholastic Aptitude Test," in *The College Board Admissions Testing Program: A Technical Report on Research and Development Activities Relating to the Scholastic Aptitude Test and Achievement Tests,* ed. William Angoff (New York: College Entrance Examination Board, 1971), p. 15.

7. Ibid., pp. 15–16.

8. Albert E. Beaton, Thomas L. Hilton, and William B. Schrader, *Changes in the Verbal Abilities of High School Seniors, College Entrants, and SAT Candidates between 1960 and 1972* (Princeton, N.J.: Educational Testing Service, 1977), p. 21.

9. College Entrance Examination Board, *On Further Examination,* p. 4.

10. Ramist et al., "Predictive Validity of the ATP Tests," table 8.17.

11. See, for example, S. Suslow, "A Report on an Interinstitutional Survey of Undergraduate Scholastic Grading: 1960s to 1970s," (Berkeley, Calif., Office of Institutional Research: University of California, 1976); R. Singleton and E. Smith, "Does Grade Inflation Decrease the Reliability of Grades?" *Journal of Educational Measurement* 15 (1978); and Isaac Bejar and Edwin Blew, "Grade Inflation and the Validity of the Scholastic Aptitude Test," *American Educational Research Journal* 18 (1981).

12. Bejar and Blew, "Grade Inflation," p. 151.

13. See William B. Schrader, "The Predictive Validity of College Board Admissions Tests," in *The College Board Admissions Testing Program: A Technical Report on Research and Development Activities Relating to the Scholastic Aptitude Test and Achievement Tests*, ed. William Angoff (New York: College Entrance Examination Board, 1971), p. 130.

14. Bejar and Blew, "Grade Inflation," pp. 143–56.

15. Ibid., p. 151.

16. Ramist et al., "Predictive Validity of the ATP Tests," table 8.17. The actual values of the correlation from 1964 to 1982 are 0.52, 0.54, 0.52, 0.52, 0.52, 0.51, 0.49, 0.48, 0.49, 0.49, 0.50, 0.48, 0.47, 0.49, 0.46, 0.47, 0.46, 0.47, and 0.47.

17. Bejar and Blew, "Grade Inflation," figs. 7 and 8.

18. See Ramist et al., "Predictive Validity of the ATP Tests," table 8.17. Ramist reports correlations between math plus verbal SAT scores and freshman grades each year between 1964 and 1982 of 0.41, 0.38, 0.38, 0.39, 0.40, 0.40, 0.38, 0.37, 0.40, 0.42, 0.46, 0.44, 0.44, 0.43, 0.41, 0.41, 0.41, 0.38, and 0.40.

19. Bejar and Blew, "Grade Inflation," p. 153.

20. Ramist et al., "Predictive Validity of the ATP Tests," table 8.17. The increments in multiple correlation when the SAT is added to the high school record each year from 1964 to 1982 are 0.08, 0.06, 0.06, 0.05, 0.07, 0.06, 0.06, 0.06, 0.07, 0.08, 0.08, 0.08, 0.09, 0.07, 0.08, 0.08, 0.08, 0.07, and 0.07.

21. The 1980 High School and Beyond (HSB) survey is a stratified, two-stage national probability survey designed to inform federal and state policy in the 1980s. It is also designed to parallel the 1972 National Longitudinal Study to ensure comparability in the analysis of educational and postsecondary trends. HSB obtained data on over 28,000 seniors enrolled in 1,015 public and private high schools in the base-year survey administered in the spring of 1980. Survey data were obtained from school administrators, students, parents, and teachers. Overall, the response rate for the first stage (schools) was 91 percent (1,015 out of 1,118, including substitutions). For the second stage (seniors), the response rate overall was 82 percent. The total response rate is, therefore, (.91)(.82) = 75 percent.

HSB also obtained SAT scores from the Educational Testing Service for base-year respondents who had taken the SAT. SAT scores are provided by HSB on a separate data file, which we merged with matching cases on the HSB senior file.

HSB selected 11,500 students from the 28,000 available seniors for the first HSB followup administered in the spring of 1982. The first followup retains the multistage, stratified design of the base-year survey. All base year respondents had a probability of inclusion in the first follow-up, and unequal probabilities were compensated by weighting. Our analyses are restricted to those seniors who participated in both the base year and first follow-up surveys (N = 10,815). Of these 10,815 students, 2,553 took the SAT.

The sample design of the HSB requires all analyses to be weighted. After selecting the sample of interest, we obtained the mean weight of the appropriate HSB weight variable and then constructed a new weight that divided the HSB weight by the mean for that sample. Thus, all statistical analyses yield the same values as the weighted ones, but a sample size equivalent to the unweighted analysis.

22. There is actually only a slight change in SAT variance from the HSB to the NLS. The SAT variance is 202 in the HSB sample and 197 in the NLS sample.

23. The predicted grade distributions summarized in table 7.2 are a composite from NLS or HSB applicants to many American colleges and universities, but are probably quite similar to those at individual American colleges. We discuss our reasons for this conclusion in chapter 3. As an additional check for the HSB survey, we constructed versions of the predicted grade cross-tabulations for HSB applicants to highly selective, selective, and less selective colleges. The separate tables do not differ in important ways from the composite versions we used to construct table 7.2.

24. The Project Talent survey began in the spring of 1960. The target population included over 400,000 students in grades nine through twelve of 1,063 public, private, and parochial high schools in the United States. All students took about six hours of tests covering sixty nominally distinct skills or varieties of information. They also completed three questionnaires, the most relevant of which was the Student Information Blank, which asked 396 questions about family background, current activities in and out of school, current attitudes and personality, and future plans.

In the mid 1970s, ETS began to investigate empirically the decline in national SAT scores. To construct a benchmark, ETS obtained a simple random sample of 20,359 cases from the 81,175 cases available in the Project Talent twelfth grade probability sample. Since the SAT was not administered to Project Talent respondents in 1960, ETS located SAT scores in its microfilm files and merged them with the Project Talent data file. Of the sample of 20,359 twelfth grade students, about 3,600 (18 percent) took the SAT at least once. Including all cases on the one-year follow-up with freshman grades who also had SAT scores and high school grades reduced the sample size to 2,212 cases, or slightly over 10 percent of the total sample.

The major limitation of this Project Talent data is that the data file does not enable one to distinguish between four-year and two-year students. The college attendance variable used by ETS simply asked if the respondent had attended college since high school. However, most respondents who attended college probably attended four-year colleges, since two-year colleges were not as popular in the early 1960s as now. For example, there were less than 600 two-year colleges in 1960, compared to almost 900 in 1970.

Chapter 8

1. Henry Chauncey and John E. Dobbins, *Testing: Its Place in Education Today* (New York: Harper and Row, 1963), pp. 110–11.

2. Educational Testing Service, "Statement of Educational Testing Service on Certain Key Issues in *None of the Above: Behind the Myth of Scholastic Aptitude* by David Owen," p. 1.

3. Henry F. Bedford to James Crouse, 6 May 1986.

4. Owen, *None of the Above,* p. 272.

5. Peter Mueser, "Comment on James Crouse, 'Does the SAT Help Colleges Make Better Selection Decisions' " (photocopy, n.d.).

6. These effects of dropping the SAT hold for the bachelor's degree criterion as well as for freshman grades. The expected graduation rate if this hypothetical college admitted all its applicants would decline from (291 + 1592)/(2470) = 76.2 percent (table 3.7) to 73.2 percent. If the college only admitted applicants from its truncated pool with predicted grades above 2.5, based on high school rank, the graduation rate would decline from (91 + 1548)/(134 + 1918) = 79.9 percent (table 3.7) to 77.5 percent. Thus, when this college drops the SAT, its graduation rate falls by 80.0 − 77.5 = 2.5 percent, which is a larger drop than the 0.1 decline in graduation rate we estimated in chapter 3 when a college has no compositional changes in its applicant pool.

7. George H. Hanford, "Yes, the SAT Does Help Colleges," *Harvard Educational Review* 55 (1985): 331.

8. See chapter 7. Also see Ramist et al., "Predictive Validity of the ATP Tests," table 8.17.

9. Howard Wainer, "On Crouse" (photocopy, n.d.).

10. Paul Schaffner, "Competitive Admissions Practices When the SAT Is Optional," *Journal of Higher Education* 56 (1985).

11. Ibid., p. 70. The last two sentences in the quotation are revealing because they affirm that the Bowdoin admissions office staff could select qualified applicants *without* the SAT. Bowdoin typically receives over 3,000 applications annually for less than 500 places in the freshman class. About 1,000 students withhold scores. That the admissions staff could do a good job of selecting applicants without using SAT scores holds promise for other college admissions offices that might wish to try an optional SAT policy.

12. William Hiss, "Optional SATs: The First Two Years at Bates College" (Paper presented at the College Board Colloquium on Measures in the College Admissions Process, Wakefield, Mass., 16 June 1986).

13. Ibid., p. 13.

14. Colleges contemplating experiments that drop or modify use of the SAT would do well to study the history and methodology of other social experiments, giving special attention to the design of their own experiments and potential threats to internal and external validity. See, for example, the classic papers by Donald Campbell and his colleagues: Donald T. Campbell and Julian C. Stanley, *Experimental and Quasi-Experimental Designs for Research* (Chicago: Rand McNally, 1966); Donald T. Campbell, "Reforms as Experiments," *American Psychologist* 24 (1969); and Thomas D. Cook and Donald T. Campbell, *Quasi-Experimentation: Design and Analysis Issues for Field Settings* (Chicago: Rand McNally, 1979).

15. Even so, before implementing an optional SAT policy, Bates College surveyed counselors and headmasters at nearly a hundred feeder high schools to determine how the policy would be received. Elizabeth Woodcock, associate dean of admissions, Bates College, to Dale Trusheim, 27 February 1985, and "Report on the Counselor Questionnaire" (Bates College, n.d.).

16. The five broad areas (and tests) are: English (English composition, literature); foreign languages (French, German, Hebrew, Latin, Spanish); history and social studies (American history and social studies, European history and world cultures); mathematics (mathematics level 1, mathematics level 2); and sciences (biology, chemistry, physics).

17. Jackson, "Scholastic Aptitude Test," pp. 383, 388.

18. College Entrance Examination Board, *About the Achievement Tests (1984–85)* (New York: CEEB, 1984), p. 4.

19. For more information on the Academic Growth Study, see Thomas L. Hilton, "ETS Study of Academic Prediction and Growth," *New Directions For Testing and Measurement* 2 (1979).

20. Karl Alexander, Martha Cook, and Edward McDill, "Curriculum Tracking and Educational Stratification: Some Further Evidence," *American Sociological Review* 43 (1978).

21. Christopher Jencks and Marsha Brown, "The Effects of High Schools on Their Students," *Harvard Educational Review* 45 (1975).

22. Quoted from Stephen H. Ivens, "SAT—Achievement or Aptitude Testing?" (speaking notes for American Educational Research Association Symposium, Los Angeles, 1981).

23. Barbara L. Heyns, *Summer Learning and the Effects of Schooling* (New York: Academic Press, 1978).

24. Jackson, "Scholastic Aptitude Test," p. 383.

25. Dean K. Whitla, "The Admissions Equation," *Change*, November/December 1984, p. 25. Whitla repeats this same finding in *Measures in the College Admissions Process,* p. 10. As far as we know, Whitla has never published the analyses upon which this finding is based. When we wrote him and asked for more detailed information, he did not answer our letters.

26. Bates College, "Review of Bates College Research: 1980–84" (Lewiston, Maine: Admissions Office, Bates College, photocopy, n.d.).

27. Ramist et al., "Predictive Validity of the ATP Tests," table 8.19.

28. Because they did not admit many students with low SAT scores, SAT scores do not explain as much of the variation in freshman grades at these colleges as they do at less selective colleges. The admissions process restricts the range of SAT scores more than the range of achievement scores, although the high correlation between SAT and achievement scores means that the difference is not likely to be appreciable. On the other hand, selective test taking may restrict the range of achievement scores relative to SAT scores. Furthermore, the fact that some students took only one or two achievement tests may make achievement scores less reliable than SAT scores in this sample. Thus, achievement scores could predict freshman

grades either slightly better or slightly worse than SAT scores if we had equally reliable scores on samples with equally restricted ranges.

29. About a quarter of the initial sample returned a mail follow-up. Project Talent drew 3 to 4 percent subsamples of nonrespondents each year and followed them up intensively, obtaining data from 80–85 percent of these individuals. Our sample includes 3 to 4 percent of the initial mail respondents and all those in the subsample that was followed up intensively. The effective response rate is thus (0.25) + (0.75) (0.83) = 87 percent.

30. Because the reading comprehension test is longer than the other two and had a larger standard deviation, it dominates the aptitude composite. Christopher Jencks, James Crouse, and Peter Mueser ("The Wisconsin Model of Status Attainment: A National Replication with Improved Measures of Ability and Aspiration," *Sociology of Education* 56 [1983]) show, however, that this fact does not account for the aptitude composite's weak relationship to educational attainment.

31. Our "English" score includes not only knowledge of English literature but mastery of "proper" English, measured by tests of punctuation, capitalization, usage, and the like. Dropping the "proper" English component of the composite slightly increased its correlation with eventual educational attainment among eleventh graders. Jencks, Crouse, and Mueser, "Wisconsin Model of Status Attainment," give additional details on the construction of the composites and their correlations with other variables.

32. The aptitude composite also correlates more highly than the achievement composite with race ($r = 0.29$ versus 0.25), father's education ($r = 0.22$ versus 0.21), father's occupational status ($r = 0.25$ versus 0.23), and mother's education ($r = 0.20$ versus 0.19). If the Project Talent "aptitude" and "achievement" composites are good proxies for the SAT and achievement tests, these correlations further support our conclusion earlier that race and socioeconomic status affect achievement tests no more than they do the SAT.

33. Because Project Talent asked high school students to report their own grades since ninth grade, table 8.2 most likely underestimates the correlation of high school grades with other variables.

34. ETS also has not examined the relationship of its achievement tests to adult economic success. Jencks, Crouse, and Mueser ("Wisconsin Model of Status Attainment") show, however, that the Project Talent "aptitude" and "achievement" composites we have just described are equally good predictors of adult economic success. If this were true for ETS tests as well, colleges could substitute conventional achievement tests for the SAT without any loss of information about applicants' future economic prospects.

35. Chauncey and Dobbins, *Testing,* p. 31.

36. M. R. Katz, *You: Today and Tomorrow* (Princeton, N.J.: Cooperative Test Division, Educational Testing Service, 1959), pp. 14, 30.

37. Samuel Messick, "Issues in Effectiveness and Equity in the Coaching Controversy: Implications for Educational and Testing Practice," *Educational Psychologist* 17 (1982): 69.

38. Samuel Messick, "Abilities and Knowledge in Educational Achievement Testing: The Assessment of Dynamic Cognitive Structures" (ETS Research Report, 1982), pp. 13, 19, and 21.

39. Harold Stevenson and his colleagues report some quantitative data for kindergarten and elementary school children in the United States, Japan, and China. They find for selected schools in both Sendai and Taipei that, compared to Minneapolis, more time is spent in school on academic work, more time is spent doing homework, and mothers express a stronger belief in the value of hard work. They do not, however, control for socioeconomic differences in the backgrounds of the children between schools and cities. See Harold W. Stevenson, Shin-Ying Lee, and James W. Stigler, "Mathematics Achievement of Chinese, Japanese, and American Children," *Science* 231 (1986).

40. For more on Japan's national obsession with university admissions tests and their impact on high schools and students, see Thomas Rohlen, *Japan's High Schools* (Berkeley and Los Angeles: University of California Press, 1983).

41. Quoted from Barbara Lerner, "The War on Testing: David, Goliath, & Gallup," *Public Interest* 60 (Summer 1980): 122. For additional evidence, see Walter M. Haney, "College Admissions Testing and High School Curriculum: Uncertain Connections and Future Directions" (paper presented at the College Board Colloquium on Measures in the Admissions Process, Wakefield, Mass., 16 June 1986).

42. See, for example, George Madaus, "Public Policy and the Testing Profession—You Never Had It So Good?" *Educational Measurement: Issues and Practice* 4 (1985), and Norman Frederiksen, "The Real Test Bias: Influences of Testing on Teaching and Learning," *American Psychologist* 39 (March 1984).

43. See, for example, the excellent discussion by Madaus, "Public Policy and the Testing Profession," and the references cited therein.

44. Owen, *None of the Above,* chap. 13.

45. See Owen, *None of the Above,* pp. 278–81. Also see Daniel P. Resnick and Lauren B. Resnick, "Standards, Curriculum, and Performance: A Historical and Comparative Perspective," *Educational Researcher* 14 (April 1985): 14–18.

46. "Highlights, 1985 Survey of Advanced Placement Teachers" (photocopy, n.d.), p. 1.

47. Ibid., pp. 1–3.

48. ETS–Golden Rule Insurance Company settlement (Circuit Court of the Seventh Judicial Circuit, Sangamon County, Illinois, no. 419-76, 20 November 1984). This settlement requires ETS to follow prescribed procedures to eliminate potentially racially biased items from the Illinois Insurance Agent Licensing Test.

49. College Entrance Examination Board, *On Further Examination,* p. iii.

Select Bibliography

Aiken, Wilford M. *The Story of the Eight Year Study*. New York: Harper and Brothers, 1942.

Alexander, Karl; Martha Cook; and Edward McDill. "Curriculum Tracking and Educational Stratification: Some Further Evidence." *American Sociological Review* 43 (1978): 47–66.

American College Testing Program. *Executive Summary: National ACT Assessment Results, 1984–85*. Iowa City: ACTP, n.d.

———. *25 Years of Service to Education: 1984 Annual Report*. Iowa City: ACTP, n.d.

Arbeiter, Solomon. *Profiles, College-bound Seniors, 1984*. New York: College Entrance Examination Board, 1984.

Astin, Alexander W. *Predicting Academic Performance in College*. New York: Free Press, 1971.

Astin, Alexander W.; Kenneth C. Green; William S. Korn; and Marilynn Schalit. *The American Freshman: National Norms for Fall 1985*. Los Angeles: UCLA Higher Education Research Institute, December 1985.

Baird, Leonard L. "Relationships between Ability, College Attendance, and Family Income." *Research in Higher Education* 21 (1984): 373–95.

Barron's Educational Series. *Profiles of American Colleges*. Woodsbury, NY: Barron's Educational Series, 1985.

Bates College. "Review of Bates College Research: 1980–84. "Lewiston, Maine: Admissions Office, Bates College, n.d. Photocopy.

Beaton, Albert E; Thomas L. Hilton; and William B. Schrader. *Changes in the Verbal Abilities of High School Seniors, College Entrants, and SAT Candidates between 1960 and 1972*. Princeton, NJ: Educational Testing Service, 1977.

Bejar, Isaac, and Edwin Blew. "Grade Inflation and the Validity of the Scholastic Aptitude Test." *American Educational Research Journal* 18 (1981): 143–56.

Berk, Richard. "An Introduction to Sample Selection Bias in Sociological Data." *American Sociological Review* 48 (1983): 386–98.

Bracey, Gerald W. "ETS as Big Brother: An Essay Review of *None of the Above*." *Phi Delta Kappan* 67 (September 1985): 75–79.

Breland, Hunter. "An Examination of State University and College Admissions Policies." Research Report RR-85-3. Princeton, NJ: Educational Testing Service, January, 1985.

———. "Population Validity and College Entrance Measures." College Entrance Examination Board Research Bulletin. New York: College Entrance Examination Board, November 1978.

Breland, Hunter M.; Gita Wilder; and Nancy J. Robertson. *Demographics, Standards, and Equity: Challenges in College Admissions*. N.p.: AACRAO, American College Testing Program, CEEB, ETS, and National Association of College Admissions Counselors, 1986.

Brigham, Carl Campbell. *A Study of American Intelligence*. Princeton, N.J.: Princeton University Press, 1923.

Brill, Steven. "The Secrecy behind the College Boards." *New York*, 7 October 1973, pp. 67–75.

Campbell, Donald T. "Reforms as Experiments." *American Psychologist* 24 (1969): 409–29.

Campbell, Donald T., and Julian C. Stanley. *Experimental and Quasi-Experimental Designs for Research*. Chicago: Rand McNally, 1966.

Campbell, John P. "Psychometric Theory." In *Handbook of Industrial and Organizational Psychology*, edited by Marvin Dunnette. Chicago: Rand McNally, 1976.

Chauncey, Henry, and John E. Dobbins. *Testing: Its Place in Education Today*. New York: Harper and Row, 1963.

College Entrance Examination Board. *About the Achievement Tests (1984–85)*. New York: College Entrance Examination Board, 1984.

———. *About Your 1983 PSAT/NMSQT Scores*. New York: College Entrance Examination Board, 1983.

———. *Guide to the College Board Validity Study Service*. New York: College Entrance Examination Board, 1982.

———. *National College-Bound Seniors, 1982*. New York: College Entrance Examination Board, 1983.

———. *National College-Bound Seniors, 1985*. New York: College Entrance Examination Board, 1985.

———. *1983–84 Student Bulletin*. New York: College Entrance Examination Board, 1983.

———. *On Further Examination: Report of the Advisory Panel on the Scholastic Aptitude Test Score Decline*. New York: College Entrance Examination Board, 1977.

———. *Profiles, College-Bound Seniors, 1981*. New York: College Entrance Examination Board, 1982.

———. *6 SATs*. New York: College Entrance Examination Board and Educational Testing Service, 1982.

———. *Taking the SAT: A Guide to the Scholastic Aptitude Test and the Test of Standard Written English*. New York: College Entrance Examination Board, 1978.

———. *Undergraduate Admissions: The Realities of Institutional Policies, Practices, and Procedures*. New York: College Entrance Examination Board, 1980.

———. *Validity Study Service Data Analyses and Interpretation*. New York: College Entrance Examination Board, n.d.

———. *The Work of the College Entrance Examination Board: 1901–1925*. Boston: Ginn and Co., 1926.

Cook, Thomas D., and Donald T. Campbell. *Quasi-Experimentation: Design and Analysis Issues for Field Settings*. Chicago: Rand McNally, 1979.

Davis, Bernard. "Neo-Lysenkoism, IQ, and the Press." *Public Interest* 73 (1983): 41–59.

Donlon, Thomas F., ed. *The College Board Technical Handbook for the Scholastic Aptitude Test and Achievement Tests*. New York: College Entrance Examination Board, 1984.

Donlon, Thomas F., and William H. Angoff. "The Scholastic Aptitude Test." In *The College Board Admissions Testing Program: A Technical Report on Research and Development Activities Relating to the Scholastic Aptitude Test and Achievement Tests*, edited by William Angoff. New York: College Entrance Examination Board, 1971.

Educational Policies Commission. *Education for All American Youth*. Washington, D.C.: National Education Association, 1944.

Educational Testing Sevice. *Accountability, Fairness, and Quality in Testing*. Princeton, N.J.: Educational Testing Service, 1980.

———. *Annual Report, 1949–50*. Princeton, N.J.: Educational Testing Service, n.d.

———. *Annual Report, 1950–51*. Princeton, N.J.: Educational Testing Service, n.d.

———. *Annual Report, 1957–58*. Princeton, N.J.: Educational Testing Service, n.d.

———. *Annual Report, 1960–61*. Princeton, N.J.: Educational Testing Service, 1961.

———. *Annual Report, 1973–74*. Princeton, N.J.: Educational Testing Service, n.d.

———. *Charter and Bylaws*. Princeton, N.J.: Educational Testing Service, 1984.

———. *Developing a Test*. Princeton, N.J.: Educational Testing Service, 1983.

———. *ETS International Activities*. Princeton, N.J.: Educational Testing Service, n.d.

———. *ETS Standards for Quality and Fairness*. Princeton, N.J.: Educational Testing Service, 1983.

———. *1983 Annual Report*. Princeton, N.J.: Educational Testing Service, 1983.

———. *1985 Annual Report*. Princeton, N.J.: Educational Testing Service, 1985.

———. *Report of the 1985 ETS Visiting Committee, n.p.*, June 1985.

———. "Statement of Educational Testing Service on Certain Key Issues in *None of the Above: Behind the Myth of Scholastic Aptitude* by David Owen." Princeton, N.J.: Educational Testing Service, 18 April 1985 Photocopy.

———. *Test Scores and Family Income: A Response to Charges in the Nader/Nairn Report on ETS*. Princeton, N.J.: Educational Testing Service, 1980.

———. *Test Use and Validity: A Response to Charges in the Nader/Nairn Report on ETS*. Princeton, N.J.: Educational Testing Service, 1980.

———. *Trustees' 1984 Public Accountability Report*. Princeton, N.J.: Educational Testing Service, 1984.

———. *What the Polls Say*. Princeton, N.J.: Educational Testing Service, n.d.

Flanagan, John C.; F. B. Davis; J. T. Dailey; M. F. Shaycroft; D. B. Orr; I. Goldberg; and C. A. Neyman, Jr. *The American High School Student*. Palo Alto, Calif.: American Institutes for Research, 1964.

Ford, S. F., and S. Campos. "Summary of Validity Data from the Admissions Testing Program Validity Study Service." Princeton, N.J.: College Entrance Examination Board, 1977.

Frederiksen, Norman, "The Real Test Bias: Influences of Testing on Teaching and Learning." *American Psychologist* 39 (March 1984): 193–202.

Fuess, Claude M. *The College Board: Its First Fifty Years*. New York: Columbia University Press, 1950.

Goertz, Margaret E., and Linda M. Johnson. "State Policies for Admission to Higher Education." College Board Report No. 85–1. New York: College Entrance Examination Board, 1985.

Gould, Stephen J. *The Mismeasure of Man*. New York: Norton, 1981.

Haney, Walter M. "College Admissions Testing and High School Curriculum: Uncertain Connections and Future Directions". Paper presented at the College Board Colloquium on Measures in the Admissions Process, Wakefield, Mass. 16 June 1986.

———. "Trials of Admissions Testing." Paper presented at the annual meeting of the American Psychological Association, Montreal, 1 September 1980.

Hanford, George H. Memo to the members. New York: College Entrance Examination Board, April 1985.

———. Memo to the members. New York: College Entrance Examination Board, May 1985.

———. *Testing the Tests*. New York: College Board, n.d. Adapted from a speech to the Middle States Regional Assembly of the College Board in Philadelphia, 6 February 1980.

———. "Yes, the SAT Does Help Colleges." *Harvard Educational Review* 55 (1985): 324–31.

Hartnett, R., and D. Feldmesser. "College Admissions Testing and the Myth of Selectivity: Unresolved Questions and Needed Research." *AAHE Bulletin* 32 (March 1980): 3–6.

Heckman, James. "The Common Structure of Statistical Models of Truncation, Sample Selection, and Limited Dependent Variables and a Sample Estimator of Such Models." *Annals of Economics and Social Measurement* 5 (1976): 475–92.

———. Sample Selection Bias as a Specification Error." *Econometrica* 47 (1979): 153–61.

Heyns, Barbara L. *Summer Learning and the Effects of Schooling*. New York: Academic Press, 1978.

"Highlights, 1985 Survey of Advanced Placement Teachers." Photocopy, n.d.

High School and Beyond, 1980, Senior Cohort First Followup (1982): Data File User's Manual. Washington, D.C.: National Center for Education Statistics, 1983.

Hilton, Thomas L. "ETS Study of Academic Prediction and Growth." *New Directions For Testing and Measurement* 2 (1979): 27–44.

Hiss, William. "Optional SATs: The First Two Years at Bates College." Paper presented at the College Board Colloquium on Measures in the College Admissions Process, Wakefield, Mass. 16 June 1986.

Hunter, J. E., and F. L. Schmidt. "Fitting People to Jobs: The Impact of Personnel Selection on National Productivity." In *Human Performance and Productivity: Human Capability Assessment*, edited by M.D. Dunnette and E.A. Fleishman. Hillsdale, N.J.: Lawrence Erlbaum Associates, 1982.

Jackson, Rex. "The Scholastic Aptitude Test: A Response to Slack and Porter's 'Critical Appraisal.' " *Harvard Educational Review* 50 (1980): 382–91.

Jencks, Christopher. "Declining Test Scores: An Assessment of Six Alternative Explanantions." *Sociological Spectrum* 1 (December 1980): 1–16.

Jencks, Christopher, and Marsha Brown. "The Effects of High Schools on Their Students. *Harvard Educational Review* 45 (1975): 273–324.

Jencks, Christopher; James Crouse; and Peter Mueser. "The Wisconsin Model of Status Attainment: A National Replication with Improved Measures of Ability and Aspiration." *Sociology of Education* 56 (1983): 3–19.

Jensen, Arthur. *Bias in Mental Testing*. New York: Basic Books, 1980.

———. "The Debunking of Scientific Fossils and Straw Persons." *Contemporary Education Review* 1 (1982): 121–35.

———. *Straight Talk about Mental Tests*. New York: Free Press, 1981.

Kahneman, Daniel; Paul Slovic; and Amos Tversky, eds. *Judgment under Uncertainty: Heuristics and Biases*. Cambridge: Cambridge University Press, 1982.

Kamin, Leon J. *The Science and Politics of IQ*. Potomac, Md.: Lawrence Erlbaum, 1974.

Karier, Clarence, ed. *Shaping the American Educational State: 1900 to the Present*. New York: Free Press, 1975.

Katz, M. R. *You: Today and Tomorrow*. Princeton, N.J.: Cooperative Test Division, Educational Testing Service, 1959.

Klitgaard, Robert. *Choosing Elites*. New York: Basic Books, 1985.

Lagemann, Ellen. *Private Power for the Public Good: A History of the Carnegie Foundation for the Advancement of Teaching*. Middletown, Conn.: Wesleyan University Press, 1983.

Lerner, Barbara. "The War on Testing: David, Goliath, & Gallup." *Public Interest* 60 (Summer 1980): 119–47.

Levine, David O. *The American College and the Culture of Aspiration, 1915–1940*. Ithaca, N.Y.: Cornell University Press, 1986.

Levinsohn, J. R.; L. B. Henderson, J. A. Riccobono; and P. Moore. *National Longitudinal Study Base Year, First, Second, and Third Followup Data File Users Manual*. Research Triangle, N.C.: Research Triangle Institute, 1978.

Linn, Robert L. "Range Restriction Problems in the Use of Self-selected Groups for Test Validation." *Psychological Bulletin* 69 (1968): 69–73.

———. "Selection Bias: Multiple Meanings." *Journal of Educational Measurement* 21 (1984): 33–47.

McKown, Harry. "The Trend in College Entrance Requirements, 1913–1922." Department of Interior Bureau of Education Bulletin no. 35. Washington, D.C.: Government Printing Office, 1925.

Madaus, George. "Public Policy and the Testing Profession—You Never Had It So Good?" *Educational Measurement: Issues and Practice* 4 (1985): 5–11.

Manning, Winton H., and Rex Jackson. "College Entrance Examinations: Objective Selection or Gatekeeping for the Economically Privileged." In *Perspectives on Bias in Mental Testing*, edited by Cecil R. Reynolds and Robert T. Brown. New York: Plenum Press, 1984.

Manski, Charles, and David Wise. *College Choice in America*. Cambridge, Mass.: Harvard University Press, 1983.

Mare, Robert. "Change and Stability in Educational Stratification." *American Sociological Review* 46 (1981): 71–87.

Messick, Samuel. "Abilities and Knowledge in Educational Achievement Testing: The Assessment of Dynamic Cognitive Structures." ETS Research Report. Princeton, N.J.: Educational Testing Service, 1982.

———. "Issues in Effectiveness and Equity in the Coaching Controversy: Implications for Educational and Testing Practice." *Educational Psychologist* 17 (1982): 67–91.

Moll, Richard. *Playing the Private College Admissions Game*. New York: Times Books, 1979.

Mueser, Peter. "Comment on James Crouse, 'Does the SAT Help Colleges Make Better Selection Decisions.' " Photocopy, n.d.

Nairn, Allan, and associates. *The Reign of ETS: The Corporation That Makes Up Minds*. Washington, D.C.: Ralph Nader, 1980.

Olson, Craig A., and Brian E. Becker. "A Proposed Technique for the Treatment of Restriction of Range in Selection Validation." *Psychological Bulletin* 93 (1983): 137–48.

Owen, David. "The Last Days of ETS," *Harper's*, May 1983.

———. *None of the Above: Behind the Myth of Scholastic Aptitude*. Boston: Houghton Mifflin, 1985.

———. "Response to ETS's Response to *None of the Above*." Photocopy, n.d.

Pearson, Karl. "Mathematical Contributions to the Theory of Evolution, XI: On the Influence of Natural Selection on the Variability and Correlation of Organs." *Philosophical Transactions of the Royal Society*, ser. A, 200 (1903): 1–66.

Pritchett, Henry. "Has the College Entrance Examination Board Justified Its Quarter-Century of Life?" In College Entrance Examination Board, *The Work of the College Entrance Examination Board: 1901–1925*. Boston: Ginn and Co., 1926.

Ramist, Leonard, W. H. Angoff, I. L. Broudy, N. W. Burton, T. F. Donlon, J. Stern, and Peggy A. Thorne. "The Predictive Validity of the ATP Tests." In *The College Board Technical Handbook for the Scholastic Aptitude Test and Achievement Tests*, edited by Thomas F. Donlon (New York: College Entrance Examination Board, 1984).

Resnick, Daniel P., and Lauren B. Resnick. "Standards, Curriculum, and Performance: A Historical and Comparative Perspective." *Educational Researcher* 14 (April 1985): 5–20.

Response Analysis Corporation. *SAT Monitor Program: High School Students View The SAT and College Admissions Process*. Princeton, N.J.: Response Analysis Corporation, 1978.

Rock, Donald A., and Charles E. Werts. "Construct Validity of the SAT across Populations—An Empirical Confirmatory Study." Research Report RR-79-2. Princeton, N.J.: Educational Testing Service, 1979.

Rohlen, Thomas. *Japan's High Schools*. Berkeley and Los Angeles: University of California Press, 1983.

Samelson, Franz. "H. H. Goddard and the Immigrants." *American Psychologist* 37 (1982): 1291–92.

Saretzky, Gary. "Carl Campbell Brigham, the Native Intelligence Hypothesis, and the Scholastic Aptitude Test." Research Memorandum. Princeton, N.J.: Educational Testing Service, December 1982.

Schaffner, Paul. "Competitive Admissions Practices When the SAT Is Optional." *Journal of Higher Education* 56 (1985): 55–72.

Schrader, William B. "The Predictive Validity of College Board Admissions Tests." In *The College Board Admissions Testing Program: A Technical Report on Research and Development Activities Relating to the Scholastic Aptitude Test and Achievement Tests*, edited by William Angoff. New York: College Entrance Examination Board, 1971.

Schudson, Michael S. "Organizing the 'Meritocracy': A History of the College Entrance Examination Board." *Harvard Educational Review* 42 (1972): 34–69.

Silverman, Bernie; Florence Barton; and Mark Lyon. "Minority Group Status and Bias in College Admissions Criteria." *Educational and Psychological Measurement* 36 (1976): 401–7.

Singleton, R., and E. Smith. "Does Grade Inflation Decrease the Reliability of Grades?" *Journal of Educational Measurement* 15 (1978): 37–41.

Slack, Warner, and Douglas Porter. "The Scholastic Aptitude Test: A Critical Appraisal." *Harvard Educational Review* 50 (1980): 154–75.

Snyderman, Mark, and Richard Herrnstein. "Intelligence Tests and the Immigration Act of 1924." *American Psychologist* 38 (September 1983): 986–95.

Stedman, Lawrence, and Carl Kaestle. "The Test Score Decline Is Over: Now What?" *Phi Delta Kappan* 67 (November 1985): 204–10.

Stevenson, Harold W.; Shin-Ying Lee; and James W. Stigler. "Mathematics Achievement of Chinese, Japanese, and American Children." *Science* 231 (1986): 693–99.

Suslow, S. "A Report on an Interinstitutional Survey of Undergraduate Scholastic Grading: 1960s to 1970s." Berkeley, Calif.: Office of Institutional Research, University of California, 1976.

Synnott, Marcia Graham. *The Half Opened Door: Discrimination and Admissions at Harvard, Yale, and Princeton, 1900–1970*. Westport, Conn. Greenwood Press, 1979.

Terman, Lewis M. *Intelligence Tests and School Reorganization*. New York: World Book Co., 1923.

Thorndike, Robert L. *Personnel Selection: Test and Measurement Techniques*. New York: John Wiley and Sons, 1949.

Tyack, David, and Elisabeth Hansot. *Managers of Virtue*. New York: Basic Books, 1982.

U.S. Department of Education. *Fall Enrollment in Higher Education, 1982*. Washington, D.C.: U.S. Department of Education, 1982.

U.S. Department of Health, Education and Welfare. *Digest of Education Statistics*. Washington, D.C.: Government Printing Office, 1976.

Valentine, John A. *The College Board and the School Curriculum*. New York: College Entrance Examination Board, 1987.

Venti, Steven, and David Wise. "Test Scores, Educational Opportunities, and Individual Choice." *Journal of Public Economics* 18 (1982): 35–63.

Wainer, Howard. "An Exploratory Analysis of Performance on the SAT." *Journal of Educational Measurement* 21 (1984): 81–91.

———. "On Crouse." Photocopy, n.d.

Wechsler, Harold S. *The Qualified Student*. New York: John Wiley and Sons, 1977.

Weitzman, R. A. "The Prediction of College Achievement of the Scholastic Aptitude Test and the High School Record." *Journal of Educational Measurement* 19 (1982): 179–91.

Whitla, Dean K. "The Admissions Equation." *Change* (November/December 1984): 21–30.

———. "Using Tests in Admissions and Other Related Matters." In *Measures in the College Admissions Process: A College Board Colloquium*. New York: College Entrance Examination Board, 1986.

Wigdor, Alexandria, and Wendell Garner, eds. *Ability Testing: Uses, Consequences, and Controversies*. Washington, D.C.: National Academy Press, 1982.

Willingham, Warren W. *Success in College: The Role of Personal Qualities and Academic Ability*. New York: College Entrance Examination Board, 1985.

Willingham, Warren W., and Hunter M. Breland. *Personal Qualities and College Admissions*. New York: College Entrance Examination Board, 1982.

Willingham, Warren W., and Leonard Ramist. "The SAT Debate: Do Trusheim and Crouse Add Useful Information?" *Phi Delta Kappan* 64 (November 1982): 207–8.

Index